The Cambridge Introduction to
The Old Norse-Icelandic Saga

The Old Norse-Icelandic saga is one of the most important European vernacular literary genres of the Middle Ages. This *Introduction* to the saga genre outlines its origins and development, its literary character, its material existence in manuscripts and printed editions, and its changing reception from the Middle Ages to the present time. Its multiple sub-genres – including family sagas, mythical-heroic sagas and sagas of knights – are described and discussed in detail, and the world of medieval Icelanders is powerfully evoked. The first general study of the Old Norse-Icelandic saga to be written in English for some decades, the Introduction is based on up-to-date scholarship and engages with current debates in the field. With suggestions for further reading, detailed information about the Icelandic literary canon, and a map of medieval Iceland, this book is aimed at students of medieval literature and assumes no prior knowledge of Scandinavian languages.

MARGARET CLUNIES ROSS is Emeritus Professor of English and Honorary Professor in the Centre for Medieval Studies at the University of Sydney. She has published widely on Old Norse-Icelandic literature and culture, especially Old Norse mythology, Icelandic sagas, Old Norse-Icelandic poetry (especially skaldic poetry) and poetic theory.

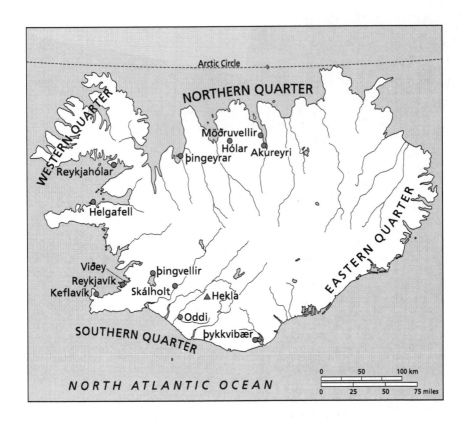

Arctic Circle

NORTHERN QUARTER

WESTERN QUARTER

Möðruvellir
Hólar
þingeyrar   Akureyri

Reykjahólar

Helgafell

EASTERN QUARTER

Viðey
Reykjavík   þingvellir
Keflavík   Skálholt   ▲Hekla

Oddi

SOUTHERN QUARTER   þykkvibær

NORTH ATLANTIC OCEAN

0   50   100 km
0   25   50   75 miles

The Cambridge Introduction to
The Old Norse-Icelandic Saga

MARGARET CLUNIES ROSS
University of Sydney

CAMBRIDGE
UNIVERSITY PRESS

CAMBRIDGE
UNIVERSITY PRESS

University Printing House, Cambridge CB2 8BS, United Kingdom

Cambridge University Press is part of the University of Cambridge.

It furthers the University's mission by disseminating knowledge in the pursuit of education, learning and research at the highest international levels of excellence.

www.cambridge.org
Information on this title: www.cambridge.org/9780521735209

First published 2010
Reprinted 2014

A catalogue record for this publication is available from the British Library

Library of Congress Cataloguing in Publication data
Ross, Margaret Clunies.
The Cambridge introduction to the old Norse-Icelandic saga / Margaret Clunies Ross.
    p.   cm. – (Cambridge introductions to literature)
Includes bibliographical references and index.
ISBN 978-0-521-51401-9 (hardback)
1. Sagas – History and criticism.   I. Title.   II. Title: Introduction to the old Norse-Icelandic saga.
PT7181.R67   2010
839'.6'09 – dc22   2010037675

ISBN 978-0-521-51401-9 Hardback
ISBN 978-0-521-73520-9 Paperback

Contents

Tables

A preface on practical issues

General aim of this book

The aim of this book is to offer an up-to-date analysis of the medieval Icelandic saga genre and to review major issues to do with its origins and development, its literary character and identity, its material existence in manuscripts and printed editions, and its changing reception from the Middle Ages to the present time. This book is about the saga genre in general but also about the various identifiable sub-genres that make it up. One of the book's themes is that many general books on the subject of the Icelandic saga are actually about only one sub-genre, the 'sagas of Icelanders' (*Íslendingasögur*) or family sagas, as they have sometimes been called in English. Some of the other sub-genres, like the 'sagas of ancient time' (*fornaldarsögur*) and 'sagas of knights' (*riddarasögur*) in particular, have been rather neglected during the twentieth century, for reasons that I shall try to explain. Although much of the discussion here perforce deals with sagas of Icelanders, because they have been the main subject of modern research and theorising, I have not confined myself to this sub-genre.

In the chapters that follow, I identify general characteristics of the saga genre as well as the characteristics that differentiate one sub-genre from others. I also propose that modern readers must be prepared to be flexible and non-judgemental about what I call in Chapter 6 the 'mixed modality' of much saga writing, which I argue reflects medieval attitudes rather better than a more compartmentalised distinction between 'classical' and 'post-classical', 'realistic' and 'fantastic' saga types that have been the anchor-points of much literary analysis and debate over the last one hundred years or so.

The book is written to be accessible to non-specialists like senior school students, undergraduate university students and the general reader. For that reason, I have tried as far as possible to make all the fundamental issues to do with the Icelandic saga as clear as I can, beginning with basic information, and always translating into English the titles of Old Norse-Icelandic texts, as well as giving translations of any passage from a medieval text that I quote.

When giving bibliographical references I have tried to choose accessible works in English where possible, but, if the best reference is in a language other than English (as it often is), I have not refrained from giving it, believing that English-speaking students will not mind moving out of their linguistic comfort zones and also expecting that some non-English-speaking readers may find this book useful. Regretfully, it has only been possible to refer to internet resources, of which there are many, in general terms, as the links to electronic sites tend to change frequently and are likely to be outdated quickly. In addition, the introductory nature of the Cambridge Introductions series prevents me documenting my work in as much detail as is normal in academic writing, although the Guide to Further Reading points to some of the major primary and secondary sources I have used. At the same time as I have tried to make this book accessible to beginners, I hope that specialists, by which term I mean scholars of Icelandic and medievalists more generally, will find things to hold their attention here. As they will see, I have not held back from fairly direct discussion of some of the major controversies in saga research, and they may find this interesting and provocative.

The book is arranged in the following manner. The first chapter is a general introduction to medieval Icelandic society, and gives basic information about the settlement of the island, its economic, social and political character, and how the development of the saga genre may have come about. Chapter 2 looks at definitional questions to do with what a saga is (then and now), while Chapter 3 takes up the issue of the likely origins of the saga form, and some of the main theories of saga origins, as well as the relationship between oral traditions and the written saga form. Chapter 4 looks at the thorny issue of saga chronology and poses the questions of whether we can determine the likely age of individual sagas in comparison with others and whether we can determine when specific sub-genres of the saga began in comparison with other sub-genres.

Chapters 5–7 deal with the literary character of the Icelandic saga. Chapter 5 suggests a way of using a historically and geographically articulated set of criteria to classify and describe the various sub-genres of the saga. It also indicates that such a perspective offers an integrated view of the genre as a whole. Chapter 6 looks at saga mode, style and point of view, again offering a means of understanding the varied representations of 'reality' across and within saga sub-genres. Chapter 7 analyses the structural elements of the saga genre, an issue on which a great deal has been written during the twentieth century, and proposes a number of deep structural patterns that bear the major themes of Icelandic saga writing.

Chapters 8 and 9 offer a historical perspective on the copying and transmission of Icelandic sagas down to the present time. Chapter 8 addresses the question of how the medieval sagas have come down to modern times, in what material form, and where they can now be accessed. In addition, it discusses how editions of sagas are made, what kinds of editions there are, and what editors do to the raw material they edit. Many of these issues, though well known to specialists, are, in my experience, completely foreign territory to students (and probably to the general reader), who may be unaware of the power an editor has to place his or her interpretation on a text at all levels from orthography to the choice of base manuscript for a saga text. Chapter 9 gives a brief overview of the reception of the medieval Icelandic saga and its various sub-genres from the end of the Middle Ages to the present day, both in Iceland and outside it, and suggests the ideological forces that have influenced the changing popularity of different saga sub-genres over the period from the seventeenth century to the present. It also looks at the importance of translations in making Icelandic sagas known to a wide audience outside Iceland.

Spelling conventions used in this book

This book uses Icelandic spellings of all Icelandic text, whether continuous prose or single words and phrases. The special characters used to write Icelandic are preserved here, not transliterated to an approximate English spelling. The special characters used are: the consonants þ (upper case Þ) and ð, pronounced as the first sound in English 'thin' and 'this' respectively and often spelled th or d in English transliteration; the ligatures æ and œ, approximating to the vowel sounds in English 'bat' and French 'peu'; the vowels y, as in German *kühl*, ǫ, as in English 'pot', and ø, similar in sound to œ, but shorter; and long forms of the various vowels (pronounced in Modern Icelandic as diphthongs) which are represented by an acute accent mark over the letter, like á and ó.

All Icelandic words taken from texts that are known to have existed in the Middle Ages are normalised to a 'classical', first half of the thirteenth century standard Icelandic orthography, as used by the *Íslenzk fornrit* (*ÍF*) series of editions of saga texts. This applies to personal names mentioned in sagas or other medieval works and to place names which no longer exist. Place names still in use are given a Modern Icelandic spelling (except in the Icelandic titles of sagas), unless they are Norwegian, when the Old Norse form of the name is given with the Modern Norwegian one in brackets after it. Similarly, technical

terms whose use cannot be attested from medieval sources are given in a
Modern Icelandic spelling; for example, the spelling *fornaldarsögur* 'sagas of
ancient time' is chosen rather than *fornaldarsǫgur*, because the compound is
unattested in medieval records, but *lygisǫgur* 'lying sagas' is so spelled because
the term appears in medieval texts.

   In the Guide to Further Reading and in the Notes the names of Icelandic
authors are given in the form first name last name, following the usual Icelandic
convention, e.g. Bjarni Einarsson, Sigurður Nordal. Non-Icelandic authors are
alphabetised by surname in the usual way.

Map of Iceland

The map of Iceland which forms the frontispiece to this volume is not over-
burdened with names, as it has seemed to me unnecessary to give many names
in an introductory book. Although the modern capital of Iceland, Reykjavík,
appears on the map, this is only for purposes of orientation; in the Middle
Ages there were no towns in Iceland, and Reykjavík was no more important
than other coastal locations from where ships could be launched. The map
indicates the major regions of the island, the four Quarters, the site of the
annual assembly place (*Þingvellir*), where the Alþingi or General Assembly was
held every summer, and some important farm and monastery names, locations
where literary activity is likely to have taken place.

Acknowledgements

I should like to thank the following people who read this manuscript and offered helpful comments on it: Geraldine Barnes, Hannah Burrows and Guðrún Nordal. I am also indebted to the three anonymous readers of the book's proforma that I submitted to Linda Bree at Cambridge University Press in November 2007 and to Linda herself for wise advice on matters of presentation. Orri Vésteinsson helpfully provided me with references to recent scientific studies of the genetic characteristics of early Icelanders for Chapter 1. Beatrice La Farge and Julia Zernack very kindly sent me copies of Zernack 1994 and Zernack's bibliography of German saga translations (1997), after I had made some enquiries of them about German translations of the sagas for Chapter 9. And I am grateful to my partner, Richard Green, for drawing a version of the map of Iceland that forms the frontispiece of the book.

Abbreviations

Below is a list of all non-standard abbreviations used in this book.

AM   designates a manuscript from the collection of Árni
            Magnússon, now in either Reykjavík or Copenhagen (see
            Chapter 8)
CVC   = *An Icelandic-English Dictionary.* Initiated by Richard Cleasby,
            subsequently revised, enlarged and completed by Gudbrand
            Vigfusson, M. A. 2nd edn with supplement by Sir William
            Craigie. Oxford: Clarendon. 1957.
fol   folio (refers to size of manuscript page, 28+ cm. high)
Fritzner = Fritzner, Johann. *Ordbog over det gamle norske sprog.* 3 vols.
            Kristiania (Oslo): den norske forlagsforening. 1883–96. 4th edn
            rpt 1973. Oslo etc.: Universitetsforlaget.
GKS   *Den gamle kongelige samling* 'The old royal collection', now in
            either Reykjavík or Copenhagen (see Chapter 8)
Holm   *Kungliga Biblioteket* The Royal Library Stockholm (Holm perg –
            vellum manuscripts; Holm papp – paper manuscripts from the
            Stockholm collection)
ÍF   = *Íslenzk fornrit,* vols. 1–. Reykjavík: Hið íslenzka fornritafélag
            (cited by volume and page numbers). A full list of all the *ÍF*
            volumes cited in this book can be found immediately after the
            Guide to Further Reading.
Lbs   *Landsbókasafn Íslands* Collection of the National Library of
            Iceland
NKS   *Den nye kongelige samling* 'The new royal collection' [from the
            Royal Library, Copenhagen] (see Chapter 8)
NRA   *Riksarkivet,* National Archive, Oslo
OED   *Oxford English Dictionary,* 2nd edn (on the internet)
ON   Old Norse
UUB or UppsUB *Uppsala Universitetsbibliotek* The University Library of
            Uppsala, Carolina Rediviva
$4°$ quarto (refers to size of manuscript page, 18–28 cm. high)
$8°$ octavo (refers to size of manuscript page, 9–20 cm. high)

Chapter 1

Medieval Iceland

Setting the scene

> That winter Ingólfr held a great sacrifice and sought for himself an
> omen concerning his destiny . . . The intelligence directed Ingólfr to
> Iceland. After that each of those kinsmen [Ingólfr and his brother-in-law
> Hjǫrleifr] prepared his ship for the voyage to Iceland; Hjǫrleifr had his
> war booty on board, and Ingólfr [carried] their common property, and
> they put out to sea when they were ready . . . When Ingólfr saw Iceland
> he threw his high-seat pillars overboard for good luck; he declared he
> would settle where the pillars came ashore.[1]

> Þenna vetr fekk Ingólfr at blóti miklu ok leitaði sér heilla um forlǫg
> sín . . . Fréttin vísaði Ingólfi til Íslands. Eptir þat bjó sitt skip hvárr þeira
> mága til Íslandsferðar; hafði Hjǫrleifr herfang sitt á skipi, en Ingólfr
> félagsfé þeira, ok lǫgðu til hafs, er þeir váru búnir . . . Þá er Ingólfr sá
> Ísland, skaut hann fyrir borð ǫndugissúlum sínum til heilla; hann mælti
> svá fyrir, at hann skyldi þar byggja, er súlurnar kœmi á land.

The modern visitor to Iceland from abroad usually approaches the island
from the air, very differently and much more easily than the first settlers did
as they approached an unknown land by sea on board small ships, bringing
with them some family members, their animals and some precious household
possessions, probably including some numinous object representing the power
of their gods, like the first settler Ingólfr's high-seat pillars. Travelling today

towards the almost suburban sprawl of Reykjavík from the airport at Keflavík along a metalled road and in a comfortable bus, the visitor may find it hard to imagine the privations that faced the first inhabitants of Iceland and that, indeed, continued for many of their descendants down to the twentieth century. Yet a glance outside the bus window tells the story: the landscape is in most respects as rugged, barren and striking now as it was at the time of the first settlement in the late ninth and early tenth centuries AD, and the weather is also much the same, with rain, snow or sleet, depending on the season of the year, occasional sun, and wind, almost always wind blowing.

The first historian to write in Icelandic, Ari Þorgilsson (1068–1148), claimed in his 'Book of the Icelanders' (*Íslendingabók*), written 1122–3, that at the time of the earliest settlement the island was well wooded: 'At that time Iceland was covered with trees between mountain and foreshore' (*Í þann tíð vas Ísland viði vaxit á miðli fjalls ok fjǫru*). If so, the new settlers' sheep and goats probably ate the dwarf birch trees and other shrubs that grew there within a relatively short time. Humans and European domesticated animals were intruders into this vulnerable early medieval landscape, where previously the only large land mammal was the arctic fox, though there were then, as now, sea mammals, birds and fish in abundance. Ari also said that Irish hermits, called *papar*, sought sanctuary on the island but fled when the heathen settlers appeared. These men must have been relatively few in number. The landscape itself was in some significant respects unlike the homelands of the colonists, whether they came from mainland Scandinavia, as the largest proportion probably did, or from the northern British Isles and Atlantic islands. Snow-capped mountains and fjords were familiar to them, but many of the Icelandic mountains were volcanic, and actively so. Iceland is one of the liveliest geothermal countries on earth, with earthquakes, dangerous volcanoes, hot springs, geysers (the word is Icelandic in origin) and swift-flowing rivers that descend from the barren central lava plateau to the sea, often branching into many-channelled streams that flow across black, volcanic sands.

In spite of its name, Iceland, the climate of the island is milder than would normally be expected of a place on a latitude so far north (64–6°), certainly much milder than Greenland, in spite of the latter's attractive name. This is because the Gulf Stream influences the climate and also brings an abundance of marine life there. Without this ameliorating influence, Iceland's climate would be almost too harsh for human habitation, given that 11.6 per cent of the land surface is covered by glaciers and only the coastal strips (approximately 23 per cent) are fertile enough to support crops and animals. In summer, sheep can be grazed on upland pastures that are snow-covered in winter.

The early settlers soon modified their behaviour and agricultural practices to adjust to their new environment. They found they could not grow many of the grain crops they were used to back home in their damp, cold climate, being restricted largely to hay, nor could they keep such a variety of animals. Sheep, goats, cows and pigs were kept initially, but the bones of cattle and pigs largely disappear from the archaeological faunal record during the eleventh century. Medieval Icelanders have been fittingly described by the Icelandic historian Gunnar Karlsson as sedentary pastoralists, living largely on a diet of milk products and meat. Horses were very important for human transport and as pack animals across a difficult terrain where made roads did not exist.

Building in wood, the standard material in early medieval North-West Europe, became difficult because, after the initial period when there were some trees, all wood had to be either imported, mostly from Norway, or gathered as driftwood. Hence a great many Icelandic farmhouses were structures of stones, some wood and turf, and this method of construction persisted into the modern period. A good idea of traditional farm construction methods can be gained from a visit to the reconstructed medieval farm at Stöng in Þjórsárdalur, probably built at some time in the eleventh century. This farm was buried under volcanic ash from an eruption of Mt Hekla in 1104 and later covered by a glacier. When the glacier receded in the early twentieth century, the ruins were revealed. They were excavated in 1939 and restored in 1974, as part of Iceland's celebration of its 1100th anniversary (assuming the settlement to have begun in 874). After *c.* 1200, the lack of local wood for building boats placed a severe restriction on the ability of Icelanders to travel abroad and engage in trade independently, and they became more and more reliant on foreign merchants, firstly Norwegians, later English and German traders, and finally a Danish monopoly that lasted until 1787.

Why Iceland?

Given the physical nature of the place, one might ask why people colonised such a marginal location, the last part of the European land mass to be settled by humans, aside from Greenland, which was settled from Iceland. There are several probable answers to this question. In the first place, the climate was warmer in the settlement period than it became after 1300. Secondly, the settlement of Iceland took place towards the end of a period in which colonies of mainland Scandinavians (from Norway, Sweden and Denmark) established themselves in many parts of Western, Eastern and Southern Europe in the period of the so-called Viking expansion, from the mid-eighth to the mid-eleventh centuries AD. The reasons for this large-scale movement of people are various and have been much debated. The expansion westwards was only one of the trajectories followed by Viking colonists, mostly from Norway. There were Norwegian colonies in most of the North Atlantic islands, from the Orkneys and Shetlands to the Faroes and so on to Iceland. There were also Norwegian settlements in Ireland, the Hebrides, the Isle of Man and northern parts of Scotland. Early sources tell that some of the early settlers in Iceland had already tried their luck in other Scandinavian colonies, and had decided to see whether Iceland offered better prospects. So, in this context, Iceland was just one of many, the last settled colony of the Norwegian diaspora. Early reports appear to have suggested that people could make a good living in a place where land and resources were as yet unclaimed and unexploited.

Medieval Icelandic sources themselves give another reason for the settlement, a reason that accounts for the proportion of the population that came from Norway, rather than those who came from Britain and the Atlantic islands. That reason is substantially political and to some degree economic. Again and again in the introductory sections of sagas of Icelanders (*Íslendingasögur*), sometimes known as family sagas, the narrators insist that their protagonists, or the latters' ancestors, emigrated to Iceland to escape the tyranny of the Norwegian king Haraldr hárfagri 'Fair-hair' Hálfdanarson (r. c. 870–932), who was in the process of exerting his authority over all regions of Norway and intruding upon the autonomy of local leaders, who had previously used to enjoy relative independence and political freedom. Although there is probably some truth in this claim, modern scholars have suspected that it is also to some degree ideologically motivated. As we shall see in discussing the Icelandic saga later on, medieval Icelandic society, and the literature produced by it, reveals an equivocal relationship with royalty and aristocratic authority. On the one hand, Icelandic independence and egalitarianism can be seen in the literature to be highly valued qualities; on the other, Icelanders often claimed for themselves close family relationships with Norwegian and other royal families and valued these positively. This is unsurprising in a medieval European context, when socially stratified societies ruled by kings and hereditary aristocracies were the norm. The socio-political and economic character of medieval Icelandic society was an exception to this norm and, though it survived for approximately 400 years (the so-called Commonwealth period c. 870–1262), it eventually succumbed to medieval European normality, not by electing kings from within its own people, but by bowing to the authority of the king of Norway, whose subjects the Icelanders became.

Where did the settlers come from?

According to 'The Book of the Land-Takings',[2] a record of the earliest settlers in Iceland and where they settled, several people bumped into Iceland, so to speak, before the first permanent settlement from Norway, which probably took place *c.* 870. These people were travelling by ship between the Scandinavian mainland and one or other of the Norse Atlantic island settlements. There was a Norwegian named Naddoddr and a Swede called Garðarr Svávarsson, the former blown off his course for the Faroe Islands, the latter attempting to get to the Hebrides. Another Norwegian, Flóki, with two companions, spent a winter in Iceland, and gave it its name on account of the pack-ice he could see in the spring in a northern fjord.

There were probably under 10,000 people inhabiting Iceland by the end of the period of settlement *c.* 930. Most medieval Icelandic written sources lead one to believe that the majority of those people had emigrated from various parts of Norway and that many of them belonged to the upper classes of society. The latter emphasis may well not have been entirely accurate; certainly, once they were domiciled in Iceland, the settlers' material circumstances appear to have become less affluent than those of their Norwegian counterparts, to judge by the evidence of the archaeological record. Undoubtedly, many of the socio-political institutions of the new Commonwealth were modelled on those of Norway, particularly Western Norway, including the practice of holding local open-air assemblies, called *þing*, the nature of the legal system and a number of other political institutions.

Equally important, however, were the structures that the Icelanders apparently deliberately repudiated, like the institution of kingship and a formalised social hierarchy below the king, as well as the allodial or odal system of land ownership held absolutely by families that Norwegians transferred to their other colonies, including the Faroes, Orkney and Shetland. In Iceland, different social and geographical conditions appear to have made such a system of familial land tenure and transmission unattractive. In terms of kinship and marriage, too, the Icelandic social system was based on a Germanic, more particularly Scandinavian, model with some significant modifications. And undoubtedly in terms of language, religion and culture Iceland was predominantly Scandinavian. Icelandic developed as a separate language from Norwegian during the medieval period, just as the other Norwegian colonies' languages did. The distinguishing thing about Icelandic, however, which is the reason it has been possible to write this book, is that it quickly developed a rich and varied vernacular literature, much of which has survived to the present day. While some vernacular writing, as well as texts in Latin, have survived in Norwegian, and we have reason to believe that the Faroes, and to a much greater extent, the Orkney Islands, were literary centres too, the output of the Icelanders was prodigious by comparison. The reasons behind their textual productivity will be discussed below.

While one must acknowledge the dominant demographic and cultural influence of Norway on the early settlers in Iceland, there is another ethnic group whose influence was less overt but nevertheless important. During the twentieth and twenty-first centuries, advances in genetic research have revealed just how significant the contribution of Celtic settlers and slaves from the northern British Isles, particularly females, is likely to have been. Studies of European blood groups within the ABO blood group system carried out during the twentieth century have shown that the distribution of groups within the Icelandic population has similarities to those of the British Isles rather than to mainland Scandinavia. More recently, ongoing studies of the mitochondrial DNA (that is, DNA subject to maternal inheritance) of a sample of pre-1000 Icelandic skeletons seem to point to a difference between males and females in place of origin; a much greater proportion of female settlers, estimated as 63–5 per cent, seem to have come from Scotland and Ireland and a much higher proportion of males, estimated as 75–80 per cent, from Norway or other parts of mainland Scandinavia. In addition, ongoing comparative studies of strontium isotopes in teeth and bones confirm that migrants among the earliest settlers came from several different places, without as yet being able to identify those places precisely.

'The Book of the Land-Takings' mentions a number of early settlers of Celtic or mixed Scandinavian and Celtic ancestry, and it is possible that medieval Icelandic sources somewhat downplayed the proportion of the population that was not Norse, especially if it was female and unfree, and perhaps also because some Celtic settlers were already Christian. It is known that Icelanders kept slaves, both male and female, in the early period. They are mentioned in many sagas and in legal texts from the Commonwealth period. Slavery was big business throughout Europe in the early Middle Ages, and there is every reason to suppose that Scandinavians of the Viking Age engaged in the practice of buying and selling slaves, particularly from the British Isles. It is generally accepted that Icelandic society was among the first in Europe to give up slavery, probably not out of Christian virtue but because it was of small economic benefit. In this context, we may wonder whether the representation in 'The Saga of the people of Salmon River Valley' (*Laxdœla saga*) of the relationship between Hǫskuldr Dala-Kollsson, an ambitious Icelandic chieftain of Norwegian ancestry, who buys a concubine in a market overseas and eventually discovers that she is the daughter of an Irish king, is not a deeply embedded Icelandic ethnic myth that seeks to acknowledge the Celtic connection while at the same time representing it as extraordinary and almost the stuff of wonder tales.

Medieval Iceland society

The following section gives a brief account of the history of Icelandic society in the Commonwealth period (*c.* 870–1262) and of the changes that occurred after 1262–4, when Iceland had been 'normalised' to a common late medieval governmental pattern as a distant and rather poor dependency of a sovereign state, Norway, whose king appointed local agents to rule the country and collect his taxes. It is important for anyone who wants to understand the saga literature produced in medieval Iceland to have at least a basic grasp of Icelandic economic, social and political history, although the reader should always bear in mind that there was a considerable time gap of some 200–300 years between the Age of Settlement and the likely period of saga writing. Some further background reading is suggested in the Guide to Further Reading at the end of the book, and particular institutions and social practices will be mentioned whenever they are relevant to the analysis of saga literature. Table 1 sets out a chronology of important events during the period.

I shall draw attention here to some major characteristics of Commonwealth Iceland that set it somewhat apart from other medieval societies of the period. Perhaps because it was often not possible for the early settlers to bring their extended families with them on the voyage to Iceland, compensatory stress was placed on the worth of the individual to act – or not to act – in socially acceptable ways. Family support was still very important in many respects, particularly in the prosecution of marriages and feuding, but it is clear from saga literature that an idealised personal honour was above all the currency in which the esteem of an individual was measured. Further, personal honour was only inflected for gender to a degree. The qualities that characterised a manly man, courage, reticence, calculated but not excessive aggression, physical strength and honesty to a point, were not all qualities appropriate to women, although there is a sense in which women were often judged according to the masculine paradigm, and as often found wanting. The negative side of personal honour is also a common theme of saga literature, as one might expect. Cowardice, garrulousness, treachery, physical weakness or disability were the obverse of manliness, and were often expressed in a sexualised

Table 1. Important events in the history of medieval Iceland

c. 870–930 The settlement of Iceland

c. 890–900 King Haraldr hárfagri 'Fair-hair' Hálfdanarson consolidates power in Norway

c. 930 Establishment of the Althing (*Alþingi*) or General Assembly

c. 960 Division of Iceland into Quarters

999 or 1000 Official conversion of the Icelanders to Christianity

c. 1004–30 Establishment of the Fifth Court (*Fimmtardómr*)

1056 Ísleifr Gizurarson, the first Icelandic-born bishop, consecrated in Bremen

1117–18 Writing down of the Commonwealth law code (*Grágás*) over the winter

1133 First monastery established at Þingeyrar in Húnavatnsþing

1153 Trondheim established as archbishopric for Norway and Iceland

1220–60 The Age of the Sturlungs (*Sturlungaöld*) – civil unrest in Iceland

1262–4 Icelandic chieftains swear allegiance to King Hákon Hákonarson of Norway and his son Magnús

1271 King Magnús sends new legal code, *Járnsíða* 'Ironside', to Iceland

1280 New law code, *Jónsbók* 'John's Book', sent to Iceland

1397 The Kalmar Union of Denmark, Norway and Sweden begins

idiom, in which the unmanly man could be accused of passive homosexuality or bestiality, termed *ergi*, a charge of such seriousness that it could lead to death.

The individual's possession of honour was his most important social attribute. Honour could be affected by the actions or inactions of others, particularly within the family. Any assault upon the honour of the family's female members, like an unauthorised sexual approach or encounter, was considered to reflect directly upon the honour of its male members, and there are instances in saga literature of feuds being started over women. Conflicts that resulted in injuries or killings demanded retribution on the part of the injured party or his representatives to restore honour and avoid the shame that would usually follow inaction. Family members and political associates were expected to participate in acts of vengeance in order to preserve honour and exact compensation. Each individual possessed a notional monetary value, as in other early Germanic societies, often called the wergild by modern scholars (literally 'man-payment', from Old English *wergeld*), and compensation awarded by a court for injury or death had to be distributed among the kin group in accordance with a set formula: the closer the awardee was to the deceased genealogically, the greater the compensation. If compensation could not be agreed on, the alternative was to exact physical retribution, often in the form of killing or maiming. Another extreme option for the most heinous crimes, or if negotiations for compensation broke down altogether, was outlawry, which placed an individual right outside society.

The importance of the individual's autonomous status can be seen at social levels beyond the family. The ruling social group of Commonwealth Iceland were the chieftains or *goðar*, and individual males of sufficient means entered into a personal contract with a single *goði* for protection and support for themselves and their households, a contract that either side could change if he wished. The *goðar* were supposed to represent the interests of their *þingmenn*, or supporters, at local assemblies (*þing*) and in some cases at the annual general assembly of the whole country, the Althing (*Alþingi*), at Þingvellir 'Assembly Plains' in South-West Iceland, which took place over two weeks every summer. The constitutional structure of the Icelandic Commonwealth was very complex, with the country divided into four Quarters (this division took place *c.* 960), each with its own *goðar*. The *goðar* in turn nominated judges to each of the four Quarter courts, which deliberated upon legal cases. Later (after 1004) a Fifth Court of review was added to the structure. The preservation and interpretation of the law was entrusted in large part to a lawspeaker (*lǫgsǫgumaðr*) who presided over the law council (*lǫgrétta*) and over the Althing itself.

In spite of the complex machinery of the law, the Icelandic Commonwealth had no executive arm. There was no one to implement the rulings of courts except the person or persons in whose favour they had been handed down. This meant that in most cases individuals and groups had to resort to violence or some other form of coercion in order to achieve the outcomes the courts said they should have. Although there were forces of moderation active in the society, the lack of executive power in the hands of authority meant that aggression was often the only recourse available to wronged individuals. Eventually, probably in the later twelfth century, as power became concentrated in the hands of five or six ruling families, who dominated large areas of the island, the balance between moderation and aggression was destabilised. These powerful families were able to amalgamate numbers of chieftaincies and raise what amounted to private armies. Political and social instability became characteristic of Icelandic society during the first part of the thirteenth century, the so-called Sturlung Age (named after one of the dominant families, the Sturlungar), and it was thus open to pressures exerted on its members by the then Norwegian king, Hákon

Hákonarson (r. 1217–63), to become a dependency of the Norwegian crown. In becoming a dependency of Norway, Icelandic society gained a different kind of constitution in which a new legal and judicial system was combined with the executive power of the king's representatives in the land.

Religion

Some of the first settlers who had migrated from the Celtic realms were Christians, but the Scandinavian majority were not. They adhered to a polytheistic religion, a Scandinavian version of a system of beliefs that seem to have had much in common throughout the early Germanic world. However, those Viking Age Scandinavians who travelled abroad, and indeed even those who stayed at home, are likely to have learnt something about Christian beliefs from people and Christian sacred objects they came into contact with before the official conversion period. Those who wanted to trade with Christians were supposed to have undergone a form of preliminary baptism, the *prima signatio* or marking with the sign of the cross (Old Norse *primsigning*).

On the whole, conversion to Christianity within Scandinavia was what historians call a top-down process, initiated by those in authority and then gradually accepted by the populace at large. If we can believe medieval Icelandic texts, principally Ari Þorgilsson's 'Book of the Icelanders', the conversion in Iceland took place as a rational decision of the Althing in the year 999 or 1000 and so was somewhat different from the common Scandinavian and medieval European pattern. There has been a great deal of scholarly discussion about the Icelanders' motives for such a move, most recently assessed by Orri Vésteinsson, and in the last decade or so Orri and other, mainly Icelandic, scholars have suggested that the development of the Church in Iceland was a much slower and more gradual process than had previously been thought. However, the conversion to Christianity was not simply a religious phenomenon. Its importance to a study of the Icelandic saga is partly because the Church and the culture it gave access to functioned as agents of change and the means by which a variety of new intellectual influences became available to medieval Icelanders, influences which they were able to combine with traditional, largely orally transmitted forms of expression to create new literary forms. In addition, although runic literacy must have been practised by some Icelanders from the early settlement period, literacy using the Roman alphabet, specially adapted to writing Icelandic, followed the Christian conversion, as did access to manuscript books. These subjects are treated in more detail in Chapters 2 and 3.

Why did medieval Icelanders write so much and so well?

Earlier in this chapter it was mentioned that, by contrast with the amount of written material surviving from other societies of the Norwegian diaspora, or indeed from Swedish and Danish areas as well, Icelandic textual production in the Middle Ages was copious and varied. Since medieval times people have wondered why, beginning with the early thirteenth-century Danish historian Saxo grammaticus, who saluted the Icelanders as the historians of the whole of Scandinavia and suggested that the long dark nights of winter and the barren landscape may have stimulated their literary productivity. The man who wrote the 'Book of Þórðr' (*Þórðarbók*) version of 'The Book of the Land-Takings' gave a different explanation. He recorded that people often say that writing about the settlement of Iceland (*landnám*) is irrelevant learning (*óskyldr fróðleikr*) but that to Icelanders the truth about their ancestry was highly relevant because it enabled them to refute the claims of foreigners that they were descended from slaves or wicked men, and that in any case all wise peoples want to know their origins.[3]

It is still true today that modern colonial and post-colonial societies are exercised about their origins and are frequently measuring themselves, both favourably and unfavourably, both seriously and humorously, against their parent societies. For the Icelanders this motivation must have been very strong, as the unusual nature of their kingless constitution, and perhaps the fact that some of them had actually been the descendants of slaves or relatively poor emigrants, would have made them ultra-sensitive to allegations of the kind the writer of *Þórðarbók* describes. In keeping with that writer's stress upon the importance of ancestry and social origins, a great deal of Icelandic vernacular writing from the medieval period can be connected in some way with the twin topics of genealogy and history. This nexus will be explored further in Chapters 5 and 7.

This kind of explanation for medieval Icelandic textual productivity may help us to understand why Icelanders wrote so much, but it does not account for the great variety of genres they mastered and to a large extent developed independently, nor does it account for the high literary quality of a good deal of what they wrote. Many scholars have argued that the coming together of traditional, orally transmitted literary modes with both the Latin literature of medieval Christendom and vernacular European genres, such as the romance and the chronicle, sourced from France, England and Germany, may have provided the dynamic for medieval Icelandic literary production. Others have pointed to religious genres like the saint's life as the likely stimulus. The

Icelandic scholar Sigurður Nordal, striking a practical note, proposed that a surplus of young calf skins, which had no useful purpose in the Icelandic farming economy, provided a cheap source of vellum. However, it must first be acknowledged that, without a strong textual tradition to start with (and I use the term 'textual' at this point to refer to originally oral genres), it is unlikely that the flowering of medieval Icelandic literature could have taken place. As we shall see in Chapter 2, there is good reason to believe that Icelandic society valued oral textuality particularly strongly across a variety of modes, poetic, legal and narrative. The saga genre, which, as far as the evidence allows us to see, was a predominantly Icelandic development, rests upon a foundation that includes all the traditional modes and some that were probably developed at least to some extent under the influence of non-native genres.

Chapter 2

What is an Old Norse-Icelandic saga?

The term Old Norse

This chapter will define salient terms and set the parameters for our discussion of the Old Norse-Icelandic saga. The first issue to be resolved is the meaning of the term 'Old Norse', which is a peculiar usage of the English-speaking world. Although it may have an old-fashioned ring to it, the term is a handy umbrella to be used when we want to refer to the languages, cultures and societies of Viking Age and medieval Norway and the Norwegian diaspora described in Chapter 1. In linguistic terms Old Norse most frequently refers to the West Scandinavian branch of the Scandinavian languages and their cultures, that is, Norwegian, Icelandic, Faroese, and the now defunct Orkney and Shetland Norn. It may also refer to the East Scandinavian languages and cultures, Swedish and Danish. This linguistic usage corresponds to the definition of the term Old Norse as applied to the whole of the Scandinavian language group in the second edition of *The Oxford English Dictionary*.[1]

One might ask why we need such a term. The answer is that, particularly in the period between the ninth and twelfth centuries, it is often difficult to differentiate textual and material evidence coming from specific parts of the West Scandinavian language and cultural area as belonging to this or that region. Only gradually did the individual languages that became Faroese, Icelandic and Orkney and Shetland Norn differentiate themselves from their parent language, Norwegian. In addition, and importantly, the texts that emerged during this period in written form (although they may in many cases have had oral beginnings) are not always easy to assign to one or the other cultural group. The composition of the two major kinds of poetry, eddic and skaldic,[2] is a case in point. Although a significant proportion of the poetry that has survived in written form has come down to us in Icelandic manuscripts from the thirteenth century and later, there is good reason to suppose that some poems predated the settlement of Iceland in some form or other, particularly if they have analogues in other Germanic languages like Old High German and Old English. Again, we have good reason to believe that the earliest skalds or court poets were Norwegian, but their compositions have mostly been written down in medieval Icelandic manuscripts of considerably later date.

The nub of the issue is that, whereas the major part of the textual evidence for Old Norse culture comes from Icelandic manuscripts, predominantly of the High Middle Ages and later, we know empirically that some forms of textual composition were practised in Norway and the other Norwegian colonies, but written evidence for the latter is not nearly as extensive as for Iceland. In addition, there has been a specific debate about the origins of the literary genre of the saga: was it Norwegian in origin or a genuinely original Icelandic invention?

Inevitably perhaps, feelings of national pride and ownership among both Norwegians and Icelanders coloured the scholarly debates of the nineteenth and earlier twentieth centuries on the subject of Old Norse literature and its ethnic affiliations. By using the term 'Old Norse' those of us who are not Icelandic or Norwegian partly sidestep this debate but risk offending one or other of the parties to it. That is why in recent decades the term 'Old Norse-Icelandic' has come into scholarly use in English.[3] It acknowledges the contribution of the Norwegian cultural base, while highlighting the unique and extensive contribution of Icelanders to Old Norse literature. In what follows, I shall try to give due weight to both the Norwegian and the Icelandic contributions to Old Norse-Icelandic literature, to the extent that the evidence allows, and to use the term 'Old Norse' when I refer to literature or cultural forms that are, or could be, both Norwegian and Icelandic.

What is an Old Norse-Icelandic saga?

The noun 'saga' passed into the English language from Icelandic, almost certainly in the writings of late seventeenth- and early eighteenth-century scholars who had become acquainted with early editions and translations of sagas, often into Latin. The second edition of *The Oxford English Dictionary* gives as its earliest example a passage from the work of George Hickes (1642–1715), the eminent Anglo-Saxonist, in support of a definition of the saga as 'a narration of History', a sentiment which, as we shall see, still holds good at a basic level today. Even the transferred sense of 'saga' in English[4] has a good deal in common with what I shall attempt to delineate here as characterising the Old Norse saga, although it is important to be aware of the differences as well as the similarities between the medieval saga and the modern novel.

It is methodologically appropriate to look first for a definition of the saga in medieval texts themselves, because, properly evaluated, these provide the closest evidence we can access to help us understand what medieval Norwegians and Icelanders meant by the term. Much of this vernacular evidence comes perforce from Icelandic sources, which vastly outnumber those in Norwegian. After that, we can review the internal evidence, from a survey of sagas that have survived, for what characterises a saga in a literary sense, and then proceed to look at modern generic and sub-generic divisions of the Old Norse saga.

Saga in the medieval lexicon

We begin with the etymology of the Old Norse word *saga*, a feminine noun whose nominative plural form is *sǫgur* (*sögur*). *Saga* is closely related to the common verb *segja* 'to say, tell', so its basic sense is 'something said, a tale or story'. Sometimes it may merely be equivalent to 'words', 'what someone says'.[5] From this we can deduce that in cases where the term applies to something more than one or two words or a casual utterance, a saga must have had a narrative form, even if minimal. We can assume further, if we draw on our knowledge of the advent of literacy in medieval Scandinavia (to be discussed in Chapter 3), that, as a literary genre, the saga is likely to have first taken shape as an orally generated and transmitted form which sometimes, but not always, acquired a written existence in later centuries. As a number of sagas that have not survived are mentioned by name in Icelandic written texts, we can be sure that more sagas existed in medieval Scandinavia than have been recorded and transmitted into modern times.

Although the linguistic evidence just reviewed does not strictly permit the following observation, it should be stated here, on the basis of a general knowledge of Old Norse literature, that a saga is not a poem, even though, as we shall see, sagas often contain poetry and some, like certain kings' sagas and sagas of poets, are largely based on poetry. It is important to establish this fundamental definitional divide, because there is plentiful evidence that poetry was the marked, elite form of the traditional Norse verbal arts. There are very many known technical terms for poetry, as well as a myth sourcing the art of poetry from the gods of the old religion, and numerous depictions of poets, their patrons and their poetry in the Old Norse literary record. We may say that the saga may – or may not – contain poetry, but is not defined by it. This means that the saga is not a prosimetrum in the strict sense of a text in which both prose and verse are necessary components. The saga, as a literary form, establishes itself outside the parameters of Old Norse poetics, and that must have been, in both societal and literary terms, a most significant placement, one that almost certainly ensured that its reach was inclusive rather than exclusive in social terms. This last supposition is borne out by what we know, which is admittedly less than we would like to know, about the audience of the Old Norse saga.

It is clear from the medieval lexical record that, even where the word *saga* is being used of a written text, the concept *saga* applies in most cases to more than the material record of a specific body of writing on parchment, except perhaps where reference is being made to a text of foreign, non-Norse origin. For example, Ari Þorgilsson refers to a life of the Anglo-Saxon king St Edmund of East Anglia as a *saga*, probably the Latin life by Abbo of Fleury, in the first chapter of his *Íslendingabók*: 'and that was eight hundred and seventy years after the birth of Christ, according to what is written in his [Edmund's] saga' (*en þat vas sjau tegum [vetra] ens níunda hundraðs eptir burð Krists, at því es ritit es í sǫgu hans*).

Several typical idiomatic usages imply that a saga is more than whatever has been crafted into a particular literary narrative, that there are inchoate elements of a story existing in the cultural memory that can be brought into and taken out of a narrative when and where appropriate. Included among these usages is the notion that a saga character can be introduced into a story as required with little or no literary preparation, a standard formula being 'that man is introduced to the saga, who was called X' (*sá maðr er nefndr til sǫgunnar, er X hét*). Equally, if the story has finished with the character, in the sense that he or she is no longer required for the narrative, saga writers often use the formula 'he/she is now out of the saga' (*hann/hon er nú ór sǫgunni*), and that is the last one hears of the individual. In some cases, a saga writer will comment that a saga narrative splits into two different stories at a certain point,[6] in others, as frequently in *Landnámabók*, that certain events gave rise to specific sagas, which are then named.[7] Even if they are named in written texts, this does not necessarily mean that such sagas existed in written form, although sometimes they clearly did.

To some extent the idea that sagas originated from events generated largely by people obscures or downplays the shaping role of tellers of tales and authors in their creation. Common expressions take such forms as 'from that arose the saga of Hǫrðr son of Grímkell and of Geir' (*þar hefsk [af] saga Harðar Grímkelssonar ok Geirs*) and 'from that arose the saga of the people of Þorskafjörður' (*þar af gørðisk Þorskfirðinga saga*), both citations from *Landnámabók*. Here the middle voice of the verbs *hefja* 'to raise up' and *gøra* 'to make, perform' is used to express the relationship between the genesis of saga narrative and the people whose activities gave rise to them.

Above all else, one gets the strong impression from medieval Icelandic usage that sagas are stories about people, whether about foreigners (e.g. *Trójumanna saga* 'The story of the men of Troy') or kings and other high-ranking Scandinavian leaders (*konunga sǫgur, jarla sǫgur* 'kings' sagas, sagas of jarls'), such as the kings of Norway and jarls of the Orkney Islands, or, most commonly, about named Icelandic families inhabiting a specific region of the island (e.g. *Svarfdœla saga* 'The Saga of the people of Svarfaðardalur'), or individual Icelanders (e.g. *Bjarnar saga Hítdœlakappa* 'The Saga of Bjǫrn, Champion of the Hítdœlir') or their ancestors (e.g. *Ketils saga hœngs* 'The Saga of Ketill Salmon'). Although occasionally the term *saga* is applied to narratives that are not people-focussed,[8] the term tends not to be applied to works of a non-narrative or didactic kind, and this distinction will be discussed further below.

Assuming that the literary conventions of the saga genre arose first in an oral milieu, a subject we shall discuss further in Chapter 3, it is not surprising that the sense of a saga as a text (and oral as well as written texts are intended here) that cannot be entirely dissociated from the events that gave rise to it should be perceptible in medieval Norse usage. However, it is also clear that a saga is not regarded as the same as the events themselves, in that the shaping force of the narrative requires characters to be in or out of the saga, and the narrative, as a quasi-independent entity, to turn in one direction or another and adopt certain points of view.

We know relatively little from medieval sources about the performance of sagas, assuming for the moment that for the most part they were performed orally or read aloud, nor do we have much hard evidence about who performed or created them. Unlike a large proportion of medieval Norse poetry, most sagas are anonymous, and that is another important distinction between sagas and skaldic poetry, where the tradition has preserved the names of many skalds, which probably suggests that the role of a saga author was considered less creative, more compilatory, than that of the poet.[9] A common view is that sagas were performed or read aloud to a general audience on Icelandic farms, but it is clear that some narratives that could be called sagas must have been created and possibly also read in clerical or monastic establishments, at least by the end of the twelfth century. And it is very likely that some sagas were commissioned by important people to celebrate their own or their families' deeds. Certainly, the saga of King Sverrir of Norway (d. 1202) was commissioned, and its Icelandic author, Abbot Karl Jónsson, claimed that the king stood over him while he wrote to make sure the narrative was shaped to suit the king's wishes. Half a century later, another Icelander, Sturla Þórðarson, was commissioned by King Magnús Hákonarson (d. 1280) to write the biography of his father, Hákon Hákonarson (d. 1263).

There is only one medieval Icelandic text that gives a relatively detailed presentation of aspects of a saga performance, including information about the subject matter of the sagas told and identification of the performers themselves, who, in this case, were also said to be the composers of the narratives. This is an account in 'The Saga of Þorgils and Hafliði' (*Þorgils saga ok Hafliða*), reproduced below, of entertainments at a wedding that took place in the year 1119 at the farm of Reykjahólar in the Western Fjords. Some aspects of this text have been much debated, but the information of interest to the present discussion stands largely clear of controversy. The date of composition of the saga itself cannot be precisely determined, but most recent commentators agree that it must have been written before 1250. At least one hundred years, probably more, separated the date of composition of the saga and the date the wedding entertainments took place, so it is probable that information about these entertainments came to the saga writer from local oral tradition.

> There was now noisy merriment and great joy and good entertainment and many kinds of games, both dancing, wrestling and story-telling... Something is told, though it is of little consequence, of who there provided the entertainment and what the entertainment was... Hrólfr from Skálmarnes told a story about Hröngviðr the viking and about Óláfr king of the levy and the mound-breaking of Þráinn the berserk and Hrómundr Gripsson, which included many verses. King Sverrir was entertained with this story, and he called such lying stories the most entertaining; and yet men are able to trace their genealogies to Hrómundr Gripsson. Hrólfr had composed this saga himself. Ingimundr the priest told the story of Ormr Barreyjarskáld including many verses and a good *flokkr*[10] towards the end of the saga, which Ingimundr had composed, and yet many learned men regard this story as true.

Þar var nú glaumr ok gleði mikil ok skemtan góð ok margskonar leikar, bæði dansleikar, glímur ok sagnaskemtan... Frá því er nǫkkut sagt, er þó er lítil tilkoma, hverir þar skemtu eða hverju skemt var... Hrólfr af Skálmarnesi sagði sǫgu frá Hrǫngviði víkingi ok frá Óláfi liðsmannakonungi ok haugbroti Þráins berserks ok Hrómundi Gripssyni, ok margar vísur með. En þessarri sǫgu var skemt Sverri konungi, ok kallaði hann slíkar lygisǫgur skemtiligastar. Ok þó kunnu menn at telja ættir sínar til Hrómundar Gripssonar. Þessa sǫgu hafði Hrólfr sjálfr samansetta. Ingimundr prestr sagði sǫgu Orms Barreyjarskálds ok vísur margar ok flokk góðan við enda sǫgunnar, er Ingimundr hafði ortan, ok hafa þó margir fróðir menn þessa sǫgu fyrir satt.[11]

This unique description has been much studied and contains a good deal of interesting, though to an extent puzzling, information, not least the saga narrator's comment about King Sverrir's opinion that sagas of the kind called *lygisǫgur* 'lying stories' were the most entertaining. As it is clear that this term refers here to what modern scholars call *fornaldarsögur* 'sagas of ancient time' or 'legendary sagas', in this case about stock characters, such as Vikings and berserk warriors, and typical legendary themes like breaking into the burial mounds of famous heroes to steal weapons and treasure, the information indicates that this type of saga must have already existed in the early twelfth century, at least in oral form. By King Sverrir's day, it seems, many sophisticated people, like the king himself, thought of such sagas as fantastic fictions, although there was still a body of opinion that took them at least half-seriously because individuals could trace their genealogies to some of these prehistoric characters.

What is of significance for the question of the character of the Old Norse-Icelandic saga is the information this passage contains about the oral performance of sagas along with other kinds of entertainment like wrestling and dancing, the nature of the sagas' subject-matter, and the identification of specific individuals, Hrólfr from Skálmarnes and Ingimundr the priest, as composers of these sagas. It is not clear from the description given whether the narrator of *Þorgils saga* implied that Hrólfr and Ingimundr narrated their sagas from written texts, although the circumstances of performance suggest otherwise. In a sentence not quoted here, the author of *Þorgils saga* indicates that some people had doubted the truth of his narrative; in this he may have been referring to his claims of individual authorship rather than collective transmission of these oral narratives. However, such claims of individual authorship presumably extended only to the particular version of each saga performed at a specific event like the Reykjahólar wedding and not to the traditional subject-matter of the stories, although in the second case the composition of a *flokkr* towards the end of the saga is said to be Ingimundr's own work, supporting a view held by a number of scholars that a good many of the longer poems within *fornaldarsögur* were not the compositions of prehistoric heroes, as they purport to be in the sagas, but of medieval authors.

Both Hrólfr and Ingimundr are introduced early in the narrative of *Þorgils saga* and characterised as men with special literary gifts. Hrólfr is said to be a 'composer of stories' (*sagnamaðr*), who performed skilfully, while Ingimundr is reportedly 'a great scholar' (*fræðimaðr mikill*) and 'a good poet' (*skáld gott*), whose reputation for composing verse had travelled abroad. Ingimundr was also the host at the Reykjahólar wedding. The passage thus reveals two men from the early twelfth century, one of them a priest, presented by a thirteenth-century saga writer, presumably on oral authority, as conscious shapers of traditional saga material and, at least in Ingimundr's case, composing poetry to insert into the saga of an older poet, Ormr Barreyjarskáld 'Poet from Barra [an island in the Outer Hebrides]', who is presumed to have lived in the tenth or eleventh century. Some fragments of Ormr's poetry are quoted by Snorri Sturluson in his *Edda* 'Poetics' of *c.* 1225. The saga of Ormr, whether as composed by Ingimundr or in some other version, has not survived, and we do not know whether it belonged to the *fornaldarsaga* type or to the sub-class of sagas of Icelanders called poets' sagas (*skáldasögur*), like 'The Saga of Hallfreðr' (*Hallfreðar saga*) or 'The Saga of Gunnlaugr Serpent-tongue' (*Gunnlaugs saga ormstungu*). The rather guarded comment at the end of the passage, that many learned men regarded the story of Ormr as true, suggests that it was more likely to have been a *fornaldarsaga*, as does Ingimundr's composition of a *flokkr* for the concluding section.

How are sagas different from non-sagas?

The composer of *Þorgils saga ok Hafliða*, writing in the first half of the thirteenth century, represented two gifted men of the early twelfth century composing and reciting stories of legendary heroes and a poet from the Viking Age. The term *saga* is applied to both these stories and the context indicates that they had assumed a recognisable textual form and content, which in both cases included verses (*vísur*). Within a decade or two of the Reykjahólar wedding, an anonymous Icelandic scholar was writing a treatise, usually referred to as *The First Grammatical Treatise*, on Icelandic phonology and the system of orthography fairly recently devised for writing Icelandic. In the course of explaining how the new Icelandic alphabet followed the example of the English, using Latin letters and additional symbols where needed, the First Grammarian mentioned that this system would assist people to write and read (*rita ok lesa*) in Iceland just as they do in England. He enumerated various kinds of texts then extant as 'both laws and genealogical knowledge or sacred interpretations or also that wise learning that Ari Þorgilsson has recorded in books from [his] sagacious understanding'.[12]

It is generally believed that the First Grammarian is listing here kinds of texts that had already begun to be written in the Icelandic vernacular in the early twelfth century, but sagas are significantly not among them. It seems probable that the new technology of writing was first applied to kinds of texts that were of practical usefulness to society (the laws and genealogies), were historical (Ari's learning) or were part of the Christian Church's agenda for educating people who could not read or understand Latin in the doctrine and history of Christianity. This last category would have included many priests, who needed to be trained in the fundamentals of the Christian faith, including the Church's standard rituals. We shall see in Chapters 3 and 4 that there is plenty of external evidence to back up the idea that the writing down of sagas in something like the forms we know did not begin until some point in the late twelfth century, but that is not to say that they had not, at least sometimes, assumed a conventionalised oral form already in the early twelfth century and possibly earlier than that, if the evidence about the Reykjahólar wedding in *Þorgils saga* is to be believed.

The kinds of texts listed by the First Grammarian could be called *frœði*, a term that was applied to both traditional lore and learned historical knowledge, such as Ari Þorgilsson possessed and wrote down. There is strong circumstantial evidence to suggest that the extent to which sagas could be considered to be or to contain *frœði* was a grey area in definitional terms, and one that continued to provide an element of uncertainty in Icelandic consciousness throughout the medieval period. This frequently unresolvable ambiguity has also provided the basis for modern debates on the historicity or otherwise of the sagas, a key issue that will be examined further in Chapters 3 and 4. The attribution to King Sverrir of the notion that *lygisǫgur* are the most entertaining, mentioned above, implies that some sectors of society, at least, considered certain kinds of saga as amusing fictions and predominantly works of the imagination, while the qualification that some people could trace their ancestry to the heroes of prehistory suggests that other groups resisted the fictionality even of the *fornaldarsaga*.

If fictionality implicitly differentiated the saga even in its oral form from other kinds of literature that began to be written down in the twelfth century, so too did form and content. Many of the textual kinds attested from the twelfth century, lists of lawspeakers, poets and kings, genealogies in general, even the basic form of works like *Landnámabók*, depend on the strategy of the list, and it is probably not coincidental that the usefulness of lists seems to strike societies particularly when they first adopt the technology of writing, and for obvious reasons. Things for which previously various mnemonic devices needed to be developed in order for the lists to be maintained in the cultural memory could be written down and displayed publicly or privately and consulted by figures of authority. The phenomenon of the centrality of listing to early writing systems has been observed across a number of cultural groups in a variety of geographical locations and is probably a universal testimony to the influence of the technology of writing upon human cognition.

One of the most striking things about the adoption of literacy using the Roman alphabet in Iceland, by contrast with Norway and the rest of Scandinavia, was that it was predominantly, from the beginning, literacy in the vernacular rather than in Latin. While it is understandable that texts like the laws and genealogies should be written in the vernacular, the extent of its use in Icelandic writing of all kinds was unusually high. In this respect, the saga shared a proclivity with other kinds of textual production in Iceland, and the implications of this general inclination to use the vernacular for most kinds of writing will be discussed further in Chapter 3. Vernacularity is a phenomenon that distinguishes medieval Icelandic from medieval Norwegian writing to a large extent, as well as from medieval Swedish and Danish. Although some vernacular Norwegian texts from the Middle Ages exist, they are relatively few by comparison with the output of vernacular writing from Iceland, and relatively few of them, except for histories and romances, can be classified as sagas. Norwegian vernacular texts include laws, histories, political pamphlets, didactic works of various kinds including homilies, saints' lives and translated romances (*riddarasögur* 'sagas of knights'), mostly of French or Anglo-Norman origin. It is generally believed that this translation programme was undertaken at the court of King Hákon Hákonarson in the first half of the thirteenth century, although most *riddarasögur* now exist only in Icelandic versions from the fifteenth century and later.

Some of the earliest histories of the kings of Norway, from the late twelfth or early thirteenth centuries, were written in Latin, not the vernacular, but it did not take long for the vernacular trend even in historiography to assert itself, especially in Iceland. There are several early Norwegian histories in Latin, notably the monk Theodoricus's 'Ancient History of the Norwegian Kings' (*Historia de Antiquitate Regum Norwagiensium c.* 1180) and the 'History of Norway' (*Historia Norwegiae c.* 1211). An early vernacular history is the 'Summary of the Sagas of the Kings of Norway' (*Ágrip af Nóregs konunga sǫgum*). *Ágrip* now exists only in an Icelandic manuscript of *c.* 1230, but it is generally thought to have been written originally by a Norwegian before 1200. The oldest saga of King Óláfr Tryggvason by the monk Oddr Snorrason of the monastery of Þingeyrar in northern Iceland was composed in Latin *c.* 1190, but is now only preserved in three different redactions of an Icelandic translation, all from after 1250.

To return to the definitional question with which we began this chapter, we have so far reached the conclusion from the available lexical and textual evidence that the Old Norse-Icelandic saga was a textual form that was primarily a narrative in the vernacular, probably taking formal shape (though not necessarily invariant formal shape) in oral transmission by at least the early twelfth century; it was about people, mostly Norse people, and their doings, whether these were individuals or groups; it often contained poetry, some of which could sometimes be invented by the composer of the saga, whose name was only rarely transmitted alongside the saga itself; it occupied a grey area between fact and fiction, springing in variable part from known events, but it was also shaped by the creating imagination of its composers. The relationship between any saga and the events and persons that gave it grounds for being was fluid. For the most part it was orally performed and had a high entertainment value.

The view from inside the text

A study of indigenous medieval terminology can only go so far in helping us to establish the saga's nature. Some of its characteristics emerge only from an internal analysis of saga texts, which can be contrasted with non-saga texts of approximately the same age to reveal many of the salient traits of saga writing, all of which will be explored in much greater detail in the following chapters. Here some of those defining characteristics are established by comparing and contrasting passages from a late twelfth-century historical work, the monk Theodoricus's *Historia de Antiquitate Regum Norwagiensium* 'Ancient History of the Norwegian Kings' with a passage from *Egils saga Skallagrímssonar* 'The Saga of Egill, son of Skallagrímr'. While Theodoricus's *Historia* was written in Latin, and thus stands outside the saga tradition on that ground alone, it has other features that characterise medieval historiography but that are not normally found in saga texts. *Egils saga* has been chosen here for comparison because it is one of only a very few sagas that can be proved to have had some kind of written existence before 1250. Unfortunately, that evidence is provided by a very small manuscript fragment of the text (AM 162 A θ fol of *c.* 1250), so the passage examined here, like most of the saga, is attested only from manuscripts of the fourteenth century and later. The fact that most Norse sagas are extant in manuscripts substantially later than their probable date of composition needs to be borne in mind at all times when discussing sagas (see further Chapters 4 and 8).

> There [in Upplönd] he [King Óláfr Tryggvason] came upon Óláfr [St Óláfr Haraldsson], who was then a little boy of three, but who later became a faithful martyr of Christ. He was staying with his mother Ásta, for his father Haraldr was then already dead. (Haraldr was the son of Guðrøðr sýr, whose father was Bjǫrn, who was nicknamed 'the trader' and was the son of Haraldr Fair-hair.) That Óláfr was the future propitious hope and glory of the Norwegian people. According to some, the king had him and his mother baptised then and there; others maintain that he was baptized in England. But I, for my part, have read in the 'History of the Normans' that he was baptized in Normandy by Robert, archbishop of Rouen.

> Ibique tunc puerulum Olavum trium annorum, qui postea devotus Christi martyr factus est, invenit cum matre Asta, patre iam defuncto Haraldo (hic fuit filius Goðroðar syr, cui extitit pater Berno, qui cognominatus est mercator et fuit filius Haraldi bene-comati), felicem spem et decus Norwagiensium futurum. Tunc et eum una cum matre ibidem secundum quosdam baptizari fecit; alii contendunt eum in Anglia baptizatum; sed et ego legi in Historia Normannorum, quod a Roberto in Normandia Rothomagensi metropolitano baptizatus fuerit.
>
> Theodoricus monachus, *Historia de Antiquitate Regum Norwagiensium*, Chapter 13[13]

> It is said that Úlfr was a skilled farmer; it was his custom to get up early in the day and then go about overseeing men's work or [to] where craftsmen were and take stock of his animals and fields, and sometimes he was in conversation with those men who needed his advice; he was able to proffer good advice on all matters, because he was very wise. But every day when evening drew near he became withdrawn so that few men could exchange words with him; he was evening-sleepy < and morning-wakeful>. It was the talk of men that he was very 'shape-powerful';[14] he was called Kveld-Úlfr 'Evening-Wolf'.

> Svá er sagt at Úlfr var búsýslumaðr mikill; var þat siðr hans at rísa upp árdegis ok ganga þá um sýslur manna eða þar er smiðir váru ok sjá yfir fénað sinn ok akra, en stundum var hann á tali við menn þá er ráða hans þurftu; kunni hann til alls góð ráð at leggja, því at hann var forvitri. En

dag hvern er at kveldi leið þá gerðisk hann styggr svá at fáir menn máttu orðum við hann koma; var hann kveldsvæfr <ok myrginvakr>. Þat var mál manna at hann væri mjǫk hamrammr; hann var kallaðr Kveld-Úlfr.[15]

Egils saga Skallagrímssonar, Chapter 1

These two passages have some things in common; each is a narrative focussed on individual human beings, in one case the future King Óláfr Haraldsson of Norway, who was to become one of the most important saints for the whole of Scandinavia, and in the other, Kveld-Úlfr, paternal grandfather of Egill Skallagrímsson, the main character in the saga named after him. However, it is immediately apparent that the character portrait of Kveld-Úlfr is much rounder than that of Óláfr. Both passages also display a keen interest in nicknames, a common concern of saga literature, and the *Historia* also shows an interest in genealogy. If a different passage from *Egils saga* had been chosen, it would have been easy to demonstrate an interest in genealogy there too, for this subject is undoubtedly a pervasive concern of saga literature and an important 'cement' in the establishment of personal relations between characters and many kinds of motivation, that were dependent on kinship relations, as we have seen in Chapter 1.

While it is true that each passage can be classified as a narrative broadly speaking, only part of the *Historia* extract is centrally so, namely the first part describing how King Óláfr Tryggvason came upon the 3-year-old Óláfr Haraldsson in Upplǫnd living with his mother. The proportion of authorial comment and reflection in the *Historia* is both greater and more overt than that in *Egils saga*, and this difference between standard medieval historiography and saga writing in regard to the overtness with which their respective composers articulate point of view is perhaps the single most significant compositional feature that sets saga literature apart from most other medieval texts, except perhaps some forms of annalistic writing. In the past, saga commentators have sometimes been misled by the flat, indirect narratorial positioning into thinking that sagas do not often articulate point of view, but many studies of the second half of the twentieth century have demonstrated the contrary.

It is quite uncommon in saga writing to construct clauses like 'who later became a faithful martyr of Christ' or 'That Óláfr was the future propitious hope and glory of the Norwegian people.' These are meant to signal to Theodoricus's audience his awareness of the many stories about the sanctity and miracles of St Óláfr that sprang up in Norway, both in Latin and the vernacular, not long after the king's death in 1030. They also signal the status of those stories, which pushed Óláfr into becoming a national saint for Norway. Indeed, his cult was also widely celebrated in other parts of Scandinavia, including Iceland. By contrast, the composer of *Egils saga* sets about establishing the credentials of Kveld-Úlfr in a way that suggests that they were common knowledge and available to him by report. He uses the introductory formula '[so] it is said' (*svá er sagt*) in order to present a value-judgement about Úlfr, that he was a skilled farmer and a good manager of men and property, as if it were merely an observation of common report. But in fact the character portrait of Úlfr is laden with positive ethical values that would have been shared by a medieval Icelandic audience: that it is a good thing for a man to get up early, be an efficient farm manager and have good rapport with his workmen. The narrator goes on to expand on this laudatory description by explaining that Úlfr was able to give good advice to others because he was very wise. This is not presented as the narrator's own view; rather, it is stated as a matter of fact. Further, without offering any opinion, or explaining that Úlfr had another, very different side to his personality, the narrative continues immediately to present Úlfr's werewolf-like transformation in the evenings as something that people also reported: 'it was the talk of men' (*þat var mál manna*).

It is not argued here that the presence of stylistic features such as those described above must be attributed specifically to an oral origin for the saga in its inchoate state. Its inchoate state is unknowable. What is argued here is that these features in the texts we now know send a message to their audience or readers that they are based on common knowledge and report and are not the views of a specific narrator.

Although saga narrators sometimes use more obtrusive means of shaping their narratives' point of view, the self-effacing impersonal stance illustrated here from *Egils saga* is by far the most common and contrasts markedly with the often tendentious, highly personalised stance of a large number of medieval European historians writing in Latin. In many cases, as with Theodoricus, these writers were clergymen, often monks. The unstated moral perspective from which these histories present their judgements is always that of the Christian Church and the Christian view of world history, from the Biblical creation to the present and future time, culminating for each soul in the Last Judgement and the pleasures of Heaven or the pains of Hell. In Chapter 5 the question of how a Christian view of history mapped onto an indigenous Norse historical and geographical world-view will be seen as fundamental to an understanding of saga sub-genres and saga subjects.

One other difference between the *Historia* and *Egils saga* passages requires comment. In the *Historia*, though not in *Egils saga*, the author bolsters his own opinion of where Óláfr Haraldsson was baptised by citing a written source, in this case William of Jumièges' 'Acts of the Dukes of the Normans' (*Gesta*

Normannorum Ducum).[16] While it is true that some sagas of Icelanders cite their sources (*Laxdœla saga*, for example, cites several that probably already had a written existence at the time of its composition) and many kings' sagas quote poetry to back up their narratives, for the most part sagas do not refer to written texts or are very sparing in their usage, even where it is quite likely that written sources had been influential in providing some of their subject matter. The relative scarcity of intertextual references to written (as opposed to oral) sources in saga literature gives the impression, whether true or not, that the subject matter, the physical setting, and the characters and their actions all derive from the lived experiences of early Norse society.

Theodoricus, like many medieval historians writing in Latin, also uses another kind of intertextuality which is not exemplified in the passage quoted above. This is the frequent quotation of Latin texts, usually by classical or early Christian poets and prose writers, particularly those prominent in the medieval school curriculum, or allusions to their works. It is likely, as we shall discuss further in Chapter 3, that this practice influenced early saga writers, especially writers of historical sagas, to introduce the poetry of their vernacular *auctores*, the skalds, into their sagas. This seems to have begun very early in the development of the saga, as Heather O'Donoghue has demonstrated in connection with *Ágrip*'s use of vernacular poetry.

Finally, another difference between the Norse saga and medieval historiography, which is also not demonstrated by the two passages quoted here, is the presence of both impersonal narrative and direct discourse in sagas. The direct discourse usually takes the form of dialogue between saga characters, although sometimes, particularly in kings' sagas, there are set speeches and orations. For many modern readers for whom sagas are a new experience, the often sudden slide from indirect to direct discourse and back again without warning is slightly unnerving, although one soon gets used to it. Additionally, the text may switch from present to past tenses of verbs and back again, also without warning. One can explain the tense-switching to some extent as giving immediacy to the narrative, but this cannot be the whole story. Rather, both features must have been selected, consciously or unconsciously, to maintain the stylistic impression of an orally based discourse, even after it had ceased to be so.

Kinds of sagas

So far, this chapter has been concerned to describe the salient features that are distinctive to the medieval Norse saga without indicating what sagas are about, except that they are about people, mostly Scandinavian people, and their doings. Describing what sagas are about necessarily entails discussing the different kinds of sagas that exist, and this in turn brings us to the question of classification, because there are sub-groups within the saga genre that have usually been identified by particular generic labels, both medieval and modern. However, as I shall argue in Chapter 6, the saga is a modally mixed literary form, and individual sagas cannot always be cleanly slotted into this or that sub-group, but may display characteristics of more than one.

Most of the terms used both by medieval writers and modern scholars to refer to kinds of sagas are based upon the nature of their subject-matter, although this is not always true of the medieval terminology, which will be discussed first. We have medieval written evidence for the sub-generic terms *konungasǫgur* 'sagas of kings' and *jarlasǫgur* 'sagas of jarls', the latter referring to sagas of the Jarls of Orkney and the former to sagas of the kings of Norway.[17] As mentioned earlier in this chapter, we also know the term *lygisǫgur* 'lying sagas', which is used in *Þorgils saga ok Hafliða* to refer to one of the sagas told at the Reykjahólar wedding in 1119, stories about Vikings and berserks and activities like breaking into burial mounds, probably to recover treasures or heirlooms of some kind, to judge from extant sagas in which such motifs appear. *Lygisǫgur* are most plausibly identified with what modern scholars call *fornaldarsögur*, a term translated variously into English as 'sagas of ancient time' or 'mythical-heroic sagas' or 'legendary sagas'.

The modern term is probably a development from the title given to an edition of this kind of saga made by Carl Christian Rafn in the early nineteenth century, *Fornaldar sögur Nordrlanda*, and emphasises the fact that these sagas are set in a prehistoric age. The medieval term *lygisǫgur*, by contrast, refers to a quite different property of these sagas, their relative lack of historicity, which, though entertaining, implicitly verges on the mendacious. A further inference is that these sagas deviate from a desired verisimilitude of saga composition, at least as an ideal, which tells a plain unvarnished tale about people and events of the past. Another term that is similar to *lygisaga*, though probably slightly less pejorative, is *skrǫksaga* 'fictitious story', a term sometimes used to translate the Latin *fabula* 'fable, fictitious narrative'. Although the textual evidence does not allow us to say for sure how widely used terms like *lygisaga* and *skrǫksaga* were, their presence in the medieval record betrays a cultural sensitivity about the status of fictionality, a sensitivity that, while being comparable to general medieval ideas on that subject, is probably more pronounced.

Yet another medieval term deserving of consideration here occurs in the words *stjúpmœðra sǫgur er hjarðarsveinar segja* 'sagas of stepmothers that shepherd boys tell'. The phrase *stjúpmœðra sǫgur* is employed in the prologue to the Icelandic translation of a work originally written in Latin, the monk Oddr Snorrason's 'Saga of Óláfr Tryggvason' (*Óláfs saga Tryggvasonar*).[18] Although the word *sǫgur* is used here, Oddr probably meant by it 'tales' rather than 'sagas'. It is unlikely that *stjúpmœðra sǫgur* refers to a sub-genre of the saga; rather, it is probably a derogatory reference to certain kinds of popular stories of the sort likely to be told by women and lower-class people, the kind who are represented often enough in saga literature as conveying tittle-tattle, rumour and superstition. Oddr's objection to this kind of story is that it belongs to the lower classes (he mentions shepherd boys telling the tales), its veracity cannot be established and it does not obey the rules of saga structure by ensuring that important people (in his case, King Óláfr Tryggvason of Norway) are central characters in the narrative. Thus, although *stjúpmœðra sǫgur* may not be a sub-class of the saga, Oddr's mention of the term and his discussion of what he considered wrong with such stories throws light on some of the characteristics of the saga genre that we have already established.

Modern saga classification is based on the criteria of either subject-matter or chronology. It is now customary for a distinction to be drawn between kings' sagas, a term already used in the Middle Ages, and *Íslendingasögur* 'sagas of Icelanders', a sub-genre which is often termed 'family sagas' in English, as this group deals largely with the doings of Icelandic families during the period from the settlement of the island until the time of the Icelanders' conversion to Christianity *c.* 1000, or slightly afterwards. This group of sagas is the best-known today of all saga sub-genres, although, as we shall see in Chapter 9, this was not the case during the seventeenth, eighteenth and early nineteenth centuries, when historical and legendary sagas were far more popular. It is also interesting that this sub-genre appears to have been unnamed, as a genre, in the medieval period, when reference was often made to the subjects of individual sagas of this group, like *Bandamanna saga* 'Saga of the Confederates' or *Laxdæla saga*, but not to the group itself. Modern scholars also distinguish another sub-group that deals with Icelanders and their activities on a chronological basis. The *samtíðarsögur* or 'Contemporary sagas' are so-called because they deal with persons and events that are near contemporary with the age of the saga writers themselves. Most *samtíðarsögur* were written in the thirteenth century (although they were subject to later revision) and engage with persons and events of the recent past in Iceland. The most significant saga writer of this sub-genre, Sturla Þórðarson (1214–84), was himself a participant in or at least an onlooker on many of the events he writes about in his 'Saga of the Icelanders' (*Íslendinga saga*).

Chronology is also the basis for the term *fornaldarsaga*, which has already been discussed. Considered as both a chronological and an ethnically focussed group of narratives, *fornaldarsögur* deal with the persons and events of prehistory in Scandinavia, which can be expressed more precisely as the time before Iceland was settled (i.e. before *c.* 870). The *Íslendingasögur* deal with events and persons from the Settlement Age up to and slightly later than the conversion to Christianity, while *samtíðarsögur* concern events of the twelfth and particularly the thirteenth centuries, up to the end of the Commonwealth period in 1262–4, at which point Iceland became part of Norwegian polity. These three saga sub-genres display a predominantly Icelandic perspective on time, history, persons and events, and they have no counterpart in the Norwegian literary record, whereas, as we have already seen, kings' sagas probably arose in a Norwegian-influenced milieu, and in the context of historical writings and miracle stories about Norwegian kings in both Latin and the vernacular, supported by the availability of skaldic verse by both Norwegian and Icelandic poets.

Several sub-groups of the saga deal largely with subject-matter of foreign origin. These include *riddarasögur* 'sagas of knights', derived originally from translations of French and Anglo-Norman romances made for the court of the Norwegian king Hákon Hákonarson (r. 1217–63) but later translated into Icelandic; romances with indigenous subjects; saints' lives (*heilagra manna sögur* 'sagas of holy men'), mainly of foreign saints, but including some important lives of Icelandic bishops for whom sanctity was claimed, versions of the life and miracles of the Virgin Mary (*Maríu saga*) and other hagiographical subjects, most of them based on foreign sources, in both Latin and vernacular European languages. In many cases these works appear to have been translated first into Norwegian and later into Icelandic. The extent to which translations from foreign narrative sources have been converted to the indigenous saga style and presentation is variable, but in most cases some recognisable modification of the foreign original has taken place.

Some scholars, like Kurt Schier in his excellent German study of the sagas (*Sagaliteratur*, pp. 5–6) have made a division between saga literature in a narrow sense and a broader definition. In the former category Schier included kings' sagas, sagas of Icelanders, sagas of ancient time, contemporary sagas and sagas of native bishops. In the latter category he placed sagas of knights (*riddarasögur*), indigenous romances (*lygisögur*, German *Märchensagas*), saints' lives and historical or pseudo-historical translations. In the present book a more, rather than a less, inclusive definition has been preferred because, although there is variability between the categories in terms of what has been defined in this chapter as characteristic of the Old Norse-Icelandic saga, even romances and saints' lives share some of the key qualities of the Norse saga in attenuated form.

Table 2. Sub-groups of the Old Norse-Icelandic saga

Fornaldarsögur 'Sagas of ancient time' or 'mythical-heroic sagas'
Áns saga bogsveigis 'The Saga of Án Bow-bender'
Ásmundar saga kappabana 'The Saga of Ásmundr the Champion-slayer'
Bósa saga ok Herrauðs 'The Saga of Bósi and Herrauðr'
Egils saga einhenda ok Ásmundar berserkjabana 'The Saga of One-armed Egill and Ásmundr the Berserk-slayer'
Friðþjófs saga ins frœkna 'The Saga of Friðþjófr the Bold'
Gautreks saga ok Gjafa-Refs 'The Saga of Gautrekr and Gift-Refr'
Gríms saga loðinkinna 'The Saga of Grímr Hairy-cheek'
Gǫngu-Hrólfs saga 'The Saga of Hrólfr the Stamper'
Hálfdanar saga Brǫnufóstra 'The Saga of Hálfdan, foster-son of Brana'
Hálfdanar saga Eysteinssonar 'The Saga of Hálfdan, son of Eysteinn'
Hálfs saga ok Hálfsrekka 'The Saga of Hálfr and the Hálfr champions'
Hervarar saga ok Heiðreks 'The Saga of Hervǫr and Heiðrekr'
Hjálmþés saga ok Ǫlvis 'The Saga of Hjálmþér and Ǫlvir'
Hrólfs saga Gautrekssonar 'The Saga of Hrólfr son of Gautrekr'
Hrólfs saga kraka 'The Saga of Hrólfr Pole-ladder'
Hrómundar saga Gripssonar 'The Saga of Hrómundr Gripsson' – in present form, dates from seventeenth century
Illuga saga Gríðarfóstra 'The Saga of Illugi, foster-son of Gríðr'
Ketils saga hœngs 'The Saga of Ketill Salmon'
Ragnars saga loðbrókar 'The Saga of Ragnarr Hairy-breeches'
Sturlaugs saga starfsama 'The Saga of Sturlaugr the Industrious'
Sǫrla saga sterka 'The Saga of Sǫrli the Strong'
Vǫlsunga saga 'The Saga of the Volsungs'
Yngvars saga víðfǫrla 'The Saga of Yngvarr the Widely travelled'
Þorsteins saga Víkingssonar 'The Saga of Þorsteinn, son of Víkingr'
Ǫrvar-Odds saga 'The Saga of Arrow-Oddr'

Riddarasögur 'Sagas of knights' – translated
Bevers saga 'The Saga of Bevis' – translated from lost version of Anglo-Norman *Bœve de Haumtone*
Clári saga 'The Saga of Clárus' – possibly translated from unknown Latin source, possibly an original composition
Elis saga ok Rósamundu 'The Saga of Elis and Rósamunda' – adapted from Old French *Elie de Saint Gille*
Erex saga 'The Saga of Erex' – prose version of Chrétien de Troyes' *Erec et Enide*

(*cont.*)

Table 2. (cont.)

Flóres saga ok Blankiflúr 'The Saga of Flóres and Blankiflúr' – from Old
  French romance *Floire et Blancheflor*
Flóvents saga Frakkakonungs 'The Saga of Flóvent, king of the Franks' –
  possibly adaptation of lost French source
Ívens saga 'The Saga of Íven' – prose version of Chrétien de Troyes' *Yvain* or
  Le chevalier au lion
Karlamagnús saga 'The Saga of Charlemagne' – sourced from various
  chansons de geste
Mǫttuls saga 'The Saga of the Mantle' – translation of Old French *fabliau Le
  lai du cort mantel*
Parcevals saga 'The Saga of Parceval' – prose version of Chrétien de Troyes'
  Perceval, ou Le Conte du Graal
Partalopa saga 'The Saga of Partalopi' – source possibly a French version of
  story of Partenopeus of Blois
Strengleikar 'Stringed Instruments (Lays)' – includes some *lais* ascribed to
  Marie de France
Tristrams saga ok Ísǫndar 'The Saga of Tristram and Isǫnd' – translated from
  the *Tristram* of Thomas of Britain by 'Brother Robert' at the behest of
  Norwegian King Hákon Hákonarson

Riddarasögur 'Sagas of knights' – indigenous
Adonias saga 'The Saga of Adonias'
Ála flekks saga 'The Saga of Spotted Áli'
Bærings saga 'The Saga of Bæringr'
Dámusta saga 'The Saga of Dámusti'
Dínus saga dramblátа 'The Saga of Dínus the Haughty'
Drauma-Jóns saga 'The Saga of Dreamer-Jón'
Ectors saga ok kappa hans 'The Saga of Hector and his Champions'
Flóres saga konungs ok sona hans 'The Saga of King Flóres and his sons'
Gibbons saga 'The Saga of Gibbon'
Hrings saga ok Tryggva 'The Saga of Hringr and Tryggvi'
Jarlmanns saga ok Hermanns 'The Saga of Jarlmann and Hermann'
Jóns saga leikara 'The Saga of Jón the Player'
Kirialax saga 'The Saga of Kirialax'
Konráðs saga keisarasonar 'The Saga of Konráðr, the Emperor's son'
Mágus saga jarls 'The Saga of Jarl Mágus'
Mírmanns saga 'The Saga of Mírmann'
Nitida saga 'The Saga of Nitida'
Rémundar saga keisarasonar 'The Saga of Rémundr, the Emperor's son'

(cont.)

Table 2. (*cont.*)

Samsons saga fagra 'The Saga of Samson the Handsome'
Saulus saga ok Nikanors 'The Saga of Saulus and Nikanor'
Sigrgarðs saga frœkna 'The Saga of Sigrgarðr the Brave'
Sigrgarðs saga ok Valbrands 'The Saga of Sigrgarðr and Valbrandr'
Sigurðar saga fóts ok Ásmundar húnakongs 'The Saga of Sigurðr Foot and
   Ásmundr King of the Huns'
Sigurðar saga turnara 'The Saga of Sigurðr the Jouster'
Sigurðar saga þǫgla 'The Saga of Sigurðr the Silent'
Tristrams saga ok Ísoddar 'The Saga of Tristram and Ísodd'
Valdimars saga 'The Saga of Valdimar'
Viktors saga ok Blávus 'The Saga of Victor and Blávus'
Vilhjálms saga sjóðs 'The Saga of Vilhjálmr of Sjóðr(?)'
Vilmundar saga viðutan 'The Saga of Vilmundr the Outsider'
Þjalar-Jóns saga 'The Saga of File-Jón'

**Konungasǫgur 'Kings' sagas' and other historical sagas (including
   compilations)**
Ágrip af Nóregs konunga sǫgum 'Summary of the sagas of the kings of Norway'
Bǫglunga sǫgur 'The Sagas of the Baglar'- compilation of events in reigns of
   Birkibeinar and Baglar kings of Norway
Fagrskinna 'Fair vellum' – compilation of lives of kings of Norway, possibly of
   Norwegian origin
Flateyjarbók 'Book of Flatey' – compilation, includes both historical and
   other texts
Fœreyinga saga 'The Saga of the Faroe Islanders'
Hákonar saga Hákonarsonar 'The Saga of King Hákon Hákonarson' – written
   by Sturla Þórðarson d. 1284
Heimskringla 'Circle of the World' – contains biographies of kings of Norway,
   probably written by Snorri Sturluson d. 1241
Hulda-Hrokkinskinna 'Secret and Wrinkled vellum' – compilation containing
   sagas of kings of Norway
Jómsvíkinga saga 'The Saga of the Jómsvíkingar' – legendary history of Viking
   band in Denmark and Norway
Knýtlinga saga 'The Saga of the descendants of Knútr' – Icelandic compilation
   of lives of kings of Denmark
Óláfs saga helga 'The Legendary Saga of St Óláfr' (Óláfr Haraldsson) –
   contains a great deal of hagiographical material
Magnúss saga lagabœtis 'The Saga of King Magnús the Lawmender' –
   fragments only extant, written by Sturla Þórðarson d. 1284

(*cont.*)

Table 2. (*cont.*)

Morkinskinna 'Rotten vellum' – compilation containing lives of kings of
   Norway and many *þættir*
Óláfs saga Tryggvasonar 'The Saga of King Óláfr Tryggvason' – composed by
   Oddr Snorrason c. 1190, extant as Icelandic translation of lost Latin
   original
Oldest saga of St Óláfr – extant only in fragments
Orkneyinga saga 'The Saga of the Orkney Islanders'
Separate saga of St Óláfr – by Snorri Sturluson, later incorporated into
   Heimskringla
* *Skjǫldunga saga* 'The Saga of the Skjǫldungar (prehistoric Danish kings) –
   extant only in Latin summary from late sixteenth century.
Sverris saga 'The Saga of King Sverrir Sigurðarson' – written at least in part by
   Abbot Karl Jónsson d. 1212/13

Íslendingasögur 'Sagas of Icelanders' ('Family sagas')
Bandamanna saga 'The Saga of the Confederates'
Bárðar saga Snæfellsáss 'The Saga of Bárðr, Snæfell-deity'
Bjarnar saga Hítdœlakappa 'The Saga of Bjǫrn Champion of the Hítdœlir'
Droplaugarsona saga 'The Saga of the sons of Droplaug'
Egils saga Skallagrímssonar 'The Saga of Egill Skallagrímsson'
Eiríks saga rauða 'The Saga of Eiríkr the Red'
Eyrbyggja saga 'The Saga of the inhabitants of Eyrr'
Finnboga saga ramma 'The Saga of Finnbogi the Strong'
Fljótsdœla saga 'The Saga of the people of Fljótsdalur'
Flóamanna saga 'The Saga of the men of Flói'
Fóstbrœðra saga 'The Saga of the Foster-brothers'
Gísla saga Súrssonar 'The Saga of Gísli Súrsson'
Grettis saga Ásmundarsonar 'The Saga of Grettir Ásmundarson'
Grœnlendinga saga 'The Saga of the Greenlanders'
Gull-Þóris saga (also known as *Þorskfirðinga saga*) 'The Saga of Gold-Þórir' or
   'The Saga of the people of Þorskafjörður'
Gunnlaugs saga ormstungu 'The Saga of Gunnlaugr Serpent-tongue'
Hallfreðar saga vandræðaskálds 'The Saga of Hallfreðr Troublesome-poet'
Harðar saga Grímkelssonar 'The Saga of Hǫrðr Grímkelsson'
Hávarðar saga Ísfirðings 'The Saga of Hávarðr from Ísafjörður'
Heiðarvíga saga 'The Saga of the Killings on the Heath' – Chapters 1–15
   reconstructed from notes made in eighteenth century
Hrafnkels saga Freysgoða 'The Saga of Hrafnkell priest of Freyr'
Hœnsa-Þóris saga 'The Saga of Hen-Þórir'

(*cont.*)

Table 2. (*cont.*)

Kjalnesinga saga 'The Saga of the people of Kjalarnes'

—*Kormáks saga Qgmundarsonar* 'The Saga of Kormákr Qgmundarson'

Króka-Refs saga 'The Saga of Refr the Sly'

— *Laxdœla saga* 'The Saga of the people of Salmon River Valley'

Ljósvetninga saga 'The Saga of the Ljósvetningar'

— *Njáls saga* (also known as *Brennu-Njáls saga*) 'The Saga of Njáll' or 'The Saga of Burnt-Njáll'

Reykdœla saga ok Víga-Skútu 'The Saga of the people of Reykjadalur and of Killer-Skúta'

Svarfdœla saga 'The Saga of the people of Svarfaðardalur'

Valla-Ljóts saga 'The Saga of Ljótr of Vellir'

—*Vápnfirðinga saga* 'The Saga of the people of Vopnafjörður'

—*Vatnsdœla saga* 'The Saga of the people of Vatnsdalur'

Víga-Glúms saga 'The Saga of Killer-Glúmr'

— *Víglundar saga* 'The Saga of Víglundr'

Þórðar saga hreðu 'The Saga of Þórðr the Menace'

Samtíðarsögur 'Contemporary sagas' a: *Sturlunga sögur* 'Sagas of the Sturlungs'

Arons saga Hjǫrleifssonar 'The Saga of Aron Hjǫrleifsson' – not in Sturlunga compilation, but treats related subjects

Guðmundar saga góða (*Prestssaga*) 'The Saga of Guðmundr the Good (Priest's saga)' – see under Bishops' sagas (below); oldest biography of Bishop Guðmundr

Guðmundar saga dýra 'The Saga of Guðmundr the Worthy'

Hrafns saga Sveinbjarnarsonar 'The Saga of Hrafn Sveinbjarnarson' – preserved in part in Sturlunga compilation, partly independently

Íslendinga saga 'The Saga of the Icelanders' – composed by Sturla Þórðarson d. 1284; the largest part of the Sturlunga compilation

Sturlu saga 'The Saga of Sturla [Þórðarson]'

Svínfellinga saga 'The Saga of the Svínfellingar'

Þórðar saga kakala 'The Saga of Þórðr Clay Pot'

Þorgils saga ok Hafliða 'The Saga of Þorgils and Hafliði'

Þorgils saga skarða 'The Saga of Þorgils Hare-lip'

Samtíðarsögur 'Contemporary sagas' b: *Biskupa sögur* '[Icelandic] bishops' sagas'

Árna saga biskups 'The Saga of Bishop Árni [Þorláksson]'

(*cont.*)

Table 2. (cont.)

Guðmundar saga góða 'The Saga of Guðmundr the Good' – extant in four
different versions, A–D
Jóns saga helga 'The Saga of St Jón [Qgmundarson]'
Laurentius saga biskups 'The Saga of Bishop Laurentius [Kálfsson]'
Páls saga biskups 'The Saga of Bishop Páll [Jónsson]'
Þorláks saga helga 'The Saga of St Þorlakr [Þórhallsson]'

One other indigenous medieval Icelandic literary genre that is distinct from
the saga, although often found in conjunction with it in medieval manuscripts,
is the *þáttr* (pl. *þættir*), a short prose tale with a frequently rather stereotyped
plot, in which young, male Icelanders travel abroad, usually to the court of a
Norwegian king, and gain renown or material rewards for their exploits under
duress, which often include composing poetry in praise of the king, finally
returning to Iceland, having gained honour or material success or both. The
noun *þáttr* in its literal sense means a single strand of a rope, so, transferred to
literature, it conveys the notion that a *þáttr* is part of a larger narrative whole.
It can be used of a particular section of the Icelandic legal code, for example,
and, in the case of the *þættir* mentioned above, is often found conjoined to
or inserted into historical compilations concerning the kings of Norway, like
Morkinskinna 'Rotten vellum' and *Flateyjarbók* 'The Book of Flatey'.

This chapter concludes with a table of the approximately 140 sagas known
to exist (Table 2), divided into sections corresponding to the various major
sub-groups described here. It is arranged with an eye to the sub-generic affinities implicit in the sagas themselves, as will be discussed in Chapter 5. In each
section, known members of a sub-group, excluding *þættir*, are listed alphabetically, and with occasional annotations. I have refrained from attempting a
chronological listing of these sagas according to modern views of their dates of
composition, because, as we shall see in Chapter 4, there is still a great deal of
uncertainty surrounding issues of chronology, and a great deal of subjectivity
involved in some of the arguments that have been used to support a chronological order of composition, even within a particular sub-grouping. The dividing
lines between the sub-groups are not always firm, and there are some sagas
that have been classified by scholars in more than one sub-group. Table 2 does
not include vernacular works, like *Landnámabók*, that are not sagas, nor does
it cover saints' lives, which are outside the scope of this book, nor works that
are believed to have existed but have not survived into modern times.

Chapter 3

The genesis of the Icelandic saga

In Chapter 2 I attempted to define what a saga is, and what it is not. We have now seen that there are many respects in which Old Norse sagas share characteristics with other kinds of medieval texts. There are many areas of overlap with other narrative kinds, especially with historical and annalistic writing, as many sagas are historical in a broad sense, and with didactic and educational writing, such as hagiography and biography, both major medieval narrative genres. Even the fact that most sagas were written in a Scandinavian vernacular rather than in Latin is not an absolute distinguishing feature, as we have seen that some early texts that have some similarities to the saga were written in Latin. Finally, we cannot say for certain that saga composition was originally an exclusively Icelandic practice, although it probably became so from the end of the twelfth century.

We have reviewed evidence that historical writings in both Latin and the vernacular, which have at least some major characteristics of the saga, were produced in Norway by Norwegians in the late twelfth century. However, what I have already characterised as a developed saga style, exemplified in Chapter 2 by a passage from *Egils saga Skallagrímssonar*, cannot be found in extant Norwegian writing from the medieval period. Whether it once existed but somehow did not survive is a question that we cannot answer. It seems that a great deal of the literary activity in thirteenth-century Norway was motivated directly from the court and the Church; thus the translations of romances from French and Anglo-Norman fostered by King Hákon Hákonarson did not apparently spark a wider vernacular literary movement in Norway. The Norwegian scholar Knut Liestøl made a case for the probable existence of oral family sagas in Norway in the medieval period, based on the existence of legends of comparable type and folktales recorded in Norway during the nineteenth century, but there is no evidence from the Middle Ages to support this view. In the absence of positive evidence of Norwegian saga production, then, we are justified in changing our reference from 'the Old Norse-Icelandic saga' to 'the Icelandic saga', and this change is reflected in the title of the present chapter.

Theories of saga origins

How the medieval Icelandic saga evolved in its gestational period, probably the twelfth century, is and is likely to remain something of a mystery. We can point to some of the likely factors that brought it into being; we can compare Iceland with other societies in which oral communication and textual creation were strong and gave rise to particular written textual traditions; we can undertake detailed analyses of the saga literature we know; and we can compare saga literature with other kinds of medieval European literature, especially those introduced by the Church after the Icelanders' conversion to Christianity, to see whether saga subjects, form and style were borrowed in any way from the one tradition to the other. We can do all these things, but what we cannot do is to determine without doubt exactly how and when literary conventions arose that allowed oral narrative traditions and oral poetry to be fashioned into what we now recognise as the saga genre. The creative spark that allowed this to happen cannot be recaptured at this distance in time from the precipitating circumstances. Nevertheless, we can try to come as close as possible to a reasonable hypothesis to account for the rise of the Icelandic saga, and that is the subject of the present chapter.

There have been a number of theories proposed by earlier scholars to explain how the Icelandic sagas originated. Many of these, while offering some worthwhile insights into medieval Scandinavian culture, can be shown, with the wisdom of hindsight, to have been influenced as much by their proponents' ideas about how early medieval literature ought to have developed, as by rigorous analysis of the actual evidence we possess from manuscripts, from medieval texts and, increasingly, from the archaeological record. This is by no means to repudiate everything that earlier scholars have written on this subject, but rather to accept the positive contributions they have made, while being aware of the ideological positions that have influenced some of their findings in ways that now need correction.

A fundamental advance in our understanding of the likely genesis of the Icelandic saga has undoubtedly come from research into oral traditions and oral literatures in many diverse societies around the world. Although the impulse to collect and record oral traditions can be traced back to the mid eighteenth century in Europe, as an aspect of Romanticism, it was not until researchers were able to undertake field studies of living oral traditions in the twentieth century that real advances could be made in understanding what they were and, in some cases, still are, like. What can be learnt from this research has functioned as a corrective to earlier theories of the genesis of the saga based on misunderstandings of the nature of oral traditions and of the various ways they interact with and often morph into literate traditions. There are many findings from research into oral traditions that have completely altered our understanding of some of the major issues that had been worrying saga scholars for decades. Some of the most significant of these are that oral literature is both complex and varied in form and content and that the relationship between oral and literate traditions is both variable and complex.

A major controversy in studies of saga origins: bookprose versus freeprose

The terms 'bookprose' (German *Buchprosa*) and its counterpart 'Freeprose' (*Freiprosa*) were coined by the Swiss scholar Andreas Heusler in 1913 to characterise what he saw as the two major contrasting approaches to the genesis of the Icelandic saga current in his day. He himself, as we shall see, adhered to the freeprose concept. The bookprose approach has been closely associated with an influential group of Icelandic scholars of the late nineteenth and the first part of the twentieth century, all of whom had been educated at the University of Copenhagen and either remained at the University of Copenhagen or returned to Iceland after the University of Iceland was established in 1911. Many of these men were among the most prolific editors of and writers on Old Norse literature in this period, so their influence is still widely apparent in a number of the standard editions and critical works about the Icelandic sagas available today. One of the most tangible and influential marks of the bookprose approach was the publication of a series of authoritative standard editions of medieval Icelandic texts by the Old Icelandic Text Society (*Hið íslenzka fornritafélag*), which had been founded in 1928, beginning with Sigurður Nordal's edition of *Egils saga Skallagrímssonar* (*ÍF* II) in 1933. The series (*Íslenzk fornrit*, abbreviated *ÍF*) is still ongoing. While it began with editions of sagas of Icelanders, stories about Icelanders from the Settlement Age, its more recent publications have included sagas of bishops and various historical works.

The so-called bookprose theory of Icelandic saga origins grew from a cultural milieu in which scholars expected, perhaps hoped, to find similar textual and literary complexities and sophistication in medieval vernacular texts as they found in the classics, which had formed the foundation of their education, both at school and at university. Not only did they approach the editing of Old Norse texts as if they were classical works, but they also looked to them for the same kinds of literary interrelatedness, allusion and readerly qualities that they knew and valued in the classics. In addition, the rise of the bookprose approach coincided with the push for full national independence in both Norway and Iceland, both of which were eager to shake off Danish rule and assert their own political, cultural and linguistic independence and the artistic worth of their respective literatures. Full independence came to Norway in 1905, but to Iceland not finally until 1944.

It is really inaccurate to refer to the bookprose approach as a coherent theory, although most writers do so. It is more a general orientation and a set of assumptions about the genesis of Old Norse literature, and particularly the Icelandic saga, based upon attitudes that nineteenth- and earlier twentieth-century scholars had learnt from the kind of education that was normal at that time. They assumed that the origin of the Icelandic saga, although based originally upon oral sources, was fundamentally in written sources and that saga authors crafted their narratives from a variety of written works that were available to them, including, in some cases, works in Latin or foreign vernaculars. The seminal bookprose work was probably the German scholar Konrad Maurer's study of 'The Saga of Hen-Þórir' (*Hœnsa-Þóris saga*), published in 1871. Here Maurer applied the methods of textual criticism to a short saga whose subject-matter happens also to be the subject of a narrative in Ari Þorgilsson's 'Book of the Icelanders'. As there are several points of disagreement of detail between the two sources, the text-critical approach was applied to assert the superior merits of Ari's sober, historicist account over the version of the saga, whose author was held to have based his narrative on a range of available written sources, including the 'Book of the Icelanders' and lost versions of 'The Book of the Land-Takings' (*Landnámabók*). Recently, Gísli Sigurðsson has argued that the variants in the traditions about Hœnsa-Þórir can be accounted for without the need to involve written sources for the saga.

The so-called freeprose theory is grounded in Romanticist and nineteenth-century misunderstandings, in this case about the nature of oral literature, which was largely equated with folk literature, that is, the orally performed and transmitted forms of expression current among the uneducated lower classes, forms such as folktales and ballads. We have to go back to the mid eighteenth century to understand some fundamental errors in scholars' assumptions about the nature of oral literatures and how those assumptions impacted upon theories of the origin and development of the Icelandic saga. The most important of these is the notion that oral literature, both poetry and prose, is primitive in the sense that, although it may express powerful sentiments, its means of expression are limited and lacking in precision.

Ideas such as these, in combination with the educated person's disdain for the uneducated and socially inferior products of the 'folk', probably led to the impasse in which Andreas Heusler found himself when he advocated the freeprose theory of Icelandic saga origins. It is paradoxical that, although Heusler admitted that the sagas were his first love, he nevertheless failed to produce any really influential study of the Icelandic saga, and the reason was, one suspects, that his preconceptions led him to postulate a memorised transmission from oral narratives, that had achieved artistic form at a late stage of their life, to the written forms they had assumed in the earliest saga manuscripts.

A problem for the freeprose theory during most of the twentieth century has been the vexed question of historicity. Because many of the early advocates of a largely oral development of the Icelandic saga had also insisted that the oral traditions upon which the sagas were based were historically true and had been passed down without change from one generation to the next, the bookprosists challenged them and appeared to find them wanting. The key saga text subjected to analysis in this context was 'The Saga of Hrafnkell, Priest of Freyr' (*Hrafnkels saga Freysgoða*). Two critics, E. V. Gordon and Sigurður Nordal, published analyses of this saga about the same time, arguing that it was not reliable as a historical source and that its author's aim was to create a piece of plausible historical fiction. Although Ólafur Halldórsson countered their arguments as long ago as 1976, basing himself on the likelihood of the existence of variable oral narratives about Hrafnkell, the question of whether or in what sense sagas are historically 'true' has been under continuous discussion before and since that time, and the matter remains a lively issue. Suffice it to say here, though, that both sides of the debate based themselves on misconceptions: the bookprosists on an absolute view of the nature of historicity, the freeprosists on the notion that oral traditions are unchanging.

Studies of oral cultures and their impact on saga studies

It has only been in relatively recent times that new developments in research have enabled scholars to go beyond the freeprosist stances of the first half of

the twentieth century, although their work was anticipated in several important ways by earlier writers during the 1970s. These new developments have
come from the research results of worldwide studies of orality and literacy,
on the one hand, and from performance studies, on the other. The two fields
are of course connected, as one significant dimension to the study of orally
transmitted literatures is the acknowledgement that performance and performance context play a pivotal role in performers' shaping of their material for
particular occasions. This insight can be applied, even in the absence of a great
deal of knowledge about the audiences of the Icelandic sagas, to their likely
performance contexts and to the representation of performance within the
sagas themselves, particularly to their representations of poetic performance
and the occasions that are depicted as giving rise to it.

A major finding of research into oral cultures concerns the variability and
transformability of the oral product. Until very recently, most scholars writing
about the Icelandic saga had assumed, in one way or another, that its oral
precursors were inevitably simpler and less variable than their written counterparts. To cite just one influential example, in her 1982 book *The Medieval
Saga* Carol Clover quoted with approval a number of scholars, beginning with
the Danish folklorist Axel Olrik, who have asserted that the complexities of
Icelandic saga content and structure cannot have developed during its oral life,
but must be indebted to the influence of written texts, particularly medieval
Latin works. In particular, Clover regarded the use of what she called 'stranding', that is, the interweaving of multiple storylines, as indicative of literate
composition, while oral narrative, she argued, is unilinear.

While this argument cannot be proved or disproved for the Icelandic saga,
worldwide evidence from the study of living oral cultures would tend to make
one sceptical of the proposition. Not only do we find that the content of oral
traditions is usually variable, depending on who tells the story and whose
interests he or she expresses, but variability is usually built into the structures
of oral forms, whether through the use of compositional formulae of various
kinds, or through the use of variable structures that are sensitive to specific
performance contexts, and can be included or excluded as convention and the
occasion require.

Later, in an article from 1986, Carol Clover approached what she called
'the long prose form' in a way that makes better sense of the nexus between
oral traditions and the written Icelandic saga. She argued there that in oral
societies there is rarely any felt need to narrate a complete story or myth from
beginning to end, because people already know it. However, this is not to say
that a long prose form does not exist in the communal consciousness as what
she called an 'immanent whole', parts of which can be told when occasion

demands it. She went on to suggest that it is only when the immanent whole text is written down that the narrative in its entirety achieves integrated (and therefore complex) expression. Clover's theory is a useful one and has been adopted by some researchers in the field of oral literatures. However, although it is helpful in assisting our understanding of how underlying oral complexity can achieve written form, there are some modifications that perhaps need to be made to it or at least grafted onto it. The first is that the immanent whole of any narrative is not necessarily understood in exactly the same way or with the same depth of understanding by all members of oral societies, so that, in a sense, the immanent whole exists always and only in a potential form, although many partial realisations may be produced at various times. As with all human societies, some people know more than others and individuals have different approaches to a potential narrative, depending on their social and personal connections. When they realise these background influences during the articulation of a particular immanent narrative, they often produce different versions of what they themselves recognise as broadly the 'same' story. It is not hard to see how various 'takes' on basically the same narrative, such as we find in some Icelandic sagas, most recently analysed in several important studies by Gísli Sigurðsson, can be seen as manifestations of this tendency.

In this context, one can revisit the question of the historicity of the Icelandic sagas which so exercised many twentieth-century bookprosists. If immanent forms of Icelandic sagas were variously converted to written form at varying times and by individuals with varying affiliations and agendas, it is unlikely that all would agree on all details of 'the same' narrative. We would expect to find variability in the witnesses where they overlap, and that is what we do find. Such variability does not necessarily indicate that the witnesses are fictions, merely that different versions of events were current in the oral memory. Moreover, once we add the distance in time between the written record of most Icelandic sagas and the events narrated, further, interpretative manipulation of the material on the part of the saga writer and his predecessors or informants becomes likely.

Vernacular literacy in medieval Iceland

Before they came into contact with Christianity, most of the early medieval Germanic cultures of North-West Europe could be characterised as societies of restricted literacy in their vernaculars, meaning that only specific groups of individuals were literate, while the majority were not. A form of writing, the runic alphabet, was used by some individuals for a relatively limited range of tasks, including inscriptions of funerary dedications to deceased individuals, usually men, on standing stones, especially in Denmark and Sweden, and for signs of ownership on weapons and other valued objects, as well as some magical or apotropaic purposes. Runic inscriptions have also survived on wooden staves of various kinds. Although the use of runes persisted in various parts of Scandinavia for upwards of two hundred years after the conversion to Christianity, especially in some communities, such as among the merchants and townspeople of Bergen in Western Norway, there is little evidence that runic literacy was ever seriously considered as a mainstream challenge to literacy using a modified version of the Roman alphabet, once Christian culture had made that possibility available.

Modern studies of societies whose introduction to literacy has been recent reveal that the effect of the one form of communication upon the other is a two-way and dynamic process, which both affects traditional oral forms and conditions the literate forms that are introduced to the newly literate society along with the technology of writing itself. The receiving society can never be the same again, and, while it may retain many of its old traditions, they will certainly be affected and probably modified by consciousness both of new forms, conventions and subjects made accessible by writing as well as by a new awareness of a different way of creating cultural capital and preserving it. Although we can never prove this, it is likely that early Icelandic society reacted in similar ways to the introduction of literacy, which would not have been an instantaneous matter but a process that took place over many years and touched some individuals quickly, some much more slowly, and others hardly at all.

Throughout Europe in the medieval period literacy usually meant, first and foremost, literacy in Latin, the *lingua franca* of the educated portion of the population and of the Christian Church. For a modern person, literacy has two parts, the ability to read and the ability to write, which for us usually go hand-in-hand. In the Middle Ages, probably more people could read than were able to write. Along with the skills of reading and writing went the technical apparatus of literacy: knowledge and use of the Roman alphabet and a complex set of marks of abbreviations, devised in the first instance for writing Latin; the preparation and use of parchment or vellum as a writing surface; and the availability of pens, hard-points, pencils, inks and other instruments. The technology of literacy was something usually only affordable by wealthy secular individuals and families, or by the Church in cathedral schools and monastic scriptoria, where many, probably most, manuscript books were copied by hand in the earlier Middle Ages, before specialist copying workshops were established in the major cities of European countries like France, Italy and Britain. In Iceland, a similar pattern probably applied, although, in the absence of towns, manuscript copying continued on farms and at religious foundations well beyond the Middle Ages.

Once Christianity had spread in Western Europe beyond the confines of the Romance-language-speaking parts of the Roman Empire, where it has been argued some elements of Vulgar Latin (or Popular Latin) could be understood until at least the ninth century, those who controlled the Church in those parts had a problem: if the official language of the Church was Latin, yet only a few elite individuals could understand Latin, let alone read or write it, how could the word of God be communicated to the majority of the population? The obvious answer was to use the vernacular languages of the local peoples to convey essential concepts and rituals of the Christian faith. This meant that ideas originally expressed through Latin had to be translated into the European vernaculars, an important but very complex process.

We do not know exactly when Icelanders first learnt to read and write in Latin, nor do we know when the very first translation from Latin to Icelandic was made, nor when an original vernacular composition was committed to writing for the first time. The eleventh century, the first century of Christianity in Iceland, must have been the period when these processes gradually took hold, yet our earliest actual records of such activities are reported as having occurred in the early twelfth century, while the earliest extant Icelandic manuscripts date from as late as *c.* 1200. The first Icelandic bishop, Ísleifr Gizurarson, was consecrated in 1056, while in the preceding half-century all the bishops were foreigners. Realistically, it would have taken some time to train the intellectual elite in the new latinate culture, although in eighth-century Anglo-Saxon Northumbria, for example, first-generation literates like Bede, whose parents were probably Christian converts, became outstanding scholars in an astonishingly short time.[1] Circumstances in Iceland, however, are unlikely to have been so favourable to the rapid acquisition of Latin learning, and it has been argued recently that the Church in Iceland probably did not achieve sufficient organisational strength in the eleventh century to push through coherent educational programmes or to train more than a handful of priests. Other important factors in the first century of Christianity in Iceland were the attraction to the priesthood of men of the leading families, who probably saw the role as conferring high status on them, perhaps in a similar way to the traditional roles of poet and lawspeaker, and the frequent ownership of churches by prosperous farmers.

On the basis of the Icelandic texts that have survived to us from the medieval period, one of the most striking characteristics of Icelandic textual production is its vernacularity, its use of the vernacular as the normal means of written communication. It seems that, virtually from the beginning of written textuality using manuscripts, the impulse was to translate Latin (and sometimes other languages) into Icelandic rather than to disseminate Latin texts in the original. Surviving works from the twelfth century bear witness to this impulse, and it continued throughout the medieval period. It is very likely, however, that the number of Latin texts produced in both Iceland and Norway has been seriously underestimated, and the same is probably true of Latin texts emanating from outside Scandinavia. Certainly, we know of a not inconsiderable number of lost Latin works written by Norwegians and Icelanders (some of which were also translated into the vernacular), and there are likely to have been others we do not know about, which have not survived the Reformation, a time when we can assume Latin texts were treated as the products of popery and undervalued or destroyed.

It has been commonly assumed that the reason so much foreign literature was translated into Icelandic was because most Icelandic audiences would not have known Latin and few Latin works would have been available for people to read. As we have seen above, this is likely to have been the case in the eleventh century, but this argument does not necessarily hold good during the twelfth, thirteenth and fourteenth centuries for some educated laypeople and, in particular, for religious communities where a great many saints' lives, doctrinal texts, sermons and religious poems are likely to have been composed, as well as many sagas. These religious communities would also have provided audiences for medieval Icelandic vernacular texts of all kinds. Further, the evidence of the inventories of religious houses in Iceland during the later medieval period indicates that some of them were relatively well supplied with books in Latin and some other European languages, especially German and English, and many vernacular texts reveal their authors' acquaintance at either first or second hand with a considerable variety of Latin sources. Moreover, Guðrún Nordal has proposed that medieval Icelandic schools used both Latin and Icelandic poetic examples in their textbooks, and this practice is likely to be reflected in the so-called 'grammatical treatises' produced between the twelfth and fourteenth centuries. These unique products of vernacularity bear witness to the transformation and appropriation of Latin culture and its incorporation into a cultural product that combined Latin and traditional learning in a new synthesis.

The virtual ubiquity of the Icelandic vernacular for writing, whether in translations or indigenous compositions, suggests that the process of creating written texts joined other vernacular arts of a more traditional, oral kind, like the composition of skaldic poetry, the maintenance of genealogies and lists of lawspeakers, as part of what distinguished the intellectual elite. In the context of our discussion of the origin and development of the Icelandic saga, it is important to note that those early Western European societies that made use of the vernacular to translate key Christian texts also began to record their own vernacular literature in writing. The use of the vernacular for translation of Latin enhanced the status of the vernacular generally as a means of written expression, although the written texts that resulted from this process were not untouched by either the new written medium or the culture of Christian Latinity. We see this phenomenon among the Anglo-Saxons and among the Irish as well as the Icelanders. It is surely no accident, then, that, although the first Icelandic texts that we know of were historical works or translations from Latin, the earliest sagas probably followed quite quickly after that.

Medieval Icelandic written textual culture is largely a phenomenon of the later Middle Ages and seems not to have taken off until the twelfth century. This places it it in the context of the vigorous textuality, both in Latin and the various European vernaculars, that flourished throughout Western Europe in the twelfth to fourteenth centuries, and that led to many new developments in textual cultures and communities of that period. Within the field of literature, new vernacular genres evolved, many in prose, such as the romance and the chronicle, and these provide an interesting parallel to the development of the prose saga, both chronologically and in terms of compositional technique. This does not mean to say that the Icelandic saga genre is a clone of the romance or the prose chronicle; clearly, it has its own very distinctive character and ideology and its own way of memorialising the past. However, the rise of the Icelandic saga shortly after the rise of new genres of historical writing and the courtly romance is unlikely to be fortuitous; the *Zeitgeist* reached to Norway and to Iceland, and Icelandic creativity responded with its own version of historicism and memorialising of both past and present.

Reflecting back on ideas of oral composition and the genesis of the Icelandic saga, discussed in this chapter, in the context of an assessment of early Icelandic literacy and writing, it is worth emphasising here that the advent of literacy was probably a gradual process and one that was not distributed very evenly throughout society. Even by the end of the Middle Ages, there were probably many Icelanders who were unable to read or write. It is therefore likely that oral communication and oral composition remained important artistic means of expression during the whole of the medieval period and beyond, and that these oral traditions influenced the written texts produced by literates at every step of the way. One of the important insights of Gísli Sigurðsson's research into the medieval saga and oral tradition is precisely this: that oral traditions continued to feed into written ones throughout the period of Icelandic saga composition. One might add that the notion of continuous interaction also allows for variability in the character and quantity of influence from the side of the written record as much as from the oral one.

The growth of saga conventions

In earlier sections of this chapter we have seen how, in various ways, many earlier scholars have been reluctant to attribute artistic form and complexity to the oral traditions and textual forms that are likely to have laid the foundations for the coming into being of the written Icelandic saga. While the evidence of early historical writings, both in Latin and the vernacular, indicate that some aspects of the art of saga writing took time to develop, there would be few scholars nowadays who would concur wholeheartedly with Gabriel Turville-Petre's famous aphorism in his *Origins of Icelandic Literature* that native traditions taught the Icelanders what to write, but foreign literature taught them how to write it.[2] Rather, the view being put here is that the Icelandic saga is likely to have developed under the dual influence of indigenous traditional textual forms, which are presumed to have been both artistically complex and to have adhered to established artistic conventions, and the new Christian culture and technology of writing that was introduced to Iceland at the beginning of the eleventh century and gradually impressed itself upon Icelandic society during the following 150 years. It is also accepted that, in all probability, there was no immediate cessation of oral narrative forms but that they continued to feed into literate ones until the end of the medieval period, and indeed well beyond the end of the Middle Ages. Of course, this set of assumptions about the development of the saga is to some extent hypothetical, as any theory of its origins will always be in the absence of evidence for what actually happened, but it is based upon comparative evidence from other human cultures as well as the evidence of medieval Norwegian and Icelandic texts of various kinds.

There is one outstanding issue that has been mentioned earlier in this chapter but needs to be addressed more fully. This is the argument of Carol Clover that 'the long prose form' is unlikely to have existed in the oral traditional stories from which written sagas took their inspiration and their subject-matter. She bases her position upon the absence of long prose forms in other cultures round the world. However, if we were to change the object of the search to long oral forms that combine prose with poetry or song, we would have no difficulty in establishing that oral cultures can and do use long textual forms in formal performance situations. In fact, it is likely that poetic texts with some admixtures of prose are among the commonest formal artistic genres in primary oral societies, while narrative that does not incorporate poetry, song or chant is quite uncommon. In this respect the Icelandic saga conforms to the norm of oral societies, in that for the most part it consists of prose and verse, in varying proportions. While it is true that some sagas include very little or no poetry, the majority use both prose and poetry. There have been long-continuing debates about the relationship between verse and prose in saga literature, but it seems most likely that the mixing of verse and prose was a traditional compositional habit, although one that was probably inflected in certain ways after the Icelanders became acquainted with Latin writers' use of poetic quotation to corroborate or ornament a prose narrative and give it authority. By the early twelfth century, according to the testimony of *Þorgils saga ok Hafliða* that we reviewed in Chapter 2, individuals were composing texts that included both prose and poetry, whether the latter was of earlier origin than the prose or the work of the saga author himself.

In the introduction to his 2006 book, *The Growth of the Medieval Icelandic Sagas*, Theodore Andersson sets out seven categories of narrative that he argues must have existed in the oral tradition because they occur with such frequency in written sagas. Most of these categories are particularly relevant to the sagas of Icelanders, but apply also to some extent to other saga sub-genres, especially kings' sagas. The first is a biographical tradition or mode, in which the life-histories of individuals or groups of people are laid out, something that, as we saw in Chapter 2, is one of the main characteristics of the saga form. Secondly, he argues that there must have been ghost and sorcerer stories, because these crop up very frequently in saga narrative and often, in his view, have no role in the development of the story's main plot. The third category is likely to have been genealogical traditions, because genealogies are central to Icelandic sagas and, as we shall see in Chapter 7, can be the basis for the interrelatedness of sub-genres of the saga and the dominant overview of history that emerges from them. Andersson further identifies regional traditions or traditions about particular families as the basis of saga narratives, together with traditions about lawsuits, fights and feuds, and place names. The last category could be extended to include a range of aetiological stories, which explain how certain features of the landscape or other natural phenomena came into being.

At a less global level, scholars have been able to identify a large number of narrative conventions of saga writing that are likely to be traditional. These relate to what Lars Lönnroth, in his 1976 study of 'The Saga of Njáll' (*Njáls saga*) has called 'the building blocks' of the saga genre, and include stock scenes, stock descriptions, action patterns, particular narrative segments that join one episode to another, specific combinations of motifs used to characterise certain character types, who are represented as acting in typical ways, and a range of kinds of background knowledge about the saga world that would have been conventional wisdom for the medieval saga audience, but that the modern reader has to learn. These will be investigated in more detail in Chapters 5–7.

It is also possible to identify certain narrative modes and stylistic conventions that are likely to have existed in early Norse oral textual forms. One of the most striking of these is the use of dialogue in saga narrative, where direct speech in either prose or poetry or both is attributed to saga characters. Frequently, characters break into direct speech at points in the narrative when they are engaged in stressful situations in which they are required to act agonistically: to provoke others by means of taunts or insults, to persuade others of the rightness of their cause, to justify themselves or to express their reasons for acting in a particular way.

Concepts of authorship

It was noted in Chapter 2 that most of the Icelandic sagas are anonymous works. If people knew who wrote the texts we now possess, they evidently did not think it worthwhile setting down that knowledge in the written record. In this respect, sagas differ from much skaldic poetry and from some other vernacular works, like the *Edda* of Snorri Sturluson, whose composers are known by name. The anonymous status of the sagas is probably a pointer to a concept of authorship that medieval Icelanders applied to such texts which differs from modern ideas about how literary works are created. In Chapter 2 we saw that the verb *samansetja* or *setja saman* 'to bring together, compile' was frequently applied to the act of creating a particular text, even in cases when the authorship of the work was known, as in the rubric that prefaces one version of Snorri's *Edda*. The use of this verb suggests that people recognised that those who created written sagas and other works brought together and arranged various kinds of information in a new synthesis, not that they were engaged in creating a text that was completely or even largely new. This concept was entirely appropriate to the business of producing a written narrative out of pre-existing stories, poems and other kinds of information, which might include foreign literature as well as traditional lore. It was also appropriate to a genre that created something new out of immanent narratives that most members of Icelandic society would have known in some form or other and that, in many cases, they regarded as having actually happened.

Whether or not the anonymous status of medieval Icelandic sagas was influenced by more learned medieval concepts of authorship, the fact is that the notion of saga creation as compilatory in kind rather than inventive or fictive has a parallel in medieval concepts of authorship that relate to religious writing, especially in the Latin commentary tradition, where writers glossed and enlarged on the interpretations of Scripture contained in the writings of earlier authorities, the so-called Fathers of the Church. Here the concept of the authority possessed by the Church Fathers was paramount; they were the giants upon whose shoulders later dwarf-like commentators stood. The ideology underlying this frequently used image was that it was only through the increased elevation they thus obtained that scholars of a later day could offer anything new in the interpretation of the sacred page. In the case of the Icelandic sagas, the rationale for regarding compilation as the saga writer's working method was somewhat different. It was doubtless the perception that the events of history, however understood and interpreted, were primary and the literary activity of the saga writer secondary that led to his being regarded as a compiler of material that already existed and existed already in some kind of artistically shaped form. We can see that this understanding has largely broken down or been parodied in some of the later indigenous *riddarasögur*, where the saga writers archly invoke all kinds of implausible written sources for their narratives, from stone walls to streets. For the most part, however, the stance of the Icelandic saga writer, consonant with his role as a compiler, is self-effacing, as we have seen in Chapter 2. This is an ideologically motivated position, however, and it must not be confused with the very real abilities of saga writers to shape their narratives using a variety of literary conventions, something that will be analysed further in Chapter 6.

Chapter 4

Saga chronology

In Chapter 3 we reviewed the likely circumstances in which the Old Norse-Icelandic saga came into being and assumed written form, noting that this must have been a gradual process and one that could have involved a number of possible connections between oral narrative, oral poetry and written texts. It seems that the beginnings of the textualisation process lay in the twelfth century, although much of what we know was written then either no longer exists or exists in manuscripts of later, sometimes much later date. We saw also that many of the earliest kinds of written texts attested, laws, genealogies and historical or didactic works, could not be classified as sagas, although they might have some saga-like characteristics. The question uppermost in Chapter 4 follows on from the findings of Chapter 3 and deals with the thorny issue of saga chronology. If we postulate that the earliest saga texts took shape in Iceland in the last decades of the twelfth century, can we say which they were? Can we then plot the chronological development of the saga? Can we say for how long the practice of composing sagas continued? Did some sub-groups of the saga genre begin earlier than others and possibly influence the latter's development? Can we date individual sagas, even approximately, and can we establish the place of individual sagas on some kind of chronological continuum? What criteria can be used to date sagas, given that these are anonymous works about whose authorship and circumstances of composition very little can usually be discovered? And does it matter whether or not we can return reliable answers to these questions?

All these are hard questions, and in recent years some of the seeming certainties underlying established views of the growth of saga writing and the relative chronology of saga texts have been subjected to critical scrutiny, to such an extent that one recent study presents itself as an attempt 'to overcome the chronological impasse'.[1] Another possible approach is experimenting with alternative criteria, such as the presence or absence of skaldic verse and the different ways in which the settlement of Iceland is depicted, as a means of dating sagas of Icelanders. Some people now believe that it is not possible to establish a firm chronology for the whole literary phenomenon of saga composition, and this is by and large the view put forward here, though with some qualifications.

In fact, opinions about the dating of the Icelandic sagas have changed quite a lot over the last 200 years, that is, since roughly the beginning of the nineteenth century, when printed texts of Icelandic sagas started to become accessible to readers beyond a small group comprising Icelanders and non-Icelandic scholars who had access to manuscripts and were able to read them. In the nineteenth century, it was believed by many that the twelfth century was the great age of saga composition, while in the twentieth, particularly during the period of dominance of the Icelandic school of bookprosists, the most active period was pushed forward to the thirteenth century, particularly to the period before or close to the loss of Icelandic independence to Norway in 1262–4. Few sagas were assigned to the end of the thirteenth century and even fewer to the fourteenth or fifteenth centuries. In the early twenty-first century, a good number of scholars are now tending to move the period of active saga composition forward into the fourteenth and even the fifteenth centuries. And it is now recognised that certain kinds of sagas, notably indigenous romances, continued to be composed well beyond the Middle Ages.

As Table 2 indicates, there are in total well over 100 medieval Icelandic sagas now known to us, across at least seven sub-groups – kings' sagas and other historical sagas, sagas of Icelanders, contemporary sagas, mythical-heroic sagas, translated romances, indigenous romances and saints' lives, including sagas of native bishops. However, most attempts to establish a chronology of saga composition deal only or largely with sagas of Icelanders, although kings' sagas are also considered because the earliest examples of this sub-group are usually thought to have antedated the earliest sagas of Icelanders and provided a model for them. Very few scholars, if any, have attempted an integrated chronology of saga writing, incorporating all the sub-groups into a consolidated list, although Kurt Schier comes close in his *Sagaliteratur*. As soon as one tries to do this, one point becomes immediately apparent: in a small and not very well-off society of no more than 50,000 people, where could sufficient saga composers, not to speak of scribes and surplus animal skins to make parchment, be found to allow all this feverish activity to take place, if most of it was squeezed into a period of fifty to seventy years? Theoretically, perhaps, such a scenario might be possible, but much more likely is a more extended period of composition, beginning in the late twelfth century and continuing, if one takes reworking of earlier material into consideration, into the later fourteenth and fifteenth centuries. As we shall see below, such a revision makes better sense in the context of what we know of manuscript copying.

The politics of saga chronology

Many scholars have already drawn attention to one of the fundamental premises of the writings of the Icelandic bookprosists of the first half of the twentieth century, namely that there was a connection between the advent of the saga as a developed literary form and the period of the thirteenth century up to the end of the Icelandic Commonwealth in 1262–4. Writing in the 1940s and 1950s, Icelandic scholars such as Einar Ólafur Sveinsson and Sigurður Nordal considered there was a causal relationship between the nature of Icelandic society and its problems in the first half of the thirteenth century, the so-called Age of the Sturlungs (*Sturlungaöld*), and the literary representation of the Icelanders of the Saga Age (*c.* 930–1000) in sagas of Icelanders. They emphasised the tensions of the thirteenth century, between the Church and the laity, between wealthy chieftains and free farmers, between those who acted to bring about Norwegian rule and those who opposed it, as a catalyst that led saga writers of the period to probe the discords and tensions of their own age dressed up as the moral and material conflicts of two hundred or more years earlier.

Literary excellence in saga writing was thus associated with a chronological period in which, it was argued, Icelanders experienced radical change in their society and its government. Out of the stresses of that age, the first half of the thirteenth century, grew great literature which reached its maturity at a time coinciding with the impending fragmentation of independent, Commonwealth Iceland. Beyond that time, it was held, decline started to set in. The decline was political, with Iceland's loss of independence, and it was also social, in that the loss of independence led to a loss of a feeling of personal and national self-worth and direct engagement with the world at large. Feelings of powerlessness arguably led Icelanders then to resort to the escapist literature of romance and fantasy, which was also considered inferior in kind to the gritty realism of the sagas composed during the Sturlung Age.

Following the implications of this argument, it was held by many that most of the sagas of Icelanders were composed during the Sturlung Age or shortly after it, and that most romances and mythical-heroic sagas were composed later, along with some late sagas of Icelanders, like 'The Saga of Bárðr

Snæfell-deity' (*Bárðar saga Snæfellsáss*) and 'The Saga of the men of Flói' (*Flóamanna saga*), that share an interest in the fantastic and the supernatural. The sagas that were supposedly composed during the Sturlung Age showed superior literary merit, it was held, manifested most clearly by being realistic and historically aware in their presentation, compared with those that were composed after the 1260s, which were more inclined to abandon the realistic mode. Thus there arose a chronology of saga writing, linked to a particular view of Icelandic politics and particular tastes in literature, that postulated first a few early sagas, which betrayed a stylistic uncertainty reminiscent of learned, latinate writing (like 'The Saga of the Killings on the Heath' (*Heiðarvíga saga*) or 'The Saga of the Foster-brothers' (*Fóstbrœðra saga*), although the early dating of both has been challenged), then a 'classical' period in which most of the good sagas were written (this period largely coinciding with the Sturlung Age), followed by a decline into a 'post-classical' fantastic group of sagas that largely lost touch with historicity and realism and were generally of inferior literary merit.

A modified version of this view of the subject still holds sway and has been most carefully articulated in recent years by the Icelandic scholar Vésteinn Ólason. Vésteinn's tentative dating allocates more sagas to the early period, which for him extends to *c.* 1280, and more to the late period, which stretches between 1300 and 1450. Only eight sagas are classified as 'classical', and their period of composition is given as between 1240 and 1310, thus allowing for overlap between the categories. For purposes of comparison, the text box sets out Vésteinn's classical sagas and the group that Kurt Schier thought likely to have been composed roughly within the period 1240 and 1310.

According to Vésteinn Ólason 'Family Sagas' (2005)

Classical sagas, composed between 1240 and 1310, are:

'The Saga of the Confederates' (*Bandamanna saga*), 'The Saga of the inhabitants of Eyrr' (*Eyrbyggja saga*), 'The Saga of Gísli Súrsson' (*Gísla saga Súrssonar*), 'The Saga of Gunnlaugr Serpent-tongue' (*Gunnlaugs saga ormstungu*), 'The Saga of Hrafnkell priest of Freyr' (*Hrafnkels saga Freysgoða*), 'The Saga of Hen-Þórir' (*Hœnsa-Þóris saga*), 'The Saga of the people of Salmon River Valley' (*Laxdœla saga*) and 'The Saga of Njáll' (*Njáls saga*).

According to Kurt Schier, *Sagaliteratur* (1970)

The following sagas of Icelanders are likely to have been written between 1230 and 1280:

'The Saga of Killer-Glúmr' (*Víga-Glúms saga*), 'The Saga of the people of Reykjadalur' (*Reykdœla saga*), 'The Saga of the Ljósvetningar' (*Ljósvetninga saga*),

'The Saga of Ljótr of Vellir' (*Valla-Ljóts saga*), 'The Saga of the sons of Droplaug' (*Droplaugarsona saga*), 'The Saga of the people of Vopnafjörður' (*Vápnfirðinga saga*), *Gísla saga Súrssonar*, *Laxdœla saga*, *Eyrbyggja saga*, 'The Saga of Eiríkr the Red' (*Eiríks saga rauða*), 'The Saga of the Greenlanders' (*Grœnlendinga saga*) and 'The Saga of the people of Vatnsdalur' (*Vatnsdœla saga*).

And an additional five between 1270 and 1290:

Gunnlaugs saga, *Hœnsa-Þóris saga*, *Bandamanna saga*, *Hrafnkels saga* and *Njáls saga*.

In all probability there is some broad truth in this presentation of the chronology of sagas of Icelanders, but it is important to recognise the premises that underpin it, some of which are unable to be verified. Firstly, few historians or literary scholars now subscribe to the idea that the Sturlung Age was so radically different from the periods before and after it as the bookprosists held. Rather, they see a much more gradual development of some of the social and political tendencies that manifested themselves in the thirteenth century, like, for example, the concentration of power in the hands of a small number of dominant families. Thus the notion that the Sturlung Age was a period of extreme tension unlike the ages before and after it and that this was the catalyst for the mature saga style is very questionable and of course incapable of proof.

Another dimension of the bookprosist argument that needs careful examination is its underlying concept of literary development as applied to the Icelandic saga. Leaving aside the questionable notion that ages of significant socio-political change produce significant literature, there has been an unexamined privileging of realistic writing which invokes historicity, whether real or fictitious, over writing in other literary modes or in mixed modes, reflecting the literary tastes for realism in modern fiction that were dominant in the early part of the twentieth century. The former has been and still is termed 'classical', the latter 'post-classical'. Such terms are heavy with value judgements: 'classical' is associated with high culture and high literary value, 'post-classical' with a decline from a peak of achievement, with something secondary and inferior. The premises upon which such value judgements are based will be examined further in Chapter 6, where it will be proposed that very few sagas are solely realistic, and that earlier scholars' emphasis on realism has overlooked the modally mixed character of a majority of sagas. Further, it will be argued there that non-realistic modes are by no means necessarily inferior literature.

A further caveat is that the theory outlined above only really applies to kings' sagas and sagas of Icelanders. If one tries to fit other sub-genres of the saga into this picture of saga chronology and literary development one arrives at the view that the majority of the mythical-heroic sagas (*fornaldarsögur*) and romances (*riddarasögur*), whether translated or indigenous, must have come into being in the 'post-classical' period because of their non-realistic literary character, although there is evidence to show that, in Norway at least, *riddarasögur* were being translated from French and Anglo-Norman in the 1220s for the court of King Hákon Hákonarson. Some of the subject-matter of *fornaldarsögur* is also demonstrably very old, as witnessed by references to it embedded in Viking Age poetry, although the versions of these sagas that survive date from the late medieval period. Further, the theory effectively downplays the literary artistry of the contemporary sagas (*samtíðarsögur*), which we know to have been composed in the thirteenth century about events that were more or less contemporary. Although recent research has revalued the literary artistry of the contemporary sagas, especially Sturla Þórðarson's *Íslendinga saga*, earlier writers tended not to see these works as on a literary par with sagas of Icelanders, viewing them as similar to annalistic writing and lacking the chronological tension produced by the disparity between Saga Age and Sturlung Age that seemed to be necessary for the creation of great saga literature.

The evidence of the manuscripts

To understand the following section, it is necessary to know that manuscripts, unlike printed books, are normally classified alphanumerically, although many Old Norse-Icelandic manuscripts also have names, conferred mostly after the Middle Ages, like *Möðruvallabók* 'The Book of Möðruvellir'. A short form of reference to manuscripts (their sigla, from Latin *siglum* 'sign') incorporates an abbreviation for the library collection to which they belong (e.g. AM = Arnamagnæan collection, now in either Copenhagen or Reykjavík; GKS = *Den gamle kongelige samling* 'Old royal collection', now split between the Royal Library, Copenhagen and the Arnamagnæan Institute for Icelandic Studies, Reykjavík) and a specific number or number plus letter assigned to the manuscript (e.g. 1009 or 162 A θ), together with another abbreviation that denotes its size, e.g. fol = folio, 4° = quarto, 8° = octavo. Most manuscripts of Icelandic sagas are now in libraries in Iceland and other Scandinavian countries, but there are also some in collections in other countries, like Germany and the United Kingdom. A list of major collections and their sigla can be found in Chapter 8, where the subject of saga manuscripts and their history will be treated in greater detail.

A fundamental reason why we must exercise caution in discussing the likely chronology of Icelandic saga production is provided by the material evidence of the manuscripts in which sagas have been written down. It is an incontrovertible fact that very few manuscripts of any saga survive that can be dated to the thirteenth century or earlier, and these are mostly fragments. In Chapter 2 mention was made of the earliest fragment of a saga of Icelanders, AM 162 A θ fol, which contains a small portion of *Egils saga*. This is the earliest, and one of very few extant thirteenth-century manuscript fragments of a saga of Icelanders, the sub-genre that most people consider to be the highlight of thirteenth-century saga composition. There are a small number of manuscripts or manuscript fragments of sagas of Icelanders dating from between 1300 and 1350, but the majority of these works are extant only in manuscripts of *c.* 1350 or later, sometimes much later. Because vernacular texts continued to be copied by hand in Iceland until relatively recent times, there are cases where a medieval work is extant only in paper copies from a much later period, the medieval exemplars having been destroyed, often by fire. A good example is Ari Þorgilsson's *Íslendingabók*. No medieval manuscript of this presumed twelfth-century work survives. Two paper copies of a lost medieval manuscript were made in Iceland in the seventeenth century by Jón Erlendsson of Villingaholt. *Hrafnkels saga Freysgoða* is another work that survives only in post-medieval copies, the earliest dating to *c.* 1500. The oldest manuscripts of the majority of sagas of Icelanders date from the period *c.* 1350–1500. A significant number of them were collected together in compilations during the fourteenth and fifteenth centuries, as we shall investigate further in Chapter 8.

The state of affairs regarding historical works, especially kings' sagas, is a little less discrepant, but not much. A considerable number of early historical works, that medieval writers report to have been written in the twelfth century or the very early thirteenth, no longer exist. These include an account of Norwegian history, probably in Latin, by Sæmundr inn fróði 'the Wise' Sigfússon (1056–1133); an account of kings' lives (*konunga ævi*) by Ari Þorgilsson; a work named 'Back Piece' (*Hryggjarstykki*), attributed to an Icelander named Eiríkr Oddsson and thought to have been written *c.* 1160; at least one early saga of St Óláfr, of which a few manuscript fragments remain, probably composed before 1200; and a life of St Óláfr by the Icelander Styrmir Kárason, prior of the monastery on the island of Viðey. There were reportedly two Latin lives of King Óláfr Tryggvason (r. 995–1000) written by Icelanders, the earlier by Oddr Snorrason (probably between 1180 and 1200), the later by Gunnlaugr Leifsson (d. 1218/19). Both these men were monks from the northern Benedictine monastery of Þingeyrar. Oddr's life was translated into Icelandic, it is not known precisely when, and exists in two manuscript versions and a fragment of a third, the earliest dated to *c.* 1250–75.

Many kings' sagas exist in large, named compilations, which cover the reigns of a number of Norwegian, or in a few cases, Danish kings. The surviving compilations often appear to have used many of the earlier collections, some of which have again not survived. Consequently, the manuscript history of kings' sagas is very complex and depends on close, comparative study of variant manuscript versions of the lives of individual kings and on an assessment of the debt of later to earlier works, both on the basis of textual criticism and bearing in mind what sources medieval writers reported themselves that they had used or revealed a debt to in their writings. Many of the main manuscripts of kings' sagas used by textual scholars are, in fact, post-medieval paper copies of lost medieval exemplars.

One of the oldest Icelandic compilations, 'Rotten vellum' (*Morkinskinna*), is thought to have existed in an older version, composed sometime between 1217 and 1222, and now no longer extant. The version we now have is from about 1275, extant in one manuscript, GKS 1009 fol, of Icelandic provenance. Recent studies have argued that this manuscript is closer than previously thought to the older version. At the same time, studies of later compilations, like the manuscript 'Fair vellum' (*Fagrskinna*, usually dated *c.* 1220) and Snorri Sturluson's compilation named 'Circle of the World' (*Heimskringla*, *c.* 1230), indicate that these later writers must have had access to the older version of *Morkinskinna*. Allowing for the gaps and uncertainties in the manuscript record, modern studies of kings' sagas suggest a period of intense creative and compilatory activity between 1180 and 1230, with another, less intense period of creativity after 1250, the latter mostly comprising the work of the Icelander Sturla Þórðarson (The 'Saga of [King] Hákon Hákonarson' (*Hákonar saga Hákonarsonar*) and 'The Saga of Magnús the Lawmender' (*Magnúss saga lagabœtis*)) and the anonymous author of the Danish royal history 'The Saga of the descendants of Knútr' (*Knýtlinga saga*). The majority of manuscripts containing kings' sagas date from after 1300, although a few fragments are earlier.

When it comes to a consideration of the texts of *fornaldarsögur* and *riddarasögur*, none of them are extant in manuscripts from earlier than 1300. However, some Norwegian translated romances exist in earlier manuscripts. For example, a text of *Strengleikar*, literally 'Stringed Instruments', translations of French *lais*, exists in the Norwegian manuscript now Uppsala University Library (UUB) De la Gardie 4–7 of *c.* 1270, which also contains part of *Elis saga*, a translation of the *chanson de geste Elie de Saint Gille*. The oldest Icelandic manuscripts to contain sagas of these sub-classes are the compilations *Hauksbók* 'The Book of Haukr [Erlendsson]' (*c.* 1300–25), *Flateyjarbók* 'The Book of Flatey' (1387–95) and MS Holm perg 7 4° in the Royal Library

Stockholm (1300–25). A few sagas are found in manuscripts of the fifteenth century, like 'The Saga of the Volsungs' (*Vǫlsunga saga*), which occurs in NKS 1824 b 4° of *c.* 1400, and 'The Saga of Hálfr and the Hálfr champions' (*Hálfs saga ok Hálfsrekka*), which is extant in GKS 2845 4° of *c.* 1450, as well as in over forty paper manuscripts. Many sagas of these sub-classes are to be found in large numbers of paper manuscripts from the sixteenth century and later. This reflects the great popularity these non-realistic sagas continued to have in the late medieval period and the period after the fifteenth century.

What conclusions can we reasonably draw from the disparity between the dates of the manuscript witnesses to Icelandic sagas and the postulated dates of composition of the sagas themselves? Playing devil's advocate to some extent, Örnólfur Thorsson argued that we might conclude from the evidence of the manuscripts themselves that the saga was predominantly a fourteenth- and fifteenth-century literary phenomenon rather than one whose apogee was in the thirteenth century. Certainly, given the paucity of pre-1300 manuscripts, the versions of sagas that survive to us do belong to the later medieval period or later than that, and, as we shall see in Chapter 8, it is in fact very difficult, if not impossible, to restore saga texts to a putative thirteenth-century format and style, even though a normalised spelling, such as that of the *Íslenzk fornrit* series, is employed. In cases where variant versions of saga texts exist, there has been a good deal of debate about which versions are earlier, which later, but in almost no case can we restore an 'original' text such as the anonymous author or compiler might have written down in a manuscript that no longer exists.

Is it then necessary to reject the standard view of Icelandic saga composition as mainly a phenomenon of the thirteenth century, with some extension backwards into the late twelfth and forwards into the fourteenth and fifteenth? The standard view is based largely on arguments (to be discussed below) that are mostly incapable of proof. Some are plausible, others are not. In no way, however, can they add up to any certainty about saga chronology except in a few rare cases. Thus it seems safest to keep an open mind about the place of any saga on a chronological continuum and to entertain the view that the continuum may well have extended forwards in time beyond the early fourteenth century to a somewhat greater extent than many scholars have been willing to accept until recently. However, the possibility that earlier versions of sagas may have existed, in written or in oral form, is a reasonable hypothesis, and not necessarily controverted by the fact that most surviving manuscript versions are from a later period. Similar time lags appear in other medieval European literatures. Most Anglo-Saxon manuscripts, many of them compilations, date from the latter part of the tenth century and the first half of the eleventh, yet some at least of the works contained within them are usually thought to be older, although how much older remains a matter for surmise in many cases, just as it does for Icelandic saga texts.

Dating criteria

In order to give the reader some idea of the kinds of arguments that have been used to place particular sagas in a chronological relationship with one another and within the genre as a whole, consideration will be given here to several typical test cases which invoke specific kinds of dating criteria. These will be evaluated individually and some generalisations drawn from the exercise that apply across the board. There are two basic kinds of dating criteria usually applied to saga literature: external and internal. External criteria are extra-textual, that is, they provide information pertinent to the dating of a particular saga or sagas from outside the saga itself. For example, there may be information in other, unrelated texts that tells us something about the composer of a saga, about when he lived or the people to whom he was related, or a known and datable event may be referred to in the saga text. For example, one of the reasons why *Njáls saga* is usually dated to the period *c.* 1275–85 is because the saga writer appears to be familiar with the legal code 'Iron-side' (*Járnsíða*), which was not introduced to Iceland from Norway until 1271. Although this kind of information is usually considered accurate, one has to be careful when assessing how far it can be relied on in dating a saga to which it relates.

Internal criteria are those that can be deduced from the saga text itself and are of two basic kinds, each of which involves both literary or textual analysis and some elements of value judgement. Many internal criteria involve assertions of literary borrowings of motifs or actual scenes from one saga to another, the presumed direction of borrowing usually being relied upon to establish a chronological relationship between saga A and saga B. Other internal criteria are dependent on thematic, stylistic, lexical and structural analysis; saga A may be deemed to be early because in a certain critic's opinion, it is lacking a tightly integrated plot or contains long, learned-sounding passages, while saga B is tightly constructed and uses an economical and objective style. The internal criteria of both kinds have been the most subject to contradictory interpretations, and it is not difficult to see why: they depend upon prior assumptions about the direction of the literary development of the Icelandic saga, and for the most part they depend upon it being uniform. Neither of these premises can be fully substantiated.

There is a special type of criterion that requires mention here, and that is the evidence provided by poetry quoted within saga texts. Like the internal criteria, but for different reasons, poetic evidence is or may be equivocal, and in fact can be classified as both internal, because it is part of the saga prosimetrum, and external, because it belongs to a second-order narrative and/or has been imported into the saga text from outside, as an already existing poetic text presumed to have been created before the saga text itself came into being. In many instances, the dates ascribed to poems and individual stanzas (the so-called *lausavísur* 'free-standing verses'), so often put into the mouths of saga characters, are and remain uncertain. While it is possible to date poetry based on linguistic and metrical criteria, more often than not an individual stanza will not display appropriate diagnostic features, so the exact date of composition remains moot. This is a particular problem for poetry quoted within sagas of Icelanders, within Snorri Sturluson's *Edda* and in *fornaldarsögur*, while the poetry cited within kings' sagas, often as evidence to support the prose narrative, has usually been considered more reliable chronologically, because its subject-matter can be connected with specific historical events and persons. The question of the relationship between prose and poetry in saga texts will be taken up again in Chapter 6 in the context of the saga's mixed modality.

External criteria

Let us consider an interesting example of external evidence about a specific individual, which may link two sagas, apparently of quite disparate kinds, and offer a chronological and thematic connection between them. I use the verb 'may' here because it cannot be absolutely certain that the same individual is being referred to in each case, although the bulk of the evidence points in that direction. The two sagas are the saga of the Norwegian king Óláfr Tryggvason, attributed to the monk Oddr Snorrason, as mentioned earlier in this chapter, and 'The Saga of Yngvarr the Widely travelled' (*Yngvars saga víðforla*), a narrative certainly in part based on historical events datable to the early eleventh century. *Yngvars saga* gives an account of a Swedish expedition through Russia to a place called Serkland, led by one Yngvarr Eymundsson.

'The monk Oddr' from Þingeyrar monastery is mentioned several times in various manuscripts of the Icelandic version of the saga of Óláfr Tryggvason and in a longer saga on the same subject. Evidence that this man was Oddr Snorrason is provided by 'The Book of the Land-Takings' (*Landnámabók*).[2] The two extant, fifteenth-century manuscripts of *Yngvars saga* conclude with a statement that the saga is based on a book 'that the monk Oddr the Wise had caused to be written based on the telling of the wise men whom he himself mentions in his letter that he sent to Jón Loptsson [d. 1197] and Gizurr Hallsson [d. 1206]'. This statement limits the period of composition of the saga to before

1206, the date of Gizurr's death, and presumably to the time before Jón's death in 1197, seeing that one does not normally write letters to men who have died.

In 1981 Dietrich Hofmann published an article arguing that the *Oddr munkr inn fróði* 'the monk Oddr the Wise' mentioned in the colophon to *Yngvars saga* was one and the same as Oddr, author of the Latin text of the saga of Óláfr Tryggvason. Although not all scholars have agreed with this, most have accepted Hofmann's argument that the extant Icelandic versions of *Yngvars saga* derive from an Icelandic translation made before 1200 of a Latin original composed by Oddr Snorrason. There are also similarities between passages in both sagas that list Oddr's oral informants. If the Oddr of the original *Yngvars saga* was indeed the same monk as Oddr, author of the Latin saga of Óláfr Tryggvason, then this man was the creator of two sagas which, in their extant forms, appear rather different. In its present form, *Yngvars saga* contains numerous exotic elements that have led many scholars to classify it as a *fornaldarsaga*, but it has been suggested that at its core is a tale of a Christian prince from Sweden who travels east to Russia and beyond as a missionary. In parallel fashion, it could be argued, Óláfr Tryggvason sets about the conversion of the pagan Norwegians.

If the attribution of the original *Yngvars saga* to Oddr Snorrason can be accepted (although it cannot be so without reservation), we can see that a work which appears in its fifteenth-century dress as a *fornaldarsaga* probably took shape in the late twelfth century as a more sober chronicle of what must have been an extraordinary expedition. The evidence for this comes from external information that is impossible to refute. There are no fewer than twenty-six runestones standing today in the Södermanland and Uppland regions of Sweden that commemorate men who had travelled east with an Yngvarr and died abroad. The inscriptions on these stones are so similar that it seems reasonable to conclude that the Yngvarr (usually written Ingvarr) they name is the same man also commemorated in *Yngvars saga*. Scholars have debated both the actual date of Yngvarr's expedition, although 1041 is still the most likely,[3] and the identity of his final destination, Serkland, a place mentioned five times in the runic inscriptions, and most plausibly to be identified with the environs of the Caspian Sea.

What are the chronological implications of the interrelationship of the two sagas attributed to Oddr Snorrason, if he was indeed the composer of both, as seems likely? The evidence shows that an Oddr, reliant on the oral evidence of wise men (and in the case of the saga of Óláfr Tryggvason, wise women also), composed two chronicles before 1200, probably in Latin, which were later translated into Icelandic and took on somewhat different forms, although in fact each could be considered a conversion narrative. This evidence is valuable because it shows, particularly in the case of *Yngvars saga*, that the subject-matter that came to be associated with *fornaldarsögur* was already available for literary development in the late twelfth century. There is no reason to suppose that the same situation did not apply to other nascent sagas of the *fornaldarsaga* sub-genre, and in fact we reviewed evidence in Chapter 2 that described the recital of two sagas arguably of this type at the Reykjahólar wedding in 1119. In his 2002 study of the *fornaldarsaga*, Torfi Tulinius has reviewed the evidence that makes it likely that legendary material, probably available in some cases in poetic form, was being shaped into saga form in the late twelfth century, alongside other narrative genres.

The evidence of both the colophon to *Yngvars saga* and additional information in the main manuscript of Oddr's *Óláfs saga* (AM 310 4°) also provides interesting evidence of how Oddr submitted his manuscripts for approval to two secular leaders known to have had intellectual interests, Jón Loptsson and Gizurr Hallsson. Oddr's near-contemporary and fellow monk, Gunnlaugr Leifsson, also showed his life of Óláfr Tryggvason to Gizurr. This information is reminiscent of the evidence Ari Þorgilsson provided in the preface to his *Íslendingabók*, revealing that he had revised an earlier version of his history at the suggestion of Sæmundr Sigfússon and the bishops Þorlákr and Ketill. Each writer is also scrupulous to name his oral informants. The practice of checking and vetting material by both secular and ecclesiatical authorities in these early Icelandic writings suggests a process of verification of evidence in the absence of written sources and a desire to 'get it right'.

Internal criteria – literary borrowings

A good example of the difficulty of establishing the direction of literary borrowing from one saga to another and thus the chronological relationship between two or more sagas is provided by comparable scenes in two different family sagas, one in 'The Saga of Gísli Súrsson' (*Gísla saga Súrssonar*), the other in 'The Saga of the sons of Droplaug' (*Droplaugarsona saga*). In fact, in connection with the notion of literary intertextuality, it is necessary to question whether modern concepts of literary borrowing, which involve the direct influence of one written text in terms of content and style upon another written text, are fully applicable to Icelandic sagas, in which there is always likely to have been an interplay between oral traditions and written texts.

The two scenes are Chapter 16 of *Gísla saga* and Chapter 13 of *Droplaugarsona saga*, as these sagas are usually divided in modern editions and translations.[4] In each case a man is stabbed to death in his bed closet,[5] where he is sleeping with his wife, by another man who enters the victim's house in his underclothes, not wearing shoes, and via the cowshed, where he (or another man) has tied all the cows' tails together, presumably to prevent people following him if he escapes from that direction. In each case the assailant first disturbs the victim before killing him. In *Gísla saga*, Gísli, the assailant, gropes inside the bed closet and touches the breast of the victim's wife, who happens to be his own sister, Þordís. She wakes, thinks the man who has touched her is her husband, Þorgrímr, who is wanting to make love to her, and they speak briefly but both settle down to sleep again. Gísli then warms his hand in his shirt and gently wakes Þorgrímr up again, only to kill him with a special family heirloom, the spear Grásíða 'Grey flank', which had been reforged from an original sword. He then exits the house via the cowshed, going home by the path he had previously taken, which involves wading through a stream, and so covering his tracks.

In *Droplaugarsona saga* the assailant Grímr has a companion, Þorkell, and they have been hiding in a passage leading from the cowshed into the living quarters of the victim's farm. Grímr gets Þorkell to fetch a sword from inside the house that belonged to his dead brother, Helgi, whose death he is in the process of avenging. Grímr enters the bed closet of his intended victim, Helgi Ásbjarnarson, and the latter's wife, Þordís, and removes the bed covers from Helgi, who wakes and thinks his wife has touched him. He complains that her hand is very cold. However, she denies having touched him, says she has a sense of foreboding about the meaning of the event, and they go back to sleep. Grímr then removes Þordís's arm from over Helgi and thrusts the sword through him. Helgi tries to sound the alarm with his men in the hall, but Grímr had taken care of them by throwing a stick into a pile of firewood, which collapses with a clatter, leading Helgi's men to rush in the wrong direction. Meanwhile, Grímr makes to escape by the same route he had entered, but he is grabbed by a blind man, Arnoddr, who is, however, misled by feeling that Grímr was shoeless and in undergarments into thinking that he might be one of the household.

Many saga scholars have written about these two scenes and have assumed that the similarities between them derive from literary borrowing, holding that the original author of saga B (allowing for the moment the concept of an original author) borrowed a scene from saga A, which already existed in written form. Thus a written form of saga A must have predated a written form of saga B, according to this line of argument. The discrepancies between the two scenes and what commentators have regarded as ill-fitting or superfluous motifs in one or other of the sagas have then come about, the argument goes, because not all details of the scene set out in saga A fitted the narrative context of saga B.

So far, so good, but the problem is that scholars have not been able to agree on which saga of the two in question in this case is saga A, and which saga B. Furthermore, after deciding which way round the borrowing has gone, analysts have then tended to justify their chronology in terms of the supposedly earlier and later saga's alleged literary qualities. The majority of those who have discussed this matter have held that *Droplaugarsona saga* is saga A and *Gísla saga* saga B and have presumed that the former is a fairly early saga while the latter, as we have seen, is usually held to have been one of the major 'classical' sagas of Icelanders. It is possible, though, to argue for the reverse direction of borrowing, on the ground that a number of the common elements in the two sagas are better motivated in *Gísla saga* than in *Droplaugarsona saga*, and that therefore the latter is likely to have borrowed from the former. Such elements include the tying of the cows' tails, the wearing of undergarments, the open bed closet and the assailant's waking of the victim and his wife before the lethal attack.

There has been a majority view among scholars that *Gísla saga* is a work of literary sophistication and psychological depth and that the scene of Gísli's killing of Þorgrímr gives a powerful clue to the former's strong sense of family honour as well as his ambivalent attitudes towards his blood relations, including his sister Þórdís, on the one hand, and his strong support for his relations by marriage, on the other. The place in the scene discussed here where he puts his hand on his sister's breast can be construed as betraying his incestuous desire for her or jealousy of her husband, Þorgrímr, whom he is about to kill in revenge for Þorgrímr's killing of Gísli's wife's brother, Vésteinn.

There is no doubt that these sexual elements are present in *Gísla saga*, at least in the version found in *Möðruvallabók*. At the same time, it does not necessarily follow that this saga adapted a scene from a written *Droplaugarsona saga* to deepen the psychological complexity of the relationships between its characters, which were already largely dictated by the saga's main plot. By contrast with *Gísla saga*, there has been relatively little literary analysis of *Droplaugarsona saga*, much of it in fact undertaken by those who wish to demonstrate that *Gísla saga* must have borrowed from it. There has been an obvious circularity of argument here which has usually been to the detriment of the supposedly earlier work. It has been characterised as episodic and mechanical. However, these attributes have not really been demonstrated by close literary analysis of the text of *Droplaugarsona saga*, and the evaluation prefacing that saga's most recent translation into English, that of Rory McTurk, seems to have a good deal of merit when it argues that the saga 'combines a well-knit structure with revealing character portraits'.

In spite of the various arguments for and against the borrowing of motifs, no clear direction of borrowing can be established between *Droplaugarsona saga* and *Gísla saga*. It is equally possible that the similarities between them could have derived from the existence of an orally transmitted scene that maybe did not originally 'belong' to either saga. Critics have noted that the two sagas come from opposite sides of Iceland, *Droplaugarsona saga* from the east, *Gísla saga* from the west, making the likelihood of written borrowing perhaps less plausible than it might have been if they were from the same Quarter of the island. Thus it does not seem that the evidence presented by the two similar scenes can be used with confidence to establish a chronological relationship between *Droplaugarsona saga* and *Gísla saga*.

A second example of how arguments based largely on internal evidence are inconclusive is provided by an unresolved scholarly debate about the place of 'The Saga of the Foster-brothers' (*Fóstbrœðra saga*) in the chronological sequence of saga composition. Is it an early saga from the beginning of the thirteenth century, as Sigurður Nordal and Sven B. F. Jansson and many later writers have thought, or is it a work from the last decades of the thirteenth century, which was the conclusion arrived at by Jónas Kristjánsson, in a detailed study of the manuscript evidence, the style and literary relations of this saga with others? Or is it rather a relatively early saga whose author bucked the developing trend of composing sagas in an impersonal, self-effacing and not overtly Christian mode and produced a work characterised by an authorially engaged, stylistically baroque and learned presentation, that manifests features that Jónas classified as late, but that may in fact be found in some Norse vernacular literature of an earlier date?

There is no doubt that *Fóstbrœðra saga* has affinities of both subject-matter and manuscript preservation with sagas about St Óláfr, on the one hand, and a sub-group of sagas of Icelanders who were court poets, the so-called 'poets' sagas' (*skáldasögur*), on the other. The *skáldasögur* comprise narratives about the adventures of these poets when they were off duty, as it were, both in Iceland and in other places away from the Norwegian royal retinue. Most of the sagas in this latter group, whose core comprises 'The Saga of Hallfreðr Troublsome-poet' (*Hallfreðar saga vandræðaskálds*), 'The Saga of Kormákr, son of Ǫgmundr' (*Kormáks saga Ǫgmundarsonar*), 'The Saga of Bjǫrn Champion of the Hítdœlir' (*Bjarnar saga Hítdœlakappa*) and 'The Saga of Gunnlaugr Serpent-tongue' (*Gunnlaugs saga ormstungu*), have generally been considered early and to have evolved in the wake of the development of sagas about the Norwegian kings, like Óláfr Tryggvason and Óláfr Haraldsson (St Óláfr), whom they served. The main characters in *Fóstbrœðra saga*, the foster-brothers Þormóðr Kolbrúnarskáld 'Kolbrún's Poet' Bersason and Þorgeirr Hávarsson, the former in particular, were known as court poets of St Óláfr, and in two of the main manuscripts, *Flateyjarbók* and *Bæjarbók*, the saga is interwoven into a saga about their patron. In two other manuscript compilations, *Hauksbók* and *Möðruvallabók*, the saga has an independent existence.

All who have studied the various extant versions of *Fóstbrœðra saga* have agreed that the text in *Hauksbók*, which was written by Haukr Erlendsson himself together with another scribe, is shorter and more concise than that found in the other versions, although Jónas Kristjánsson offered the important reservation that this shortening only occurs in the part that Haukr wrote himself. Haukr's work can be dated to the years 1302–10, and possibly more narrowly than that, to 1306–8. The weight of recent opinion is that the shortened version is an adaptation of the text to suit more 'classical' tastes, as all the other manuscripts, which belong to two main classes, manifest the learned and engaged style of writing described above.

The majority of commentators on *Fóstbrœðra saga* have not been favourably disposed to the saga's dominant mode, reflecting the common modern valorisation of the impersonal saga style and its presumed development from early insecurity to classical certainty of expression. An earlier view held that the passages in a 'non-classical' style were interpolations, but, as Jónas Kristjánsson's detailed 1972 study demonstrated, they are thoroughly integrated into the fabric of the narrative at a thematic level and are therefore most unlikely to be the interpolations of a later redactor. Nevertheless, most analysts, including Jónas himself, have used the misnomer 'digressions' (Icelandic *klausur*, literally 'clauses' or *útúrdúr*) to refer to passages in the saga text that depart from what have been held to be the norms of saga writing, whether in terms of *Fóstbrœðra saga*'s ornate, rhetorical style, or in terms of the theological reflections and learned speculations upon the relationship between mind and body that characterise this saga. In many places, the saga writer's presentation of his characters and their motivation (a topic not usually discussed overtly in Icelandic sagas) is informed by medieval medical and physiological theories about the relationship between the human body and its various organs and the traits of mind and disposition that express an individual's character. It is highly likely that whoever wrote this saga was acquainted with learned literature on this subject, which, as Lars Lönnroth and, after him, Jónas Kristjánsson have shown, was available in the form of *florilegia* and other encyclopedic works derived from the writings of Lactantius, Isidore of Seville, Bede and others.

Although Jónas concluded that the writer of *Fóstbrœðra saga* may have derived his learning from a work, the *Regimen Sanitatis Salernitanum*, that was probably not known in Iceland before the later thirteenth century, there is no inherent reason he could not have become acquainted with earlier works on the subject and thus composed his saga in the earlier, rather than the later, part of the century. He also pointed out that *Fóstbrœðra saga* shows the influence of the chivalric romance and followed a general opinion that chivalric elements do not begin to appear in sagas of Icelanders until the middle of the thirteenth century at the earliest, presumably thinking of a saga like *Laxdœla saga*, which is generally dated to the mid century. However, as we know that the programme of translating romances into Old Norse began in the 1220s at the court of King Hákon Hákonarson, there is in principle no reason why their influence could not have been felt by at least the 1230s in Iceland, and many scholars have detected the influence of the romance on the poets' sagas, most of which are probably of early date.

Some tentative conclusions

The foregoing analysis of various external and internal criteria for the establishment of a continuum along which we can plot the chronological development of the Icelandic saga has not encouraged any assurance that such a sequence can be established. There are, of course, some points of certainty, mainly supplied by external data, but in the main they are not sufficiently numerous to be generally helpful. Rather than throw up our hands in despair, however, at the failure of conventional methods of literary analysis to establish a firm saga chronology, we have the option of finding such a failure liberating from the preoccupations and presuppositions of earlier scholarship. Most of the examples reviewed in this chapter have revealed underlying assumptions about the nature of the saga and its evolution over time which are open to challenge. They include the idea of virtually uniform development from an early type of saga still tied to the hagiographic mode of early kings' sagas through a central classical phase of impersonal, realistic saga writing to a post-classical interest in the fantastic and the supernatural. This view usually involves some form of value judgement about the relative literary merits of the various modes, something that is rarely subject to critical scrutiny and is to some extent subjective.

Another conventional way of trying to establish chronological and literary relationships between one or more sagas has been the search for intertextual literary borrowings (Icelandic *rittengsl*, literally 'connection of literary works'). Establishing *rittengsl* has been a major preoccupation of the Icelandic school of saga studies and of many non-Icelandic scholars during the twentieth century, but several of its underlying premises can be queried. One of them is the presumption that literary borrowings are from one written, fixed text to another, whereas, as Gísli Sigurðsson and others have indicated, just because one saga text mentions another saga, this need not imply that written text was transferred from saga A to saga B or indeed that saga A existed at a particular time in written form. The reference could equally well be to the immanent form of saga A, even if the wording of the two sagas in their extant forms is similar, and thus cannot be used with certainty to establish a chronology of the written sagas we know.

Liberation from some of the views of the past may well permit us to develop a more pluralistic model of the sequence of saga writing, in which we can allow that the different sub-groups of the Icelandic saga are quite likely to have developed alongside one another and in interaction with one another instead of in a single sequence that privileges sagas of Icelanders above all other sub-genres. Equally, styles other than the realistic may become more acceptable in time and be recognised as a legitimate part of the Icelandic saga tradition. This may help us to appreciate the mixed modality of the Icelandic saga, and not to dismiss or relegate to a 'post-classical' turn writing of a kind that does not conform to the impersonal, concise, tight-lipped style that has been generally preferred by many modern scholars and that was clearly a convention of much saga writing. Through much of the twentieth century and still today, such sagas as 'The Saga of the inhabitants of Eyrr' (*Eyrbyggja saga*) and 'The Saga of the people of Vatnsdalur' (*Vatnsdœla saga*) that do not conform to this model have sometimes been marginalised or dismissed, even though the arguments presented for doing so are often quite subjective.

To return to one of the examples discussed in this chapter, a number of the so-called digressions in *Fóstbrœðra saga* can be understood as both moving and highly effective in conveying both characterisation and authorial point of view, though in a way that is different from the hard-boiled style of many sagas. It is not necessary to find them jarring or excrescent, as many scholars have. While recognising that particular literary tastes are at least partly subjective, it is also possible to point to the way in which the saga writer has used these passages to deepen his characterisation of the saga's protagonists. A case in point is the description of the 15-year-old Þorgeirr's reaction when he learns of his father's slaying:

> News of Hávar's death spread quickly, yet when Þorgeirr learned that his father had been slain he showed no reaction. His face did not redden because no anger ran through his skin. Nor did he grow pale because his breast stored no rage. Nor did he become blue because no anger flowed through his bones. In fact, he showed no response whatsoever to the news – for his heart was not like the crop of a bird, nor was it so full of blood that it shook with fear. It had been hardened in the Almighty Maker's forge to dare anything.

> Víg Hávars spurðisk skjótt víða um heruð, ok er Þorgeirr spurði víg fǫður síns, þá brá honum ekki við þá tíðenda sǫgn. Eigi roðnaði hann, því at eigi rann honum reiði í hǫrund; eigi bliknaði hann, því at honum

lagði eigi heipt í brjóst; eigi blánaði hann, því at honum rann eigi í bein reiði, heldr brá hann sér engan veg við tíðenda sǫgnina, því at eigi var hjarta hans sem fóarn í fugli; eigi var þat blóðfullt, svá at þat skylfi af hræzlu, heldr var þat hert af inum hæsta hǫfuðsmið í ǫllum hvatleik.[6]

The standard saga description of a man's reaction to such news, which brings with it the obligation to take vengeance sooner or later (usually later), is impassive and terse. Here, however, as Lars Lönnroth demonstrated by a triangulation of this scene with the Old Norse translation *Alexanders saga* 'The Saga of Alexander [the Great]'[7] and a passage from *Njáls saga*, the saga writer is using what Lönnroth calls 'clerical style' to place Þorgeirr's typically Icelandic reaction in the context of medieval theories about human nature. He shows that the author of *Njáls saga* has been able to harmonise his references to medieval humour theory with the objective saga style, whereas the writer of *Fóstbrœðra saga* either could not or would not. This can be interpreted, as Lönnroth did, as a lack of literary skill; alternatively, it could be interpreted as an active preference for the overt Christian style, given the significant number of comparable passages in *Fóstbrœðra saga*.

Saga subjects and settings

This chapter is concerned with the subject-matter treated in sagas and will show that we can distinguish broadly between sub-genres of the saga on the basis of their subject-matter, which in its turn is related to the specific historical and geographical settings of the various sub-genres. The narrative mode and style of these sub-genres is the main subject of Chapter 6; in Chapter 5 the subject-matter and its setting in time and space will be the centre of attention. This chapter will propose that both chronology and geography can be seen to act as consistent markers of sub-generic identity in the literary world of the medieval saga and must have been perceived by their contemporary audiences as indicators of generic affiliation and thus of the range of interpretative possibilities available to them. As we shall see, these constituent elements of saga writing function, just as much as characterisation, as determiners of presumed medieval audience and modern readerly response, without their creators having to invoke specific cultural assumptions directly.

Time and place in the saga world

In terms of the medieval Icelandic perspective on world history, saga time ranges from prehistory to the present time, seen from the saga audience's viewpoint, while saga geography extends from Iceland to the rest of Scandinavia, then west to the British Isles, the North Atlantic, Greenland and North America, and south and east to the Mediterranean world, Russia and the

Middle East. These historical and geographical settings map onto specific saga sub-genres.

Thus, to begin with prehistory, *fornaldarsögur* are set in times before the settlement of Iceland and usually take place in greater Scandinavia; their protagonists are heroes and figures of the past, often with supposed Icelandic descendants. Romances (*riddarasögur*), whether translated or indigenous, normally present non-Scandinavian nobles or knights in European settings, although they often range much further afield to include parts of Asia. Their time-setting is usually non-specific, as far as Icelandic chronology is concerned, but in the translated *riddarasögur* it is normally linked to the days of the legendary British King Arthur. Exotic saints' lives (*heilagra manna sögur*) tend to mirror the settings of their exemplars, which are usually Latin texts or texts in other European vernacular languages translated from Latin. Such settings frequently involve early Christian society, often in some part of the Eastern Mediterranean region.

Kings' sagas, as their name implies, deal with the acts and reigns of the kings of Norway, to some extent those of Denmark, and with the jarls of the Orkney islands. The settings of these sagas are in the historical world of the Scandinavian diaspora during the Viking Age and up to the late thirteenth century in Scandinavia, the British Isles, Europe and the Middle East. Sagas of Icelanders (*Íslendingasögur*) are largely set in Iceland during the so-called Settlement Age and the period just before and just after the conversion to Christianity. They deal with Icelandic families at home on their farms interacting with their fellow Icelanders, but can follow their characters' forays into Norway and other parts of Scandinavia, as well as to parts of Europe and the Middle East and, sometimes, westwards to Greenland and North America. Contemporary sagas (*samtíðarsögur*), including the sagas of Icelandic bishops, are also largely set in Iceland during the late twelfth and thirteenth centuries, and deal with the conflicts and other activities of the most powerful Icelandic families of this period.

Although there is some blurring of the sub-generic categories, especially within the sagas of Icelanders, by and large each sub-genre keeps to its own conventions of setting, both historical and geographical, and of subject-matter. These conventions depend upon a largely stable set of beliefs and assumptions that we can characterise as a medieval Icelandic world-view. Such a world-view included both indigenous elements, deriving from the Icelanders' actual geographical location on an island in the North Atlantic ocean and the historical circumstances of their settlement there, together with a knowledge of all that had happened to them since that time. They were also in possession of knowledge of legends, probably in the form of both poetry and prose narratives, that allowed them to think in certain ways, often mythical, about the past and about their Scandinavian and Celtic forebears who lived before the settlement of Iceland.

On the other hand, the medieval Icelandic world-view came to incorporate elements from the wider European culture to which the Icelanders also belonged. To some extent, contact with that wider culture would have been furthered by various individuals' engagement with outsiders, whether in Iceland or abroad; however, the most potent agent of cultural contact with mainstream Europe was the Christian Church and the technology of literacy that it controlled. Even though the medieval Church in Iceland may have taken a good century to confirm its position, there is plenty of evidence that Christian ideology, Christian books and Christian practices were well established in Iceland by the time of the presumed beginnings of saga writing in the later twelfth century. By this time, therefore, we can assume that the Icelandic world-view combined traditional knowledge and attitudes with those attributable to mainstream medieval Christianity. Thus, whether a saga is set in prehistoric times, in the tenth or the thirteenth century, one can expect that both the composer and his audience will have approached the processes of saga creation and interpretation with some combination of traditional Nordic and Christian attitudes. It will be assumed here that these attitudes are encoded and detectable in the saga texts we know today.

Considered as a whole, the conventions of Icelandic saga writing present a view of both history and geography that is compatible with medieval Christian ideology, though inflected to present a specifically Icelandic outlook on the events of past and present. This is so even in cases of some sagas that seem to be largely secular in their outlook, because the underlying premises upon which their actions are founded are compatible with Christian ideas. Further, the conventions of each sub-genre, considered together, answer to the Christian understanding of the whole of history as divided into successive ages, each dependent on the central events in the history of God's relationship with humanity, which was to culminate in the Last Judgement. Likewise, in terms of geography, indigenous concepts of the cardinal directions marry with medieval Christian views which held the centre of the world to be at Jerusalem, with the various key narratives of Christian history, including the lives of saints and the Crusades, taking place predominantly in the Eastern Mediterranean and the Middle East.

The Icelandic saga world, which was traditional in its basic conceptualisation of history and geography, is inflected to express the time scale and historical consciousness that was standard in medieval Christendom. The Christian concept of time depended absolutely, as Beryl Smalley put it, upon a religious conviction that 'time existed only between the Creation and the Last Things'.[1] Furthermore, Christians divided history into several time-bands that corresponded to the major events attested in the Old and New Testaments of the Christian Bible, which ended with the Last Judgement. According to St Augustine of Hippo (d. 430) there were six ages of the world and a seventh, ushered in by the Last Judgement, which marked the transition from chronological time to eternity.

Early medieval historians like Eusebius (d. *c.* 341) and Orosius (d. *c.* 418) created narratives that gave room for the historiography of human societies outside the orbit of Christendom, although the histories of such groups were largely significant in the eyes of these writers because they came into contact with Christians and either resisted Christianity or converted to it. Nevertheless, with the model of Orosius's *Historia adversum paganos* 'History Against the Pagans', a kind of world history that took account of the presence of non-Christian societies came into existence and could be used by later medieval writers as a basis for narratives of the lives and beliefs of peoples in pagan times. Probably the first early medieval vernacular ethnography to represent pagan Scandinavia was the insertion into the Old English translation of Orosius's history, usually thought to have been produced during the reign of King Alfred (871–99), of a first-hand account from two traders, named as Ohthere and Wulfstan, working in Scandinavia and the Baltic, of the geography, economy, navigation routes and rituals of peoples living there during the ninth century.

A great deal has now been written about how medieval Icelandic writers accommodated texts representing the pre-Christian societies of Scandinavia within Christian accounts of the history of the last, sixth age of the world, which began after the birth of Christ and was to end at the eschatological millennium. A number of these accommodations asserted that the pre-Christian dynasties and other ruling families of Scandinavia could trace their ancestry to the old pagan gods, to figures from the Book of Genesis or to ancestral tribes or heroes known from classical literature, particularly from the story of the fall of Troy. Other strategies were of a typological nature and implicitly argued that the events of the pre-Christian past could be paralleled with the events of Christian history. Still others focussed on the period of conversion (*siðaskipti* 'change of customs') when the tyrannical rule of demons and other devilish forces in Scandinavia was brought to an end by the power of Christianity and its agents. It is argued here that the literary representation of the saga world across the corpus of Icelandic sagas, considered both in their sub-generic parts and as a whole, fills out the ethnographic picture of what it was like to live in the world's sixth age as experienced in Scandinavia and as considered from an Icelandic perspective.

The world of the *fornaldarsögur*

The world of the *fornaldarsögur*, as their modern Icelandic name implies (literally 'sagas of the old time'), is prehistoric, considered from an Icelandic point of view, that is, it implicitly belongs to a period of history before the settlement of Iceland and before the conversion to Christianity. This circumstance is rarely indicated explicitly in any saga, although a relative chronology may be given, but it can be deduced from several features of *fornaldarsaga* narratives. In the first place, Iceland is never the setting for any saga of this sub-genre, and yet many of its protagonists are said to have been born in Norway and to have had Icelandic descendants, some of whom are mentioned in *Landnámabók*. One such example was named in Chapter 2: Hrómundr Gripsson was one of the subjects of the entertainment provided to the wedding party at Reykjahólar in 1119, and it is mentioned in *Þorgils saga ok Hafliða* that some people in Iceland were able to trace their genealogies to him. *Landnámabók* also names Hrómundr as a historical person, whose two sons migrated to Iceland.

Similarly, a group of *fornaldarsögur* about men from the Norwegian island of Hrafnista (Ramsta), off the coast of Naumudalr (Namdal), including 'The Saga of Ketill Salmon' (*Ketils saga hœngs*), 'The Saga of Grímr Hairy-cheek' (*Gríms saga loðinkinna*), 'The Saga of Án Bow-bender' (*Áns saga bogsveigis*) and 'The Saga of Arrow-Oddr' (*Qrvar-Odds saga*), include protagonists who share their ancestry with the paternal kin of Egill Skallagrímsson. Other *fornaldarsaga* characters are said to come from more distant parts of Norway, Sweden or Denmark, but rarely, if ever, do they originate from outside Scandinavia, although they often travel to exotic destinations in the course of their adventures.

A number of *fornaldarsögur* represent a world of Scandinavian royal and heroic dynasties in which the lives of several generations of legendary royal houses are traced from mythical beginnings and are linked to historical Scandinavian families. Chief among them are 'The Saga of Hervǫr and Heiðrekr' (*Hervarar saga ok Heiðreks*), 'The Saga of Hálfr and the Hálfr champions' (*Hálfs saga ok Hálfsrekka*), 'The Saga of Hrólfr Pole-ladder' (*Hrólfs saga kraka*), 'The Saga of Ragnarr Hairy-breeches' (*Ragnars saga loðbrókar*) and 'The Saga of the Volsungs' (*Vǫlsunga saga*). The kind of legendary material preserved in these sagas is similar to legendary material that prefaces some kings' sagas, like Snorri Sturluson's *Ynglinga saga* 'Saga of the Ynglingar', the legendary kings of Sweden, which introduces the compilation *Heimskringla*, or the introductory chapters to other historical narratives, like 'The Saga of the Orkney Islanders' (*Orkneyinga saga*), and may well have its origins in a common tradition of legendary dynastic history. This kind of *fornaldarsaga*, termed by Torfi Tulinius 'the Matter of the North', has affinities with the kind of legendary history being composed in other parts of Europe in the twelfth century, particularly with Geoffrey of Monmouth's *Historia de regum Britanniae* 'History of the kings of Britain' (*c*. 1136), which brought the Arthurian legend into aristocratic consciousness and stimulated the rise of the romance. Geoffrey's work was translated into Icelandic, possibly first via Norwegian, as *Breta sögur* 'The Sagas of the British', with *The Prophecies of Merlin* rendered metrically in *fornyrðislag* 'old story metre' as *Merlínusspá*. This poem is ascribed by manuscripts of *Breta sögur* to the Icelandic monk Gunnlaugr Leifsson (d. 1218/19).

One characteristic of a good many *fornaldarsögur* is their prosimetrical character. However, unlike other saga sub-genres, which include predominantly skaldic verse, *fornaldarsögur* preserve verse almost exclusively in eddic metres. This exclusiveness is entirely appropriate to their genre as one anchored in Scandinavian prehistory. Eddic poetry, particularly its dominant metre *fornyrðislag*, was considered to be an older verse-form than the main skaldic measure *dróttkvætt*, and, although some poetry found in *fornaldarsögur* was probably of quite recent origin, it purported to be old, and in some cases probably was old, like the subject-matter of the sagas in which it was embedded. *Völsunga saga*, for example, is clearly based on a group of poems, recorded in the Codex Regius collection of the Poetic Edda, that celebrate the life and deeds of the legendary hero Sigurðr Fáfnisbani 'Slayer of Fáfnir'. Others, like *Hervarar saga ok Heiðreks*, are built around several different poetic corpora, including: a dialogue between a mound-dwelling dead father, Angantýr, and his daughter Hervǫr, who is intent upon recovering the family's cursed, ancestral sword Tyrfingr; a set of riddles; and a heroic poem celebrating the ancient encounter between Gothic and Hunnish tribesmen.

Just as the protagonists of many *fornaldarsögur* are said to have connections with individuals who lived in historical times, so the kind of world that they inhabit is half familiar in terms of Icelandic social conventions, although in many cases it is distinctly aristocratic and in that respect unlike Icelandic farm culture. These characters marry, have children and live lives that involve everyday tasks like cutting hay, driving cattle into a byre and catching fish. Yet at the same time strange things happen to them, and they frequently interact with beings that are not fully human, such as dwarves, trolls, mound-dwelling heroes of a past age, giantesses, a poetry-spouting mountain and a merman. They also range over a wide geographical area in their adventures, moving with ease from Scandinavia to points east and west, and sometimes to mythical countries, like Risaland 'Giantland'. Both the personae of the *fornaldarsaga* and the geographical settings in which they move must have signalled to the medieval audience that the action of this saga sub-genre was removed from the world of the everyday, at least in part, but not so fully removed that its subject-matter could not be meaningful to them.

The prevalence in *fornaldarsögur* of beings and events from beyond the world of the everyday is another indication of these narratives' chronological setting at a time before the settlement of Iceland and, importantly, when Scandinavia was still pagan. Before the powers of Christendom could eradicate the dangerous illusions and manifestations of Satan, these devilish forces had free rein. Such ideas form the conceptual background, not only to *fornaldarsögur*, but to sagas and *þættir* about the evangelising journeys into the pagan Norwegian backwoods of the missionary kings Óláfr Tryggvason and Óláfr Haraldsson, who often encounter hostile beings and their sorcery. These beings are either explicitly or implicitly interpreted as demonic and capable of creating illusions of pagan deities and their powers, as well as various kinds of magical illusions. Such representations thus conform to the second of the two kinds of magic recognised by medieval thinkers, natural and demonic: 'Natural magic was not distinct from science, but rather a branch of science. It was the science that dealt with "occult virtues" (or hidden powers) within nature. Demonic magic was not distinct from religion, but rather a perversion of religion. It was religion that turned away from God and toward demons for their help in human affairs.'[2]

In conformity with such views, Oddr Snorrason's saga of Óláfr Tryggvason has the king encounter and rout the pagan deities Óðinn and Þórr, apparently disguised as ordinary humans, though with give-away attributes of the old gods, the former as a one-eyed old man who tries to poison the king's food, the latter as a red-bearded man who boasts of his prowess in killing giantesses and then dives off the king's ship.[3] In both cases the king understands the figures as manifestations of the Christian devil. The episode of King Haraldr hárfagri's 'Fair-hair's' spellbinding by the Saami woman Snæfriðr, which caused him to neglect his royal duties for three years after her death, is another example of the medieval attitude to demonic magic, in this case attributed to the non-Norse Saami, who could apparently preserve a corpse to arrest its decay. This phenomenon could perhaps be attributed to natural magic, but the tenor of the description of this event in Snorri's 'The Saga of Haraldr Fair-hair' (*Haralds saga ins hárfagra*) in *Heimskringla* makes its clear that demonic magic was thought to be the cause, as there is a description of how all kinds of evil creatures, such as adders, frogs and toads, crawled from Snæfriðr's corpse once the illusion had been broken. The multiplicity of abnormal and grotesque beings and strange events that populate many *fornaldarsögur* are also symptoms of life in an age lacking the benefits and regularity of Christian revelation. The often flippant tone of such sagas is of course completely different from that of the kings' sagas just mentioned, as befits their different saga sub-genre, but the cultural framework in which each must be understood is the same.

Two *fornaldarsögur*, 'The Saga of Arrow-Oddr' (*Qrvar-Odds saga*) and 'The Tale of Nornagestr' (*Nornagests þáttr*), depend in a different way upon the sub-genre's chronological setting in the pre-Christian age in Scandinavia to develop narratives of characters who live well beyond a normal human life-span and so, because they bridge the pagan and Christian worlds, have some insight into Christian revelation as what Lars Lönnroth has identified as 'noble heathens', that is, people who have an understanding of the basic tenets of Christianity before their community has experienced Christian conversion. In the case of the Methuselah-like Nornagestr, he is over 300 years old and appears at the court of the missionary king Óláfr Tryggvason, still a pagan but having undergone preliminary baptism (*primsigning*, Latin *prima signatio*). Qrvar-Oddr, on the other hand, is a pagan who instinctively distrusts the practices of paganism, including the prophecy of a 'prophetess and sorceress' (*völva ok seiðkona*) named Heiðr. He refuses to listen to her account of what the future holds in store for him, so she lays a curse on him to the effect that he will lead a life of wandering but will be killed at home by the skull of his own horse, Faxi. In the course of his many adventures, undertaken in part to frustrate Heiðr's prophecy, Oddr comes into contact with Christians in France and is offered baptism, which he accepts on his own terms:

> He said he would do so on this condition: 'I will adopt your faith, but yet conduct myself in the same way as before. I will sacrifice neither to Þórr nor to Óðinn nor to other graven images, but I do not have a mind to remain in this country. For that reason I will wander from land to land and stay sometimes with heathen men, and sometimes with Christians.'

> Hann kveðst mundu gera þeim á því kost: 'Ek mun taka sið yðvarn, en hátta mér þó at sömu sem áðr. Ek mun hvárki blóta Þór né Óðin né önnur skurðgoð, en ek á ekki skap til at vera á þessu landi. Því mun ek flakka land af landi ok vera stundum með heiðnum mönnum, en stundum með kristnum.'[4]

In many respects, the world of the *fornaldarsaga* is close to that of the Scandinavian folktale, both in the cultural assumptions that underlie its themes and motifs, in many of its narrative patterns and in the matter-of-fact way in which its themes are deployed. Some *fornaldarsögur*, though by no means all, also show similarities to folktales in terms of characterisation, in that their protagonists move victoriously through one adventure after another in picaresque fashion. In his study of the post-classical family saga, Martin Arnold has noted similar kinds of characterisation in some of the later sagas of Icelanders, where folktale motifs occur against a realistic background of life in Iceland in the tenth century.

The group of royal and heroic *fornaldarsögur* mentioned earlier manifest a somewhat different kind of characterisation from that described above. As Torfi Tulinius has observed, the characters in these dynastic prehistories are often caught up in tortuous family problems, including legitimacy of birth and access to inheritance (*Hervarar saga ok Heiðreks*), incest and conflicts of loyalty to blood-kin versus loyalty to marriage alliances and blood-brotherhood (*Vǫlsunga saga*), transgression of gender roles, sexual jealousy, incest, interfamilial killings and homophobia (*Hrólfs saga kraka*), sexual rivalry between men for one woman, polygyny, violence as a consequence of sexual rivalry (*Hálfs saga ok Hálfsrekka*), inter-generational conflict between fathers and sons, and the status of married and unmarried women (*Ragnars saga*). In many of this group of sagas, the themes played out in these dynastic histories lead to tragic outcomes for at least some of the protagonists.

The themes, characters and the whole world of the *fornaldarsaga* lend themselves to interpretation, not as realistic narratives, but rather as subjects dealing with deep and disturbing human issues that cannot be approached from the perspective of the mundane world but must rather be enacted in a literary world in which often tabu subjects can be raised and aired, though not necessarily resolved. They may also be treated in a comic or parodic vein, as may many of the *riddarasögur*. Although, until recently, the *fornaldarsaga* sub-genre was rather neglected by saga scholars, it is significant that a new interest in these works from psychological, anthropological or religio-historical viewpoints has been productive of a number of valuable studies, which strongly suggests that at long last their *modus operandi* is becoming better understood. This issue is taken further in Chapter 6, where we see how a close reading of saga mode and style can assist our understanding of this and other sub-genres.

Riddarasögur and their world

Some of the late medieval manuscripts in which *riddarasögur* 'knights' sagas' have been recorded attest to the fact that it was King Hákon inn gamli 'the Old' Hákonarson of Norway (r. 1217–63) who commissioned a number of translations from French chivalric romances and various other French or Anglo-Norman genres, like the verse epic, the *lai* and the *fabliau*, probably beginning in the mid-1220s with a certain Brother Robert's translations of the *Tristan* of Thomas of Britain (*Tristrams saga*) and the *chanson de geste Elie de*

Saint Gille (*Elis saga ok Rósamundu*). Hákon's motivation in commissioning these translations was his ambition to bring himself, his court and Norwegian politics into the European mainstream, and his success in this goal is amply attested in the biography of this king written by the Icelander Sturla Þórðarson shortly after his death. A number of translated romances and other courtly narratives survive, many, but not all, in Icelandic manuscripts, although the original translations are likely to have been made by Norwegian clerics. However, it seems that Icelanders were fairly soon directly involved, both in the process of copying these texts, which seem to have become popular in Iceland rather quickly, and in their translation.

The Old Norse term *riddarasaga* thus covers what were a number of genres in Latin, French and Anglo-Norman, but common to all of them are their courtly setting, their interest in kingship, and their concerns with the ethics of chivalry and courtly love. It seems, however, from a comparison between the French originals and the Old Norse translations of courtly romances, such as Chrétien de Troyes' *Erec et Enide* (*Erex saga*), *Yvain* (*Ívens saga*) and *Perceval* (*Parcevals saga* and *Valvens þáttr*), that the translators who supplied King Hákon's court and others in Norway and Iceland who enjoyed such sagas offered an independent rewriting of their sources. It is notable that they did not convey a number of key aspects of Chrétien's somewhat ironic perspective on courtly society. This may well be because most of the translators were probably clerics, but it is also likely to reflect traditional Norse tastes and narrative conventions. In particular, most elements of explicit eroticism have been deleted from the *riddarasögur*, as have much comedy and irony in the treatment of the protagonists' behaviour. Instead, the narratives are largely exemplary and didactic, in large part because the Scandinavian translators refrained from using two essential narrative devices of their sources, namely the internal monologue, which conveyed the private thoughts and feelings of the characters, and the intrusive involvement of the narrator, which was a vehicle for conveying a nuanced and often ironic point of view.

The omniscient and impersonal narrator was, as we have seen in earlier chapters, one of the defining characteristics of saga narrative, so it is not surprising to find a resistance to a radically different form of narrative point of view in the translated romances. The use of internal monologue is likewise absent from the prose of saga texts. However, it had its equivalent in the poetry ascribed to the saga characters in most other sub-genres, and it is interesting that the translators refrained from using this native resource in their work. In fact, they adopted a common practice of medieval Scandinavian translators in turning verse originals, as many of their chivalric sources were, into a mannered prose, distinguished by the use of alliteration, antithesis, parallelism and rhyming word pairs, as if to signal their exoticism, and, as a further indication of foreignness, not to embed in it any indigenous poetry. The lack of verse is thus a distinguishing feature of the *riddarasögur* as a group and sets them off from all other saga sub-genres.

As might be expected from their status as translations, the *riddarasögur* mirror the settings and locations of their sources in time and space, although they usually inflect them to take account of their audiences' likely tastes and prior knowledge. Some sagas are specific about these details, others use them without explanation or introduction, as a given of the sub-genre. The opening sentences of *Ívens saga* inform the audience that the story belongs to 'the Matter of Britain', as part of the cluster of narratives associated with the court of the legendary King Arthur:

> The excellent King Arthur ruled England, as is known to many. After a time he became king of Rome. He was the most illustrious of the kings who had lived on this side of the ocean and the most popular other than Charlemagne. He had the bravest knights who lived in Christendom. It happened one time, as was customary . . .

> Hinn ágæti kóngr Artúrus réð fyrir Englandi, sem mörgum mönnum er kunnigt. Hann var um síðir kóngr yfir Rómaborg. Hann \<er\> þeira kónga frægastr er verit hafa þann veg frá hafinu ok vinsælastr annarr en Karlamagnús. Hann hafði þá röskustu riddara er í váru kristninni. Þat var einn tíma sem jafnan . . . [5]

Several characteristics of the *riddarasaga* can be learnt from this passage. In the first place the location of the action is not entirely explicit, although it can be deduced to be in Britain, seeing that the narrative goes on to describe an adventure that began at Arthur's court. However, as the narrator then informs the audience that 'after a time' Arthur became king of Rome, they might wonder whether a more continental European setting could also be possible, as long as it was 'on this side of the ocean', a reference that may have made the audience feel its own location was being brought into the sphere of the action. Secondly, although the narrator does not give a precise chronology, and the main action of the saga is timeless, he does indicate that his saga takes place in a Christian environment. This signals an important difference between the *riddarasaga* and the *fornaldarsaga*: although the plots of both abound with unusual characters and events, the world of the *riddarasaga* is within Christendom, whereas the world of the *fornaldarsaga* is not. Thus even the most improbable happenings in *riddarasögur* are subject to God's law and are said to have been influenced by God's intervention.

In *Ívens saga*, for example, one of Íven's many adventures involves his fighting a giant (*jötunn*). The lord of a certain castle appeals to the knight to help him because the giant, named 'Mountain Harper' (*Fjallsharfir*), has already killed two of his six sons and threatens to kill the others if the lord does not give the giant his beautiful daughter in marriage. Íven, as a chivalrous knight, complies with this request and ends up killing the giant. Among the details that distinguish this giant-killing episode from similar themes in *fornaldarsögur* is God's intervention in the fight. All the people in the castle pray to God before the battle to protect Íven 'against this troll' (*fyrir þessu trölli*), and God apparently heeds their prayer, so that when the giant strikes at Íven with his iron club 'God protected him so that it did not strike him so as to hurt' (*barg þá guð er eigi kom á hann svá at hann sakaði*). Numerous other apparently grotesque or abnormal beings and actions in this and other *riddarasögur* seem at first glance to be beyond nature, but are seen to be under God's control when all is revealed.

A third characteristic of the *riddarasaga* demonstrated by the opening sentences of *Ívens saga* is the nature and social station of their protagonists. Following their sources, their characters are in the main knights, nobles and kings on the one hand, and beautiful ladies and their handmaidens on the other. Typically, the knight hero is involved both in the pursuit of a lady and of adventure. Often the one motivates the other. So, in *Ívens saga*, Íven wins and marries a beautiful lady after first killing her husband in a joust, but then, somewhat inexplicably, forgets to return to her from participating in King Arthur's tournaments until the deadline for their reunion has well and truly expired. He is then forced to expiate his chivalric lapse by undertaking a great number of adventures, many of them in company with a lion he has rescued from a flame-spewing dragon.

Scholars have pointed out that the Old Norse translated romances lack the complexity of characterisation of their sources because they cut out most of the internal monologues through which the characters' inner conflicts between love and the duties of chivalry are expressed. On the other hand, King Arthur and his knights are presented as more heroic than their counterparts in the French sources, which sometimes undercut chivalrous behaviour with an ironic awareness of the distance between ideal and actual conduct. Geraldine Barnes has characterised the chivalry displayed in the *riddarasögur* as 'feudal' rather than 'courtly', with the emphasis on the virtues of courage, loyalty, piety and modesty, along with a lack of interest in the ritual and emotion of love.

Riddarasögur, like their sources, have their questing knights move in a conventionalised setting of courts and castles, where the beautiful people live, separated by thick forests and deep valleys, the homes of various threatening forces. These may be anthropomorphic beings like giants, dwarves and other misshapen creatures, or wild animals, mostly of types that would have seemed exotic to Scandinavian audiences, such as lions, leopards and dragons. The standard *mise-en-scène* of these sagas, with tournaments, jousts between the hero and an unknown knight, damsels in distress, animal companions and helpful and evil maidens also distinguishes the *riddarasaga* from other saga types. However, it should be stressed that the influence of the *riddarasaga* ideology and its interest in chivalry and kingship appears in other saga sub-genres, including sagas of Icelanders and kings' sagas.

It has been customary to distinguish the Old Norse romances that were translated from French and Anglo-Norman during Hákon Hákonarson's reign from a second group of sagas, also referred to as *riddarasögur*, that arguably came into being under their influence. These are the so-called indigenous *riddarasögur*, which have some similarities of plot and theme to the translated romances, but differ from them in that they involve characters, often with Scandinavian names, and actions that may notionally take place in a chivalric setting, in that the protagonists are usually kings' sons and daughters, but that quickly reveal themselves as dealing with central themes of Nordic saga literature, including conflicting family loyalties, whether to blood relatives, blood-brothers or affinal kin, male sexual rivalry, inheritance claims and marriage arrangements. It is often difficult to make a clean distinction between the indigenous *riddarasögur* and certain *fornaldarsögur*, and in fact some sagas, such as 'The Saga of Hrólfr son of Gautrekr' (*Hrólfs saga Gautrekssonar*), are classified by some scholars as *riddarasögur* while others treat them primarily as *fornaldarsögur*.

The indigenous *riddarasögur* can be thought of as taking inspiration from both the translated romances, in terms of their representation of the social world of their protagonists and the fact that many of them involve a man's quest for a bride, and from the *fornaldarsögur* in terms of some of the deep themes they treat, as well as the settings in which the protagonists experience a range of unusual and exotic individuals and events. The *mise-en-scène* is, however, usually closer to that of the translated romances than the *fornaldarsögur*, and the geographical settings of this group of sagas range widely from Europe to Asia. Like the translated romances, too, the indigenous *riddarasögur* are prose works, the only one to contain verse being 'The Saga of Jarl Mágus' (*Mágus saga jarls*), which includes three stanzas.

Kings' sagas

Konungasǫgur, 'kings' sagas', like saints' lives, follow a biographical and, often, a hagiographical literary pattern, that is, they share a great deal in terms of structure, conceptual background and characterisation with the medieval saint's life. Although saints' lives, of which there are a great many in Old Norse, will not be accorded separate treatment here, they were among the most popular of all medieval European literary kinds, and their influence upon other kinds of medieval writing was profound. Some scholars have regarded the saint's life as the kind of writing upon which Icelandic vernacular authors cut their literary teeth. Whether or not this was so, most scholars are of the opinion that the kings' sagas, which are closest of all the saga sub-genres to medieval European biography, were probably where the Icelandic saga-writing habit began. As we saw in Chapter 2, the composition of historical literature began during the twelfth century in both Norway and Iceland, in Latin and in the vernacular.

The term *konungasǫgur* covers a number of biographical or semi-biographical subjects. The majority of the sagas in this group are biographies of the kings of Norway, either singly, as with 'The Saga of Sverrir' (*Sverris saga*) and 'The Saga of Hákon Hákonarson' (*Hákonar saga Hákonarsonar*), or in compilations. In Chapter 4 we touched on the complex textual relationships between the great compilations, such as *Morkinskinna*, *Fagrskinna* and *Heims-kringla*. Comparative textual evidence indicates that the compilers of these compendia knew and reworked the earlier compilations and sometimes added new material to them, presumably to satisfy both their own and their audiences' changing tastes. Other compilations, such as *Hauksbók*, compiled for the Icelandic lawman Haukr Erlendsson (d. 1334), and in part by him, contain more varied material: kings' sagas and *þættir*, as well as legendary histories, like 'The Sagas of the British' (*Breta sǫgur*), and translations of geographical and scientific literature. Often the chronological period covered was extended by later writers beyond the limit reached by earlier compilers. The net result of this process of rewriting, which took place intensively in the early part of the thirteenth century, was to produce several series of biographies of the Norwegian kings, arranged in chronological order, and, in many cases, accompanied by *þættir*, or short narratives that recount information about Icelanders, often poets, who were present at these kings' courts. In the case of some kings, like Óláfr Haraldsson (St Óláfr), who came to be venerated as a saint shortly after his death, multiple biographies exist.

While the majority of kings' sagas are biographies of Norwegian kings, there was also an interest among Icelandic writers in the kings of Denmark, beginning with the now lost legendary history *Skjǫldunga saga* 'Saga of the Skjǫldungar [Danish royal house]', whose content is known from an early modern Latin epitome by the Icelander Arngrímur Jónsson (1568–1648). The late thirteenth-century 'The Saga of the descendants of Knútr' (*Knýtlinga saga*) continues this interest and narrates the histories of the kings of Denmark from the early tenth to the thirteenth centuries. By contrast, there are no separate sagas or compilations about the kings of Sweden, although the name of their royal dynasty, the Ynglingar, was subsumed into the legendary history of the kings of Norway, a position most clearly presented in Snorri Sturluson's *Ynglinga saga*, the preface to his Norwegian royal history *Heimskringla*, which draws upon a dynastic poem, 'List of the Ynglingar' (*Ynglingatal*), ascribed to the late ninth-century Norwegian poet Þjóðólfr of Hvinir, for evidence about the lives and deaths of kings who lived in the prehistoric period.

There are some other historical sagas which are usually classified with kings' sagas, although attempts have been made to distinguish them on generic grounds as 'political sagas' (without a great deal of success). Two of these, 'The Saga of the Orkney Islanders' (*Orkneyinga saga*) and 'The Saga of the Faroe Islanders' (*Færeyinga saga*), in spite of their titles, are not histories of the whole of these island societies, but rather accounts of their leaders, in the case of the Orkneys of a dynasty of Jarls, who descended from the Jarls of Møre in Norway. Yet another work, 'The Saga of the Jómsvíkingar' (*Jómsvíkinga saga*), which is a history of a group of people, the Jómsvíkingar, an all-male band of warriors associated with the fortification of the stronghold of Jómsborg, identified with Wollin in present-day Poland, is a legendary history which touches at certain points upon the military history of tenth-century Denmark and Norway. It is estimated that a version or versions of this saga had achieved written form by 1200. The texts of these three sagas are preserved partly in independent fragments, and partly in major compilations of the sagas of the kings Óláfr Tryggvason and Óláfr Haraldsson, principally the late fourteenth-century *Flateyjarbók*.

In the Middle Ages, the writing of history was classified as a branch of the subject of grammar and was not regarded as a separate subject in the educational curriculum. Consequently, those who wrote history were conscious of the necessity to follow the rules of medieval grammar (which was a much broader discipline than modern grammar and included rhetoric) in presenting their subject and to secure the authenticity of their narratives by drawing upon the evidence of trusted authorities to back them up. Such authorities could be either eyewitnesses to events or written authorities whose status was universally accepted. For many medieval European historians writing in Latin, or even sometimes in the vernacular, their authorities were earlier written texts, as we saw in Chapter 2 with the example of the Norwegian monk Theodoricus's appeal to the authority of the Norman historian William of Jumièges. The historians of Scandinavia, however, had very few written authorities to turn to. Instead, they used the most reliable and most prestigious vernacular authorities they knew, the skalds or court poets.

In his Prologue to *Ynglinga saga* in *Heimskringla,* and with slightly different wording in the Prologue to his separate saga of St Óláfr, Snorri Sturluson set out the conditions under which skaldic poetry could be regarded as authoritative for a historian:

> There were skalds with King Haraldr [Fair-hair], and people still know their poems and poems about all the kings there have since been in Norway, and we take examples mostly from what is said in those poems which were recited before the princes themselves or their sons. We take everything to be true that is to be found in those poems about their journeys or battles. Though it is the habit of skalds to praise most the one in whose presence they are, yet no one would dare to tell a prince himself about deeds of his which all those who heard them would know to be nonsense and invention, as he would himself. For that would be mockery rather than praise.

> Með Haraldi konungi váru skáld, ok kunna menn enn kvæði þeira ok allra konunga kvæði, þeira er síðan hafa verit í Nóregi, ok tókum vér þar mest dœmi af, þat er sagt er í þeim kvæðum, er kveðin váru fyrir sjálfum hǫfðingjunum eða sonum þeira. Tǫkum vér þat allt fyrir satt, er í þeim kvæðum finnsk um ferðir þeira eða orrostur. En þat er háttr skálda at lofa þann mest, er þá eru þeir fyrir, en engi myndi þat þora at segja sjálfum honum þau verk hans, er allir þeir, er heyrði, vissi, at hégómi væri ok skrǫk, ok svá sjálfr hann. Þat væri þá háð, en eigi lof. [6]

Court poets are thus Snorri's vernacular authorities, but he sets limits to the kinds of skaldic verse that can be considered authoritative, at least in theory: authoritative skaldic verse must have been recited before its royal subjects or before their sons, if the poems were composed after the kings' deaths as memorial encomia or *erfidrápur*. In practice, the writers of kings' sagas varied a lot in the extent to which they drew on skaldic authorities to support their narratives. To some extent this depended on how much poetry there was available to them, which in turn depended in part on the degree to which specific kings had cultivated court poets. Some kings, most notably King Haraldr harðráði 'Hard-rule' Sigurðarson (r. 1046–66), himself a poet, encouraged a good many skalds to compose for him and about him. Consequently, a considerable number of poems about Haraldr's life, his journeys and battles have been preserved in several historical compilations and offer illuminating evidence for the details of his reign. On the other hand, relatively little poetry has been preserved about rulers like King Sverrir Sigurðarson (r. 1177–1202), even though *Skáldatal* 'List of Poets', a table of rulers and the poets who worked for them, records that a number of skalds composed encomia about Sverrir. This may in part be because he himself did not encourage the use of poetry for historical documentation. Only seventeen stanzas are extant in *Sverris saga*, and it is recorded that Sverrir himself supervised his biographer, the Icelandic abbot Karl Jónsson (d. 1212/13), and influenced what he wrote, at least in the first part of the saga. Most of the seventeen stanzas are incorporated into Sverrir's many speeches or are used to comment on events in a manner very different from the use of poetry in earlier kings' sagas, which were often written quite some time after the events they narrated took place. Skaldic poetry is used in perceptibly different ways in kings' sagas composed after about 1250 which rarely depend on the poetry of contemporary witnesses as they did in earlier times.

It was not only the authoritative value of skaldic poetry as source material that would have appealed to the writers of vernacular kings' sagas. The ideology of these poems as royal propaganda was of immense importance in establishing one of the marks of the sub-genre, its interest in and promotion of the medieval ideology of kingship. In a series of recent studies, Ármann Jakobsson has drawn attention to the extent and intensity of medieval Icelandic interest in the subject of kingship, even though, paradoxically, Iceland was distinguished for several centuries within medieval Europe by not having kings when everyone else had them. Kings' sagas may be seen as a set of variations on the theme of kingship, good, bad and indifferent, but the tone for a great deal of the substance of these sagas was already set by the poets who composed in praise, and sometimes in criticism, of these rulers.

A good example of how moral emphases that are already present in skaldic stanzas can be expanded into the prose narratives of kings' sagas to comment on kingly behaviour is Chapter 22 of 'The Saga of Haraldr son of Sigurðr' (*Haralds saga Sigurðarsonar*) in *Heimskringla*.[7] Snorri describes how, shortly after Haraldr's return, via Sweden, from exile in Russia, he has a meeting with the Danish king Sveinn Úlfsson, who is ostensibly friendly, but in fact tries to kill Haraldr. This treacherous behaviour in a supposed ally, shortly to be a bitter enemy, is contrasted with the generosity displayed by Haraldr's nephew, Magnús inn góði 'the Good' Óláfsson, who comes to a meeting with his kinsman and offers to share the throne of Norway with him. Magnús's magnanimity and the openness of the meeting, described as a *fagnafundr* 'joyful meeting' in Snorri's prose, is backed up with a stanza from the skald Þjóðólfr Arnórsson's *Sexstefja* 'Six-Refrains', in which the poet gives as his own opinion the view 'I think that the kinsmen met there most joyfully' (*hykk, at frændr fyndisk þar hóla fegnir*, *Sexstefja* 10/6–8).[8] The following chapter shows how generosity begets generosity, when Haraldr shares his vast wealth, acquired in Byzantium, with his nephew.

Like the *fornaldarsaga* and the family saga, the historical character of the kings' sagas is critically influenced by these sagas' chronological positioning on one side or other of the divide marked by the conversion to Christianity in both Norway and Iceland. To deal with the time before the period of conversion, dynastic histories are constructed as myths, in which eponymous ancestor figures, descended from the gods, established their rule over the peoples of various parts of Scandinavia. It is likely that both indigenous and learned traditions played a part in the construction of these myths. Sagas about those kings who lived immediately before the conversion, in particular King Haraldr hárfagri 'Fair-hair' Hálfdanarson, during whose reign Iceland was settled, are presented in such a way as to suggest the imminent advent of Christendom while at the same time using mythic themes to convey the ambivalent character of lived experience for people of that liminal time.

The sagas of the two missionary kings, Óláfr Tryggvason (r. 995–1000) and Óláfr Haraldsson (r. 1015–1030), the latter later elevated to sainthood, have been mentioned earlier in this chapter as frequently instantiating the rout of the forces of the devil, often in the form of the pagan gods, in the face of the advancing power of Christianity, brought to the remotest parts of their kingdoms by the kings themselves. A great many episodes in the sagas written about these kings are of this nature. In the case of St Óláfr, there very quickly grew up miracle stories about the saintly powers of the king after death, which matched and even outdid the powers he displayed when alive. The status of the miracles was equivocal, from the point of view of the compilers of kings' sagas; some included many of them (like the so-called *Legendary Saga*), others were more circumspect (like *Heimskringla*). It is clear, though, that medieval historians generally considered some aspects of the paranormal, according to modern perspectives, to come within their purview, notably phenomena that could be classified as either miracles or manifestations of natural magic.

Sagas of Icelanders and their world

The world of the sagas of Icelanders or family sagas is more familiar to most general readers than any of the other literary environments explored in this chapter, owing to the many existing translations of works from this sub-genre and numerous studies of the Icelandic sagas which deal largely with this group of texts. During the twentieth century sagas of Icelanders have been far more intensively studied by scholars than any other sub-genre and are consequently the subjects of a great many critical studies. As far as chronology goes, these sagas are set in the period covering the first settlement of Iceland (*c.* 870–930) and the first one hundred years or so of Iceland's history, a period discussed in some detail in Chapter 1. Whereas some family sagas are set in the age before Iceland's conversion to Christianity in 1000, others carry their narratives beyond conversion to give a foretaste of the condition of life in Iceland in Christian times. A few sagas of this group, like 'The Saga of the the Foster-brothers' (*Fóstbrœðra saga*), are set wholly within the Christian period, although, as the writer of this saga expresses it, the immediate post-conversion world still held *margir gneistar heiðninnar* 'many sparks of heathendom',[9] which needed to be extinguished before a truly Christian society could be established.

As the name 'sagas of Icelanders' (*Íslendingasögur*) indicates, these narratives deal squarely with the lives of Icelanders, mostly as spent in Iceland, and are presented in a narrative mode that has appeared objective and realistic to many earlier saga critics, but that, when examined more carefully, as it will be in Chapter 6, is revealed as much more partial and accommodating to non-realistic elements than many earlier scholars have allowed. Among the principal subjects of family sagas are the generational histories of specific families settled in particular regions of the island, beginning with the first settlers and tracing the family history to the conversion and beyond, like 'The Saga of the inhabitants of Eyrr' (*Eyrbyggja saga*) and 'The Saga of the people of Vatnsdalur' (*Vatnsdœla saga*); the histories of feuds and lawsuits between rival families, which often come to involve many other parties, such as *Ljósvetninga saga* 'The saga of the people of Ljósavatn' and large parts of *Njáls saga*; and the biographies of Icelandic poets and outlaws, like *Egils saga* and *Grettis saga*. Many sagas of Icelanders begin with a prelude dealing with the fortunes of the Icelandic family's immediate ancestors in Norway; others take the protagonists overseas, often to Norway, during parts of their lives. The Vinland sagas, 'The Saga of Eiríkr the Red' (*Eiríks saga rauða*) and 'The Saga of the Greenlanders' (*Grœnlendinga saga*), constitute a special case, in that they deal with the colonisation of Greenland and explorations in parts of North America by Icelanders.

The sagas of Icelanders share with kings' sagas and *fornaldarsögur* the importance of genealogy and the biographical narrative mode, only in this sub-genre the biographies are of important Icelanders, who by definition are not royal, nor are they noble in the normal medieval European sense of being part of a hereditary or a socially recognised aristocracy. However, in many cases the protagonists of sagas of Icelanders are the ancestors of men and women who wielded great power in the period covering the late twelfth and thirteenth centuries, that is, the age during which much saga writing is thought to have taken place. In some cases, the saga writers have imbued their characters with the qualities, appearance and attributes of chivalric figures, such as we find in the depiction of Kjartan Ólafsson in *Laxdœla saga*. Thus it is likely that many sagas of Icelanders would have been considered by their original audiences as crypto-noble biographies on a par with some biographical genres that flourished about the same time in other parts of Europe. These include the ancestral and historical romance, popular in England and France during the late thirteenth and fourteenth centuries, in which legendary heroes of the past are the subjects of a narrative that explores the question of national or regional identity.

A good deal has been written about the protagonists of sagas of Icelanders considered both as individuals and as heroes. While the honour and integrity of the individual are clearly the highest ethical value represented in these texts, as we have already mentioned in Chapter 1, other virtues, such as moderation and the ability to compromise, disturb any tendency to outright heroism in family sagas. Theodore Andersson has referred to the moderation of purely heroic attitudes in these sagas as a 'displacement' of the heroic ideal to be found in Old Norse heroic poetry, for example. A number of saga writers are clearly critical of the excesses of some protagonists, such as Guðmundr inn ríki 'the Powerful' in 'The Saga of the Ljósvetningar' (*Ljósvetninga saga*), who, while occupying positions of authority, display failures of courage and intellect. Moreover, the obverse of honour, namely dishonour and a failure to live up to standards of individual probity, are mercilessly criticised in sagas of Icelanders.

Contemporary sagas

Like the sagas of Icelanders, the contemporary sagas (*samtíðarsögur*) are set in Iceland, and like them their writers espouse an objective style and deal with events and persons of Icelandic society. Unlike the family sagas, however, the chronological period covered by the contemporary sagas stretches from the early twelfth century to some time in the 1260s, a period during which Iceland had been Christian for some two hundred years. The contemporary sagas appear to have been written within a hundred years of the events they relate, and in many cases they are much closer than that to their subject-matter. This is particularly true of *Íslendinga saga* 'The Saga of the Icelanders', the major work in the compilation 'The Saga of the Sturlungar' (*Sturlunga saga*), named for the powerful family, the Sturlungs, whose members are its protagonists. *Íslendinga saga* was composed by Sturla Þórðarson (1214–84), who also wrote *Hákonar saga Hákonarsonar* on commission from Hákon's son Magnús lagabœtir 'the Lawmender', a biography of Magnús, which is no longer extant, and a version of *Landnámabók*. He composed a great deal of poetry for his biography of King Hákon as well as verse that has not survived for his saga of King Magnús. Sturla was an eyewitness to many of the events of *Íslendinga saga*, although he usually presents his narrative in an apparently impersonal manner. In spite of Sturla's closeness to the events he describes, however, we must remember that his work has not been preserved in its original form, but has come down to us in the *Sturlunga saga* compilation, probably a work of the early fourteenth century.

Most literary analysis of the contemporary sagas is fairly recent, as these works had previously been somewhat neglected or treated as less artistically sophisticated variants of the sagas of Icelanders sub-genre. This view is now changing, and in recent decades there have been some excellent studies, mainly of the *Sturlunga* compilation as a whole or specifically of *Íslendinga saga*. These sagas are both political narratives, in that they involve all the main players in Icelandic politics during the period covered, and family histories, inasmuch as struggles between members of the half dozen or so major families on the island were the chief arena within which Icelandic politics was played out. The main families at this time were: from the Southern district, the Odda-verjar, Haukdælir and Svínfellingar; from the Western district, the Sturlungar; from the West fjords, the Vatnsfirðingar; and from the Northern district, the Ásbirningar. To the extent that the Norwegian king manipulated the most powerful Icelandic chieftains of the first half of the thirteenth century in order to further his aim of bringing the country under the Norwegian crown, the action of the contemporary sagas, though set mainly in Iceland, frequently involves events that take place in Norway and protagonists based there.

The subject-matter of the contemporary sagas appears raw and often shocking because it is presented as more or less immediate in time and urgent in its implications. It sometimes makes the action of sagas of Icelanders seem mannered by comparison. One event, frequently of a violent nature, follows another in quick succession. But, in most cases, and certainly in *Íslendinga saga*, a narratorial perspective is offered on the action. As Guðrún Nordal has demonstrated in her 1998 study of this saga, Sturla Þórðarson uses a variety of literary and mythical models to shape his narrative and give it an overarching moral perspective. He is thus able to provide a complex ethical stance which acknowledges the ties and pressures of kinship and marriage, sexuality, personal ambition and the hunger for power while at the same time promoting a middle way of conciliation and peace. Such a narratorial positioning requires an author to command a complex array of literary techniques, and there is no doubt that Sturla, and to a lesser extent the authors of other contemporary sagas, possessed these skills.

An example from one of the most dramatic episodes of *Íslendinga saga*, the burning of Gizurr Þorvaldsson's farm at Flugumýrr in 1253, illustrates how Sturla, who was personally involved in the event in several ways, was able to negotiate a narratorial path that was both objective and engaged through the often minute detail of a striking and horrifying event. The background to the burning involved ongoing feuding between the Haukdælir and the Sturlungar. In an attempt to secure peace between the two families, Sturla Þórðarson's daughter Ingibjǫrg was married to Gizurr Þorvaldsson's son Hallr, and it was at their wedding feast that a plot to burn Gizurr's farm was put into effect. It has also to be understood as background to the episode that Gizurr was ultimately to emerge as the victor in the struggle for power as the Norwegian king's regent in Iceland, even though in the aftermath of the Flugumýrr burning he appears as a humiliated and pathetic, though still dignified, figure.

The final part of the Flugumýrr burning focusses on Gizurr, both on the remarkable way in which he evaded capture by his enemies and on the many personal losses he suffered, including the deaths of his wife and three of his sons.[10] From the beginning of this chapter (174), the emphasis is upon Gizurr, as the narrative makes clear with a direct opening statement: *Nú er at segja frá Gizuri Þorvaldssyni, at hann kom at skyrbúri, ok hann Guðmundr, frændi hans, fylgði honum* 'Now it is to be told about Gizurr Þorvaldsson, that he came to the *skyr*-room and his kinsman Guðmundr followed him.' Gizurr quickly gets rid of other men in order to be alone in one of the few unburnt rooms at the farm, a coolroom in which *skyr* 'curds' and whey were made and stored. His concealment from his enemies, who come looking for him there, is both audacious and ignominious. He hides in the whey vat. Sturla tells of his ordeal there in incredibly fine detail and with sympathy. Gizurr gently deflects the points of his enemies' spears as they probe the vat in case he is in there. In the process he gets many surface wounds and becomes so cold that his shivering makes ripples in the whey, but when his enemies enter the room he has such self-control that he stops shaking. Eventually he escapes from the *skyr*-room to the nearby church and is warmed between the thighs of a servant woman.

In the course of this memorable narrative, Sturla the narrator guides his audience's responses both covertly and overtly. He evaluates Gizurr's behaviour in a balanced way by commenting: *Gizurr hresstist brátt ok bar sik vel ok drengiliga eftir slíka mannraun ok harma* 'Gizurr recovered quickly and bore himself well and nobly after such humiliations and injuries.' Implicit here, as Guðrún Nordal has suggested, may be a comparison between Gizurr's ingenious but not entirely heroic escape and that of Kári Sǫlmundarson in *Njáls saga* from the burning at Bergþórshvǫll. A little further on, Sturla mentions other burnings that had occurred in Iceland previously and calls upon God in his mercy to forgive those who caused the Flugumýrr fire, thus reinforcing the traditional Icelandic abhorrence of this particular act of aggression and bringing a Christian perspective to bear on the event. At the conclusion of the episode Sturla invokes the emotion of sympathy, both for Gizurr, who turns away from the sight of his wife's and son's charred bodies with tears in his eyes (and this is said to be witnessed by a third party), and finally, but covertly, for himself and his 13-year-old daughter Ingibjǫrg, whose wedding feast has turned to tragedy with the death of her new husband and the danger and stress of the fire. Sturla comments movingly in conclusion: *Var hon mjök þrekuð, barn at aldri* 'She was quite worn out, a child in years.' Such carefully nuanced narrative with its unobtrusive manipulation of the audience's response distinguishes this contemporary saga from the more impersonal use of authorial point of view in most sagas of Icelanders.

Chapter 6

Saga mode, style and point of view

This chapter will explore the nature of the saga's modality and present it as a modally mixed genre, although conceding that some sub-genres are less mixed than others. It will demonstrate, with selected examples, that such a mixed modality is well suited to the world-view of medieval Icelanders and enabled saga authors to present their material as historically plausible, while at the same time accommodating perspectives on human experience and the natural world that modern readers would classify as fantastic or supernatural. The chapter will also explore the implications of mixed modality for saga style generally, with a close analysis of selected examples. A special aspect of the saga's mixed modality is the prosimetrical character of many, but by no means all, sagas. This important dimension of the Icelandic saga will be investigated here, as will the role of verse in sagas, a subject on which much has recently been written.

Throughout this book, the medieval Icelandic saga is treated as a specific literary genre within which a number of sub-genres can be distinguished. It was conceded in Chapter 2 that some characteristics of the saga genre are shared with other medieval literary kinds, like hagiography, for example, but there are still enough characteristics that are distinctive to the saga to allow us to recognise it with confidence as a unique literary genre or kind. At this point in our analysis it will be helpful to identify the nature of the term 'literary mode' and to establish how this concept can aid us in understanding some of the characteristics of saga literature that cannot be fully comprehended within a purely generic or structural analysis. Literary modes exist within a variety of external forms, as, for example, when a novel is described as 'comic'. This particular modal designation can be applied to a number of literary forms, dramatic, narrative or operatic. Thus, in the case of the Icelandic saga, its generic identity determines characteristics of its form, including such qualities as structure, setting, characterisation and narrative character, while its mode gives the genre its distinction of mood, its approach to the relationship between possibility and actuality as depicted in the saga world. Most modern studies of the Icelandic saga have neglected the genre's literary mode and have consequently been ill at ease with the combination of modalities sagas often display.

In earlier publications I have argued that Icelandic sagas often display a 'mixed modality', by which I meant that sagas switch more easily between a realistic and a non-realistic mode than much modern writing has done, especially before the advent of postmodernist literary genres. Thus I have argued that the saga form is characterised by multiple modalities, that is, modes of writing that present different dimensions of represented experience. There are very few examples of individual sagas that are uni-modal. Previously I have written about 'realism' and 'fantasy' in the saga as if they were two separate literary modes, but I now want to move beyond such relatively superficial distinctions, which I believe represent more of a modern approach to texts, to develop an analysis within a sense of mixed modality, which allows one to detect differences of mode or register,[1] but does not restrict one to classifying texts as one or the other. The justification for this position is that medieval texts themselves do not operate in this way.

Within a mixed modality a writer can range between what modern literary analysis is likely to classify as two or more separate modes without changing register. This facility probably reflects characteristic ways in which many medieval people thought, stemming from an ideology that did not always differentiate sharply between events and experiences that could be ascertained empirically and those that could not. The latter would usually now be classified as belonging to the dimension of the spiritual or the supernatural, depending on the extent to which the element of systematic belief applied to the phenomenon under consideration. In the Middle Ages, some of the phenomena that we would class as supernatural would have been accepted as verifiable empirically or at least sanctioned by some authority, usually divine. Thus a believing Christian, then as now, would be inclined to regard the shroud of

Turin as the result of a miracle and a sign of Christ's continuing existence, while a modern non-believer would tend to explain the marks on the shroud as the result of some physical process of staining.

As far as supernatural phenomena not directly associated with Christian belief are concerned, such as apparently magical happenings, ghosts or unusual natural events, there is again a range of modern responses, although these are not as narrowly guided by Christian doctrine as those of medieval people were, and fewer people nowadays are likely to give credence to the operation of the supernatural in their world. In this book, I have preferred to use the term 'paranormal' rather than 'supernatural' to refer to phenomena that cannot be accounted for empirically in order to acknowledge the fact that in the Middle Ages a larger number of people, perhaps most, would have admitted at least some events and experiences that we would classify as improbable or illusory into the realm of their lived experience. In all likelihood, ordinary people would have admitted more such phenomena into their world of experience than would intellectuals and clerics, whose thinking would have been more firmly guided by the Church's attitude to the supernatural, which established distinctions between those phenomena that could be attributed to the influence of the Christian God, such as miracles, those that were natural wonders or the product of natural magic, and those that were likely to be the result of the operation of demonic forces of some kind.

We saw in Chapter 5 that paranormal episodes could be presented in sagas both as the illusions of demons or the result of natural magic, that is, the operation of the laws of nature, albeit often in unusual circumstances. Some paranormal phenomena could also be accounted for as miracles, in the sense of being caused solely by God. All these types of presentation occur in saga literature of all sub-genres, although they are more frequent, as we have already seen, in sub-genres like *fornaldarsögur* and *riddarasögur* that are set outside Iceland. This is partly because these sub-genres depict the 'other worlds' of prehistory or legend in which the paranormal could be expected to play a large part and partly because saga writers felt less constrained to document the veracity of such events outside their own community. It is also likely that saga writers were very well aware of the medieval tradition, inherited from the Greeks and Romans, that situated a range of natural marvels, including strange races of humans, giants, dragons and other fabulous beings, beyond their own familiar boundaries.

In order to understand the ways in which medieval writers present human lived experience, it is always necessary for the modern reader to be aware both of the greater acceptance of the paranormal in medieval society than in our own and of the medieval Church's official attitude to it, because these views affect the ways in which the paranormal is represented in medieval texts, including Icelandic sagas. Sävborg's recent and otherwise excellent study of differences in the authorial representation of the paranormal in Icelandic sagas makes no mention at all of the influence of Christian thought upon the various ways in which supernatural events or beings are treated there, and yet it would be unusual, to say the least, if saga writers were uninfluenced by mainstream Christian thinking on the subject, the more so because they were likely to be educated men writing about traditional beliefs in their community, which would not always be in accordance with the beliefs of the educated sector of Icelandic society, nor of medieval Europe in general. As we shall see below, and as Sävborg has himself demonstrated, saga writers were well able to nuance their presentations of the paranormal by using various distancing devices, which enabled them to indicate their own perspective on such phenomena, as well as that of the characters within the sagas they were narrating.

The remainder of this chapter will be devoted to presenting a workable basis upon which we in the twenty-first century can attempt to understand how medieval Icelanders would have understood saga texts, whether they encountered them in oral or in written form. While always being mindful of the fact that we can never completely 'get under the skin' of people from a past age, the textual markers identified here are sufficiently robust to provide tangible evidence of how Icelanders are likely to have perceived saga narratives and give us a guide, using standard modern techniques of literary analysis, to how sagas 'mean' for us today.

The importance of understanding the sagas' literary mode has already been discussed. Closely related to the identification of modality is the identification of variations in saga style, because different literary styles not only contribute substantially to the creation of a particular mode, but are also accessible to close rhetorical analysis and the demonstration of the existence of specific and changing registers, lexical range and narrative points of view. Another issue that arises when one undertakes a close reading of saga texts is this: what cultural knowledge and assumptions are required of us and were required of medieval Icelanders to understand these texts? I propose to test all these issues of mode, style and cultural assumptions by means of a close analysis of four passages, three from sagas of Icelanders and the fourth from a *fornaldarsaga*, analysing them in depth in order to establish their changing modality and style and to identify the cultural knowledge needed to understand them. To evaluate modality requires cultural knowledge, something that would have been acquired in various ways by members of the medieval Icelandic community over the course of their lives, but which we can only acquire through scholarship and learning about the Icelandic version of the medieval European world.

An example of prosimetrum: *Kormáks saga*, Chapter 6

Síðan ferr Kormákr at finna Steingerði jafnt sem áðr; ok eitt sinn, er þau tala um þessa atburði, lætr hon ekki illa yfir. Kormákr kvað vísu:

> Sitja menn ok meina
> mér ásjǫnu þína,
> þeir hafa lǫgðis loddu
> linna fœtr at vinna;
> því at upp skulu allar,
> ǫlstafns, áðr ek þér hafna,
> lýsigrund, í landi,
> linns, þjóðáar rinna.

'Mæl þú eigi svá mikit um,' segir Steingerðr, 'mart má því bregða.' Þá kvað Kormákr vísu:

> Hvern myndir þú hrundar
> Hlín skapfrǫmuð línu,
> líknsýnir mér lúka
> ljós, þér at ver kjósa?

Steingerðr segir:

> Brœðr mynda ek blindum,
> bauglestir, mik festa,
> yrði goð sem gerðisk
> góð mér ok skǫp, Fróða.

Kormákr segir: 'Nú kaustu sem vera ætti; opt hefi ek hingat mínar kvámur lagðar.' Nú biðr Steingerðr Kormák stunda til fǫður hennar ok fá hennar, ok fyrir sakar Steingerðar gaf Kormákr Þorkatli gjafar. Eptir þetta eigu margir menn hlut í, ok þar kom um síðir, at Kormákr bað Steingerðar, ok var hon honum fǫstnuð ok ákveðin brullaupsstefna, ok stendr nú kyrrt um hríð. Nú fara orð á milli þeira, ok verða í nǫkkurar greinir um fjárfar, ok svá veik við breytiliga, at síðan þessum ráðum var ráðit, fannsk Kormáki fátt um, en þat var fyrir þá sǫk, at Þórveig seiddi til, at þau skyldi eigi njótask mega.

. . .

Kormákr sœkir eigi brullaupit eptir því sem ákveðit var, ok leið fram stundin. Þetta þykkir frændum Steingerðar óvirðing, er hann bregðr þessum ráðahag, ok leita sér ráðs.

Then Kormak went to visit Steingerd, just as he did before.

On one occasion, when they were discussing these events, she in no way expressed disapproval.

Kormak spoke a verse:

> Men lie in wait and deny
> to me the sight of your face;
> they have a hard fight ahead

> with the serpents of the shield.   *serpents of the shield*: swords
> For all the mighty rivers in the land
> shall sooner flow uphill
> before I forsake you, oh shining ground   *ground of ale-cups*: bearer
> of flame-gleaming ale-cups.   *of ale-cups*, woman

'Don't speak so much about it,' said Steingerd. 'There are many things that can happen to change the situation.'
Then Kormak spoke a verse:

> Which valkyrie's champion   *valkyrie's champion*: warrior
> oh goddess of the veil,   *goddess* (Hlín) *of the veil*: woman
> would you choose for your husband?
> Your soothing looks bode brightly.

Steingerd spoke:

> Ring-breaker, though he were blind,   *Ring-breaker*: generous man
> it's to Frodi's brother I'd bind me.
> For then the gods and the fates
> would despite all be treating me well.

Kormak said, 'Now you've made the right choice; I have often visited you here.'

Steingerd now asked Kormak to seek her father's friendship and obtain the promise of her hand in marriage, and for Steingerd's sake Kormak gave Thorkel gifts. After that many people were involved in the matter, and what happened in the end was that Kormak asked for Steingerd's hand, and she was betrothed to him and the wedding was arranged, and things stayed quiet for a while. Now messages passed between them, and these came to include certain disagreements about money matters, and it turned out strangely that, after the marriage was decided on, Kormak's feelings about it cooled, and this was because Thorveig worked a spell so that they would not be able to enjoy each other's love.
. . .
Kormak did not attend the wedding as had been arranged, and time passed. Steingerd's kinsmen considered it dishonourable that he should break off this engagement, and they sought a solution.[2]

Literary and cultural background

Kormáks saga is generally regarded as one of the earliest sagas of Icelanders to have achieved written form, but decisive proof of this dating is lacking. Most scholars think it was written in the early thirteenth century, although the oldest manuscript in which it is preserved complete, the saga anthology *Möðruvallabók* ('The Book of Möðruvellir'), dates from the mid fourteenth century. There is another fragmentary vellum, AM 162 F fol, of about 1400. The saga belongs to the sub-class of skalds' sagas within the sagas of Icelanders sub-genre, a group that tells of the lives and loves of individual Icelandic skalds who are mostly known as court poets in other contexts, such as kings' sagas and Snorri Sturluson's *Edda*. The poets' sagas are set in Iceland for the most part, although their authors also devote some attention to the protagonists' adventures abroad. They share a number of themes, chief of which is the poet's love for a particular Icelandic woman which is thwarted for various reasons, including the man's truculent and aggressive character, the opposition of the woman's family and rival suitors, and, in the case of *Kormáks saga*, the operation of sorcery which ensures that the couple will never marry and enjoy each other's love.

The skalds' sagas are also characterised by the nature and quantity of verses they contain. Typically, the verses express the skald's love for his chosen woman, his frustration at not being able to gain access to her or marry her, and his scorn of his rivals (some of whom *are* able to marry the woman, although she really loves the poet). According to the West Norwegian and Icelandic law codes, the composition both of love poetry and the poetry of scorn and insult was a risky business, punishable by law and able to bring death as a consequence for the poet. The reason for such a harsh attitude, in both cases, was that the composition of such personal poetry could be – or could be presented as being – an affront to the honour of an insulted man and, in the case of love poetry directed at a woman, to the honour of her family and male relatives, who had the task of ensuring that only they determined who could marry or consort with her. If a man composed poetry about her this might imply – or be construed to imply – that that man had enjoyed illicit intimacy with her. Such cultural background knowledge is required for the understanding of the narrative dynamics of all the skalds' sagas, including *Kormáks saga*, and many others.

Another area of cultural knowledge essential to the understanding of *Kormáks saga* is that which pertains to the social conventions of betrothal and marriage. In a society like that of medieval Iceland in which women's honour was controlled by their male kin, it followed that the disposal of women in marriage was also the formal responsibility of male relatives. While prospective brides could express personal views about their wooers, as Steingerðr does in the passage quoted here, the betrothal of a woman was formally a transaction between her father or brothers or other close male relatives and the male relatives of the prospective husband. There are numerous examples in saga literature of the dangers of men going ahead with betrothal and marriage arrangements without bothering to consult the woman in question – such marriages are usually represented as being doomed to failure – but the fact remained that men had the deciding vote when it came to the arrangement of a marriage and the ensuing social ties between affines that were consequent upon it. In the chapters of *Kormáks saga* leading up to the passage quoted above, Steingerðr's father Þorkell has been so upset by Kormákr's many private visits to his daughter which had not yet resulted in a proposal of marriage (he feared dishonour because gossips could insinuate that she was having an affair with Kormákr without the prospect of marriage) that he agreed to support the suit of a rascal named Narfi, whom Kormákr promptly insulted and hit with the back of an axe. Further, Þorkell incited two brothers, sons of a woman named Þórveig, to ambush Kormákr, while he shut Steingerðr up in a storeroom. The upshot of this situation was that Kormákr fought against both brothers and killed them and then refused to pay compensation for their killings to their mother, whom he threatened to drive from the district.[3]

In Chapter 5, where Þórveig and her sons are introduced into the saga, another important cultural assumption appears, namely, that some individuals, particularly older women, practised sorcery and were thereby able to influence the lives of individuals in their community. The saga narrator defines Þórveig by one personal characteristic only: *Þórveig hét kona; hon var mjǫk fjǫlkunnig* 'There was a woman named Þórveig; she was very skilled in magic.' Þórveig's revenge against Kormákr for his killing of her sons is that she will prevent him ever enjoying Steingerðr. The implication is that she will bring this about by using her powers of sorcery... *en því skal ek þér launa, at þú skalt Steingerðar aldri njóta* 'but this is how I will pay you back [for not compensating her for her sons' deaths]: you will never enjoy Steingerd's love'. The narrative does not explicitly link the power of this threat with the practice of sorcery, but it is implicit, given the identification of Þórveig as a sorceress right at the beginning of the chapter.

Although Kormákr pours scorn on Þórveig's threat, which she makes shortly before the beginning of the passage cited in the text box, the saga narrative does not actively discourage the interpretation (to be discussed below) that some at least of the events that follow and continue to prevent Kormákr and Steingerðr from living happily together were caused by her sorcery.

Below we shall consider what we can infer from this text about the saga narrator's and his society's attitude to sorcery. At this point it can be observed that many sagas include among their characters individuals who are stated to be sorcerers and who are said to bring about certain changes that do not appear to have a rational explanation. In some cases these characters have no other role in the saga; in most instances they are marginal to society in some respect, either through their ethnicity, as in the case of Saami people, to whom such powers are often attributed, or through their gender and social status, as in the case of older women like Þórveig, or through their assiduous practice of pre-Christian rituals, like Þorgrímr nef 'Beak' in *Gísla saga* or their association with the prehistoric world, like Miðfjarðar-Skeggi, who lends Kormákr his magical sword Skǫfnungr, which several other Icelandic sources claim Skeggi obtained from the legendary Danish hero Hrólfr kraki after he had broken into the latter's burial mound. In the ethnographic record from many human societies where beliefs in sorcery occur, those individuals who have a reputation for sorcery are often considered marginal in some way by the majority, a social strategy that absolves non-marginal people from blame and charges of illicit acts, should such charges be laid.

Kormáks saga contains eighty-five verses in total, the majority of which are attributed to Kormákr himself. This is a very substantial number in what is a relatively short saga and is in fact the highest number of verses to be included in any of the sagas of Icelanders, some of which contain no verses at all, others only a small number. Unsurprisingly, all the skalds' sagas contain a high percentage of verse quotation, much of it attributed to the poets themselves. There is no doubt that the combination of verse and prose, or prosimetrum, in *Kormáks saga* is important in a number of ways: it drives the prose narrative, which sometimes seems perfunctory by comparison; it enriches the narrative by revealing the inner thoughts of the speakers of the verse; it provides a literary mode and an aesthetic which is sometimes quite divergent from the more realistic mode of the prose text. We must assume, for a saga as richly laden with verse as *Kormáks saga* is, that its medieval audience understood and appreciated the intricacies of metre and diction revealed by the stanzas it incorporates.

In most instances where poetry is quoted in sagas of Icelanders the verses are *lausavísur*, literally 'loose verses' (single stanzas rather than long poems) in the prestigious skaldic *dróttkvætt* metre, originally devised for praise-poetry composed for kings and regional leaders in Norway, but, it seems, extended in Iceland and the Orkneys to non-courtly, occasional situations. Certainly the majority of verses within sagas of Icelanders are presented as the actual words of the protagonists, rather than to confirm or corroborate something mentioned in the prose text, which is frequently the way in which poetry is used in historical sagas. During the twentieth century some scholars questioned the authenticity of many of the verses in sagas of Icelanders, and there has been a keen debate about their age: could these stanzas really have been composed by skalds in the tenth century, memorised and transmitted orally from one generation to the next, and finally written down by a saga author or redactor at some time in the thirteenth or even the fourteenth century? Could the verses have been composed by the saga writer himself or possibly by some other person who was able to use what would then have been archaic linguistic and metrical forms to create supposedly tenth-century poetry? In connection with the sagas of poets, and with the extravagant love verses in *Kormáks saga* in particular, some scholars thought they detected the influence of Provençal troubadour poetry, which would of course mean that the love poetry of Kormákr and other skalds could not have originated in the tenth century but rather from almost two hundred years later. In a chapter in Russell Poole's edited volume *Skaldsagas*, Kari Ellen Gade has reviewed the arguments on both sides of this debate and has provided metrical and syntactic evidence in support of the authenticity of the stanzas in the skalds' sagas:

> Leaving the possibility open that most if not all of the *dróttkvætt* stanzas in *Gunnlaugs saga* (and perhaps a portion of the later stanzas in *Bjarnar saga*) are the work of later skalds, we must conclude that the *lausavísur* in *Kormáks saga* and *Hallfreðar saga* bear all the marks of having been composed prior to 1014. That is not to say that each and every stanza in *Kormáks saga* is authentic but, bearing in mind the large corpus of lines (616) that show few traces of later metrical and linguistic developments, we must conclude that the poetry in the oldest skald saga [*Kormáks saga*] was not composed by its thirteenth-century author.[4]

The analysis

The first thing to notice about Chapter 6 of *Kormáks saga* is how the prose and poetry of its initial section interact and produce a complex and equivocal modality by means of the pronounced differences in register and style between the two media. The two media also carry different and partially contradictory messages. The prose is blunt, impersonal and understated: it tells that Kormákr carries on with his wooing of Steingerðr even though he has just been threatened with life-long sexual and emotional frustration by Þórveig and that Steingerðr 'in no way expressed disapproval' (*lætr hon ekki illa yfir*). It also indicates, by means of Steingerðr's response to Kormákr's extravagant poetic declaration of undying love for her, that she is aware of the strong possibility that things could go badly wrong for them. Nevertheless, she is guardedly encouraging in the prose, bringing him to the point of asking her father for her hand in marriage, and, in the verse, reveals her inner feelings of love for Kormákr, even in the face of the likelihood of the adverse operation of the gods and fate (*goð ok skǫp*). Whereas in his first verse of the chapter Kormákr acknowledges the fact that hostile men stand between him and Steingerðr, and they will have to be fought off with swords, something he is rather good at, she reveals herself both in prose and verse as more aware of less tangible but more sinister forces of opposition to their love, forces that are about to be demonstrated very clearly and quickly.

The language of the three verses in this chapter transforms both Kormákr and Steingerðr and their love to a level beyond their everyday existence as two young Icelanders frustrated by jealous rival suitors, a rather stupid father and a vengeful old woman. They come to life, thanks partly to the poetic kennings, as a brave warrior and an elegant noblewoman. Steingerðr's status is particularly enhanced by her being called a 'shining ground of flame-gleaming ale-cups' (*lýsigrund linns ǫlstafns*), a phrase suggestive of a woman serving ale in a grand hall, and a 'Hlín [goddess] of the veil' (*Hlín línu*). Further, the passion they feel for one another is represented as unqualified and undying in the poetry, although the prose hints strongly at frustration and misfortune. In the half-stanza attributed to her, Steingerðr indicates her unequivocal preference for 'Fróði's brother', Kormákr, as a husband, but the most intense statement of steadfastness and devotion comes in the second half of Kormákr's first stanza in which he states hyperbolically that all the rivers in Iceland will run uphill before he forsakes Steingerðr. This half-stanza has been one of the most discussed verses in the skalds' sagas, because some scholars have argued that it shows the influence either of classical Latin or of troubadour poetry, or both, yet this now seems unlikely in view of the probable authenticity of the poetry in *Kormáks saga*.

The second section of Chapter 6 is in prose and the direct speech, in both prose and verse, that characterises the prosimetrum section is absent here. The apparently objective narrative style gives a chronologically sequential account of events that lead, or are intended to lead, to Steingerðr's betrothal and marriage to Kormákr,[5] emphasised by the use of adverbs of time (*nú* 'now', *eptir þetta* 'after that', *nú* 'now') to begin each sentence. This chronological sequence is suddenly interrupted by an impediment in the shape of 'certain disagreements about money matters' (*nǫkkurar greinir um fjárfar*). The narrative does not specify how these disagreements arose, what they were caused by, or who instigated them, thus leaving the causative agency vague at this point. It does, however, specify the consequence, that 'after the marriage was decided on, Kormak's feelings about it cooled' (*at síðan þessum ráðum var ráðit, fannsk Kormáki fátt um*). Further, after having offered the opinion that 'it turned out strangely' (*svá veik við breytiliga*), the narrator's voice concludes by firmly attributing to Þórveig and her sorcery the cause of Kormákr's strange *volte face* from ardent devotion to cool withdrawal, 'and this was because Thorveig worked a spell so that they would not be able to enjoy each other's love' (*en þat var fyrir þá sǫk, at Þórveig seiddi til, at þau skyldi eigi njótask mega*).

Although the narrator of this passage is careful about how he attributes blame for the strange happenings that caused Kormákr not to turn up to his own wedding, the audience (and the modern reader) is left in no doubt that Þórveig was the causative agent and her means of bringing about such a radical change was sorcery. The verb *seiddi* '[she] worked a spell' indicates that Þórveig practised the art of *seiðr*, a form of sorcery used by women in particular, according to saga literature, though also sometimes by men, to bring about changes either in other people, often to their disadvantage, or in the climate and weather. While it is true that the narrator of *Kormáks saga* gives no account of how Þórveig actually carried out the rites that wrecked Kormákr's marriage to Steingerðr, he does not cast doubt on the effect of her sorcery and thus on the act of sorcery itself. Nor does he introduce any distancing formulae into his account, such as 'people say', 'it is rumoured that' and so on. Indeed, the whole course of the saga narrative lends support not only to the existence of the power of Þórveig's sorcery but to that of others with magical powers in the saga, and, even though Kormákr himself at certain points scoffs at the efficacy of these powers, the net effect of the saga narrative is a cautious acceptance of the influence of paranormal forces in the human and natural world.

As we have seen earlier, such a stance is by no means unusual in medieval writings of the thirteenth and fourteenth centuries on the subject of magic and sorcery, which could be understood as demonic but could equally be considered of natural origin. The composer of *Kormáks saga*, at least in the version that we know, availed himself of the privilege of narratorial omission to avoid specifying anything about the details of Þórveig's sorcery, with regard to both the rituals she enacted to perform it and the beliefs that underpinned the rituals. However, the dramatic change in Kormákr from ardent lover and superb poet to someone who runs away from his own wedding, thereby bringing dishonour on both himself and his prospective relatives, is firmly attributed to Þórveig's sorcery in the chapter under discussion.

Valla-Ljóts saga, Chapter 4

Síðan fóru þeir upp um Hǫrðabrekku. Þá mælti Halli: 'Farið nú aptr, því at nú á ek skammt heim, ok munu nú engir fyrir sitja.' Þeir gerðu svá sem Halli mælti. Sauðahús Halla váru á gǫtunni. Þá mælti fǫrunautr Halla: 'Menn eru þar,' sagði hann. Halli svarar: 'Má vera, at þat sé Bersi, sonr minn.' Hann svaraði: 'Þat eru ekki várir menn; þeir váru tólf saman ok einn í blám kyrtli ok hefir øxi snaghyrnda í hendi.' 'Far þú heim, ok seg Bersa, at Ljótr þykkisk eiga smáørendi við mik, ok er engi þǫrf þín hér at vera.' Hinn tók þegar á rás mikilli. Halli var gyrðr í brœkr ok hafði skikkju yfir sér; hann kastaði henni af sér. Hann hafði hjálm á hǫfði ok broddstǫng í hendi, en gyrðr sverði, ok gengr í móti þeim ok hjá fram. Þá mælti Ljótr: 'Dveljum eigi við atgǫngu, ok tǫkum hann.' Þeir ráða at honum, en hann gengr snúðigt ok komsk hjá fram, er hann fór forbrekkt, ok fá þeir ekki við hann fest, er þeir gengu við brekkunni; síðan nam hann staðar á sléttu nǫkkurri. Þá mælti Ljótr: 'Nú hœlisk hann um við oss, er hann stendr hæra en vér.' Halli svarar: 'Ek mun njóta frœkleiks míns ok fráleika, en bíða eigi.' Ljótr mælti: 'Bíða myndi Karl, afi þinn, þá er hann átti inn efra hlut heimsins, ok aldri lét hann eltask sem geit.' Halli svarar: 'Staðar skal ok nema, ok berjumsk vit tveir; er þat sómi þinn, en hitt skǫmm.' Ljótr svarar: 'Eigi er á þat at líta, enda skal ok svá vera.' Halli mælti: 'Hvat gefr þú mér at sǫk?' Ljótr segir: 'Sú er sǫkin, at þú skalt eigi optar kenna mér helgihaldit. Nú ef þér hefir gott til gengit ok vili engillinn gefa þér sigr, þá muntu þess at njóta. En ef þat var með fégirnd ok ágang, þá hafðu minna hlut, ok sjái hann mál okkart, ok muntu þá vel njóta þess hálfs hundraðs silfrs, er þú tókst af mér ok [hefir] haldit síðan.' Ljótr gekk at honum með járnaðan skjǫld. Halli lagði til Ljóts í skjǫldinn, ok kom í bóluna svá hart, at sverðit festi. Ljótr snaraði þá skjǫldinn svá fast, at sverðit brast í tanganum, en síðan hjó Ljótr Halla banahǫgg. Þeir fœra hann til sauðahúss ok kómu heim á bœinn ok segja tíðendin, ok lýsti Ljótr vígi Halla á hendr sér. Bersi ferr þegar á fund Guðmundar ok sagði honum þessi tíðendi. Hann kvað þat fara eptir getu sinni. Bersi bað hann taka við málinu, – 'en ek vil fara útan.' Þá váru af tekin hólmgǫngulǫg ǫll ok hólmgǫngur.

Then they went up along Hordabrekka.

Halli said, 'Go back now, for I'm but a short way from home and no one will be lying in wait for me now.'

They did as Halli said. Halli's sheep-pens were along the path.

Then Halli's companion spoke: 'Some men are over there,' he said.

Halli responded, 'Perhaps it is Bersi, my son.'

He answered, 'Those are not our men; they are twelve in all, and one is dressed in a black tunic and has a snag-horned axe in his hand.'

'Go home and tell Bersi that Ljot thinks he has some small business with me. There's no need for you to be here.'

The other ran off in a great hurry.

Halli was clad in breeches and had a cloak over him; he threw it off. He had a helmet on his head, a pikestaff in his hand, and a sword at his belt; he went toward them and past them.

Ljot said, 'Let us delay the attack no longer: seize him.'

They rushed at him, but he moved swiftly and got past them because he was going downhill, and they could not get hold of him while they were going up the slope. Then he stopped at a level place.

Ljot said, 'Now he is boasting that he stands higher than we do.'

Halli replied, 'I will make use of my boldness and swiftness, and wait no longer.'

Ljot said, 'Your grandfather Karl would have waited, when he was above ground, and would not have let himself be chased about like a nanny goat.'

Halli responded, 'I will also stand my ground, and you and I will fight each other; that way will bring you honour, but the other way, shame.'

'That goes without saying; indeed, it shall be so.'

Halli said, 'What charge do you make against me?'

Ljot said, 'This is the charge, that you will not teach me to observe the holy days a second time. Now if you acted with good intentions and the Angel wants to grant you victory, then you will prevail. But if you acted out of greed and aggression, then you will draw the lesser share. May He watch over our struggle, and may you profit well by the half hundred of silver you took from me and have kept ever since.'

Ljot went at him with an iron-clad shield. Halli thrust out at Ljot's shield and hit the boss so hard that his sword stuck fast. Ljot twisted the shield so fiercely that the sword broke off at the hilt; and then Ljot dealt a deathblow to Halli. They carried him to the sheep-pen and then came home to the farm and told what had happened. Ljot declared himself responsible for the killing of Halli.

Bersi went off at once to see Gudmund and told him the news. Gudmund said it had gone as he had guessed it would.

Bersi asked him to take charge of the lawsuit, 'but I want to go overseas.'

At that time all the laws for duelling had been abolished, and duels themselves.[6]

Literary and cultural background

Valla-Ljóts saga 'The Saga of Ljótr of Vellir' belongs to a group of sagas of Icelanders set in the Eyjafjörður region of Northern Iceland which deal with the lives and feuds of men and women of the area, their relationships with their chieftains and the chieftains' own power politics. The main sagas of this group, aside from *Valla-Ljóts saga*, are *Ljósvetninga saga* 'The Saga of the Ljósvetningar' and *Svarfdæla saga* 'The Saga of the people of Svarfaðardalur', the latter of which is a kind of prequel to *Valla-Ljóts saga*, although it was probably a later composition, at least in its present form. The date of composition of *Valla-Ljóts saga* is unknown, but it is probably unlikely to be early in the saga-writing period. The saga has not been preserved in any medieval manuscript and is known today from numerous paper manuscripts, the oldest dating from the seventeenth century. Both *Valla-Ljóts saga* and *Ljósvetninga saga* have been the subject of an exhaustive socio-historical and literary study by Andersson and Miller, and their study includes a translation of both sagas.

One of the most striking characteristics of the group of sagas centred on the Eyjafjörður region is that several of their dominant characters appear in more than one saga, and this is particularly true of one of the chieftains, Guðmundr inn ríki 'the Powerful' of Möðruvellir, who appears in fourteen saga texts, as well as in *Landnámabók* and *Íslendingabók*. Ljótr Ljótólfsson (Valla-Ljótr), after whom the saga under analysis is named, is the descendant of characters who figure prominently in *Svarfdæla saga*, and the same is true of the other main character in this saga, Halli Sigurðarson, nicknamed Hreðu-Halli 'Disturbance-Halli', whose paternal grandfather Karl Þorsteinsson the Red is one of its protagonists. Although characters often appear in more than one saga of Icelanders, the density of the interrelationships in this group of sagas is greater than average and enabled the saga composers to draw on the audience's stock of knowledge about the actions of several generations of people and to either contrast the behaviour of one generation with its predecessors (as happens in the passage under discussion) or see the continuities in behaviour and actions from one generation to the next. Such narrative techniques may suggest that this group of sagas was composed largely for the entertainment of local audiences, and it may also indicate the closeness of the texts that have been written down to their oral antecedents and counterparts.

Valla-Ljóts saga focusses first on Halli and his two brothers shortly after the death of their father Sigurðr. Both the two elder sons, Hrólfr and Halli, are described in negative terms in the first chapter, Hrólfr being 'overbearing and greedy' (*uppivǫzlumikill ok fégefinn*) and Halli 'a reveller and a man of law, a boastful and aggressive man' (*gleðimaðr mikill ok lǫgmaðr, hávaðamaðr inn mesti*). The saga goes on to exemplify Halli's, and to a lesser extent Hrólfr's, character portrait. Halli seeks the support of Guðmundr the Powerful, who has recently assumed the position of chieftain in Mǫðruvellir from his father Eyjólfr. With Guðmundr's backing, Halli attempts to establish himself in Svarfaðardalur, where Valla-Ljótr is chieftain, without asking permission to settle there. Tension between Halli and Ljótr, and their kinsmen and supporters, escalates, and, in the chapter under analysis here, Ljótr kills Halli. The latter's case is taken over by Guðmundr after Halli's son Bersi declares he wants to go overseas, and a feud develops, with the two chieftains, Guðmundr and Ljótr, on opposite sides. In the litigation and stand-offs that follow, these two powerful men play a wary and clever game, neither wanting to lose face and influence. In this saga, unlike some others in which Guðmundr dominates, it is clear that Ljótr's combination of judicious peacemaking and aggression, when the latter is called for, gives him the upper hand.

Valla-Ljóts saga is set chronologically in the period shortly after Iceland's conversion to Christianity in 1000. There are numerous details, one of which is found in the passage under analysis here, that confirm that the saga was composed in recognition of that particular cultural context and in the knowledge that the audience of the saga would also recognise the significance of these details. Among them are a direct mention by the narrator that Icelanders had converted to Christianity not long before the action of the saga took place and that the observance of Sunday as a day free from work had been accepted into law (Chapter 3). In the same chapter mention is made of the feast of Michaelmas. The local chieftain Ljótr's division of lands on behalf of two brothers (which he marks with a cross cut in the turf) on that holy day gives rise to a lawsuit with Hreðu-Halli, who objects to the land-division, on the ostensible ground that Michaelmas should also be a day of rest for Christians, even if it does not fall on a Sunday.

Although he has been arraigned by Halli for what both the narrator and the two chieftains Ljótr and Guðmundr the Powerful regard as a minor offence, Ljótr twice invokes St Michael the archangel, on both occasions when he is implictly critical of Halli for his hawkish and immoderate aggression. St Michael was a figure of power in the conversion period in Iceland, for he was the angel who weighed the souls of the living and the dead at Judgement Day and decided whether they should be saved or damned to Hell. Icelandic belief in his role in saving the individual soul is attested in numerous and diverse sources: in a verse by the eleventh-century skald Arnórr jarlaskáld, in 'The Saga of Christianity' (*Kristni saga*), which also emphasises the observance of Michaelmas as a day of rest, and in *Njáls saga*, as well as in sermons in both Norwegian and Icelandic and in Church art, where Michael is often depicted weighing the souls on a pair of scales.

Valla-Ljóts saga is very much in the tradition of a substantial group of Icelandic sagas that are centrally concerned with the evaluation of human conduct, particularly that of men under stress and threats to their honour and status. It is clear that Halli's rashness and aggression are valued negatively by the narrator, while Ljótr's restraint and patience in most circumstances are given a positive value. There is also no doubt that the narrator of *Valla-Ljóts saga* strongly associates the character of Ljótr with the practice of the new religion of Christianity, another positive quality, given that he and presumably his thirteenth- or fourteenth-century audience would have been Christian. The narrator makes it very clear in his initial character portrait of Ljótr that this man was normally restrained and peaceable but aggressive when the need arose. At the end of Chapter 2 it is stated that Ljótr's mood changes were signalled by changes in his dress and weapons: when he was in a good mood he wore a brown tunic and carried an inlaid, double-bladed axe. When the killing mood was upon him (*er víghugr var á honum*), he wore a short black tunic and carried a snag-horned axe. The significance of this detail is activated in the passage under discussion.

The analysis

Unlike *Kormáks saga*, *Valla-Ljóts saga* contains no poetry. The narrator depends both on the resources of a third-person narrative style interspersed with sections of prose dialogue and on the audience's background knowledge of local events, local genealogies and country-wide historical events, such as the adoption of Christianity and the abolition of duelling, to convey his point of view about the action and characters of the saga. He must also have assumed that certain moral positives articulated in the saga and discussed above would have been shared by his audience.

The chapter begins with a short section that follows a well-known structural paradigm of saga literature. The narrator makes use of the audience's presumed awareness of the scene's inevitable outcome here to signal Halli's impending death. According to this stock paradigm a companion catches sight of the enemy lying in wait for his victim, but the victim seems unaware of the danger he is in, and often, as here, imagines the enemy to be a friend or kinsman. His companion, however, recognises the enemy by his appearance and describes it, in this case identifying Ljótr by his clothes and axe, so also conveying to the audience that he is in his killing mood. The victim, in spite of the danger he is clearly in, sends his companion off and faces his aggressors alone.

The style of the next section of the chapter combines a description of the antagonists and their manoeuvring for position with a dialogue between Halli and Ljótr in which each asserts his own superiority, Halli boasting of his 'boldness and swiftness' (*frœkleiks... ok fráleika*) in winning a superior position on the hillside, and Ljótr turning Halli's boast into a charge of reckless impatience (a negative quality according to Icelandic mores). He makes a telling comparison with Halli's grandfather Karl the Red, by indicating that if Karl were on higher ground, he would have waited for his assailant to come to him, a sign of fairness and honour, 'and never have let himself be chased about like a nanny goat' (*ok aldri lét hann eltask sem geit*). This insulting and provocative remark amounts to a charge of *ergi* or gross moral turpitude, suggesting a range of unmanly behaviours from passive homosexuality to cowardice. Comparing a man to a female animal was one of the commonest forms of *níð* or shaming insult, something that also underlay many of Kormákr's poems composed to insult his rivals.[7]

Halli's response to Ljótr's insult is to reassert his honour and issue a challenge to Ljótr to fight against him in single combat, claiming 'that way will bring you honour, but the other way, shame' (*er þat sómi þinn, en hitt skǫmm*). He alludes here to the fact that he is alone, whereas Ljótr is in a party of twelve men. Ljótr readily agrees to the transparency of this statement, although, as Andersson and Miller observe, giving examples from other sagas, 'in such situations it is unusual for those with numerical superiority not to take advantage of it... Ljot's action is therefore to be understood as particularly chivalrous.'[8] As with other such instances from this saga and many others, it is crucial to the audience's evaluation of the morality and etiquette of the actions described to be familiar with such social conventions, which become the saga's unstated sub-text, and the modern reader needs to be informed of them too or else the subtlety of the characters' words and actions is lost.

The final section of the chapter is devoted to the single combat between Halli and Ljótr and its motivation. Normally, a duel required a charge to be laid, and, officially, Ljótr had laid no charge. The legalistic Halli therefore asks what the charge is, and Ljótr's response is to admit implicitly to having been humiliated by Halli when the latter earlier pressed a trivial charge against him for working on a holy day, which led to his paying out a lot of money to avoid a legal summons. In his speech Ljótr indicates that Halli's motives in threatening to summons him for breaking the law forbidding work on a holy day were quite self-interested, something he had previously intimated in Chapter 3, at the time of the original incident. Ljótr's words on that occasion are repeated, with variation, in his final speech to Halli.

There is a noticeable change of literary mode to one of greater solemnity and gravity in this section compared with the previous two. The saga writer achieves this not only by having Ljótr repeat his earlier suspicion that Halli acted hypocritically out of greed and aggression, but also by invoking a specifically Christian, eschatological dimension to their encounter, unusual in such a scene from a family saga. He reminds Halli that St Michael's power is the power of last things, of spiritual life or spiritual death, and that the angel will decide the outcome of their duel, the implication of course being that Halli's soul will be found wanting. To a Christian audience, this passage invoking the power of a guardian angel must surely have been deeply significant, and the narrator puts it in a conversion-era context in the chapter's final, antiquarian sentence.

There the saga narrator draws the audience's attention to the historical dimension to his story: duels were things of the past, the duelling laws having been abolished shortly after Icelanders had accepted Christianity. In other contexts the duel (*hólmganga*) is represented in sagas as a heathen practice, but here it is clear that Ljótr understands it as transformed to a Christian purpose, with St Michael deciding the outcome. Such an understanding may be the saga writer's reconstruction of what people of his own day thought about duelling in the earlier Middle Ages, imagining it as a type of trial in which either pagan gods or the Christian deity decided the outcome. The composer of *Valla-Ljóts saga*, who may well have been a cleric, is likely to have been aware of this difference in understanding between his own time and the time of newly converted Christians like Ljótr, to whom he attributes conversion-era beliefs.

Brennu-Njáls saga, Chapter 157

Fǫstumorgininn varð sá atburðr á Katanesi, at maðr sá, er Dǫrruðr hét, gekk út. Hann sá, at menn riðu tólf saman til dyngju nǫkkurrar ok hurfu þar allir. Hann gekk til dyngjunnar ok sá inn í glugg einn, er á var, ok sá, at þar váru konur inni ok hǫfðu vef upp fœrðan. Mannahǫfuð váru fyrir kljána, en þarmar ór mǫnnum fyrir viptu ok garn, sverð var fyrir skið, en ǫr fyrir hræl. Þær kváðu þá vísur nǫkkurar:

> Vítt er orpit
> fyrir valfalli
> rifs reiðiský,
> rignir blóði;
> nú er fyrir geirum
> grár upp kominn
> vefr verþjóðar,
> er þær vinur fylla
> rauðum vepti
> Randvés bana.

[There are ten more stanzas]

Rifu þær þá ofan vefinn ok í sundr, ok hafði hver þat, er helt á. Gekk hann þá í braut frá glugginum ok heim, en þær stigu á hesta sína, ok riðu sex í suðr, en aðrar sex í norðr.

Slíkan atburð bar fyrir Brand Gneistason í Færeyjum.

Á Íslandi at Svínafelli kom blóð ofan á messuhǫkul prests fǫstudaginn langa, ok varð hann ór at fara.

At Þváttá sýndisk prestinum á fǫstudaginn langa sjávardjúp hjá altárinu, ok sá þar í ógnir margar, ok var þat lengi, at hann mátti eigi syngja tíðirnar.

On the morning of Good Friday, in Caithness, this happened: a man named Dorrud walked outside and saw twelve people riding together to a women's room, and then they disappeared inside. He went up to the room and looked in through a window that was there and saw that there were women inside and that they had set up a loom. Men's heads were used for weights, men's intestines for the weft and warp, a sword for the sword beater, and an arrow for the pin beater. The women spoke these verses:

> A wide warp
> warns of slaughter;
> blood rains
> from the beam's cloud.   *beam's cloud*: the threads hanging from the crossbeam on a loom
> A spear-grey fabric   *spear-grey fabric*: battle ranks
> is being spun,
> which the friends
> of Randvér's slayer   *Randvér*: son of Ermanaric (fourth
> will fill out   century), hanged or killed by Odin himself;
> with a red weft.   *friends of his slayer*: valkyries

[There are ten more stanzas]

The women then pulled down the cloth and tore it to pieces, and each of them kept the piece she was holding in her hand.

Dorrud then went away from the window and back home, and the women climbed on their horses and rode away, six to the south and six to the north.

A similar event occurred to Brand Gneistason in the Faroe Islands.

At Svinafell in Iceland blood appeared on the priest's cope on Good Friday, and he had to take it off.

At Thvotta river on Good Friday a priest thought he saw a deep sea next to the altar, and he saw many terrifying sights in it, and it was a long time before he was able to sing mass again.[9]

Literary and cultural background

Njáls saga, or *Brennu-Njáls saga* 'The Saga of Burnt-Njall', is the longest of all sagas of Icelanders and is regarded by many people as the best of all sagas from a literary point of view. It begins by dealing in the *realia* of saga-age Icelandic politics and feuding, and explores the fates and friendship of the two heroes of the first part of the saga, Gunnarr and Njáll. However, it broadens out at many points into a more cosmic perspective on persons and events in both Iceland and the wider world, particularly through two sections, often termed the Conversion and Clontarf episodes (Chapters 100–5 and 154–7), which indicate that fate and the Christian God are directing events. Part of the second of these two episodes is the subject of the present analysis.

Njáls saga, like all sagas of Icelanders, is an anonymous work. It is datable to the last two decades of the thirteenth century on the basis of what the saga reveals about its composer's knowledge of Icelandic culture, particularly in the field of law, where his presentation of saga-age legal process reveals an acquaintance with the legal concepts introduced from Norway in 1271 in the law code 'Iron-side' (*Járnsíða*). The earliest manuscripts of the saga date from about 1300, and there are a considerable number of medieval manuscripts of this saga, as well as later, paper versions, pointing to its early popularity in Iceland, a situation that has continued to the present day.

The passage for analysis here comes from the Clontarf episode towards the end of the saga. In earlier chapters (145–55) the saga writer has given an account of how those of Njáll's relatives and supporters who survived the burning of his farm and household at Bergþórshváll carried out vengeance on the burners, some of whom had travelled abroad after being banished from Iceland by an arbitration court. Kári Sǫlmundarson in particular, whose son died in the fire, pursues a number of the burners to the British Isles, killing one burner, Gunnarr Lambason, in Orkney (Chapter 155) and another one in Wales. Eventually, right at the end of the saga, like the chief burner, Flósi Þórðarson, Kári undertakes a pilgrimage to Rome to expiate his sins, returns to Iceland and is reconciled with Flósi.

Kári's presence in Orkney, where his killing of Gunnarr Lambason brings him to the attention of the Orkney Jarl Sigurðr, leads the saga's perspective to expand to embrace a cluster of paranormal events that signal the involvement of supernatural forces in world history. While the events in Iceland chronicled by *Njáls saga* take place on either side of Iceland's conversion to Christianity, the extraordinary events described in the Clontarf episode widen the saga's perspective to show that the defeat of Scandinavian paganism by Christianity takes place outside Iceland too and belongs to a course of world-shaping events in Christian history. The Clontarf episode in its entirety gives an account of the Battle of Clontarf, fought outside Dublin on Good Friday 1014 between the Christian Irish king Brjánn 'Brian' and a group of pagan Scandinavians led by Jarl Sigtryggr silkiskegg 'Silkenbeard' of Dublin. Jarl Sigurðr of Orkney and fifteen of the burners die among the pagans in the battle.

Many scholars have regarded the Clontarf episode as an interpolation into *Njáls saga*, postulating a lost **Brjáns saga* as its source. However, as Lönnroth demonstrated in his 1976 study of the saga, the episode is thematically and stylistically compatible with the many instances in this saga where the composer indicates that miraculous forces are at work in the world and that they signal the operation of paranormal forces in human affairs. The passage above describes only one of these happenings, which occurred at the same time that the Battle of Clontarf was being fought in Ireland. It tells of a man named Dǫrruðr at Caithness in Northern Scotland who sees through a window a group of twelve valkyries weaving a bloody web which signifies the battle itself. They use men's guts for thread and their skulls as loom-weights and are represented as reciting a series of eleven verses that indicate that they are themselves directing the course of the battle. The verses are not named in the saga text, but they have traditionally been called *Darraðarljóð* 'Song of Dǫrruðr'.[10]

The analysis

The style and mode of the first paragraph of this passage is factual: it indicates the timing of the event ('on the morning of Good Friday'), the place ('in Caithness') and the name of the man whose experience is recounted. The narratorial positioning is confirmatory (*varð sá atburðr* 'this happened' or, more literally, 'that event took place') and gives no indication of disbelief in Dǫrruðr's experience. It is significant that the prose text uses the noun *atburðr* 'occurrence, event' to describe Dǫrruðr's experience, as the word often refers to an unexpected or supernatural happening. It is true, as Daniel Sävborg has recently noted, that a distance is established between Dǫrruðr as the viewer of these events through a window (*hann sá* 'he saw' is repeated three times) and the purported events and participants themselves. Further, the narrator is somewhat imprecise about the identity of the participants. He reports that Dǫrruðr saw 'twelve people riding together' (*menn riðu tólf saman*) to a women's room. The use of the Icelandic word *menn* 'men, people' suggests a group of men, but the fact that they were riding to a women's room, where female activities such as spinning and weaving might take place, confuses the gendering of these participants. It is left up to the audience to make the apparently logical connection between the twelve *menn* who ride up to the room and the women Dǫrruðr sees inside (*konur inni*) setting up a loom, weighted with men's heads and using men's guts for the weft and warp. These grisly details are reported quite factually by the narrator as part of what Dǫrruðr saw.

Although the narratorial positioning accepts as credible what Dǫrruðr saw, it is significant that at no point does the narrator himself identify the weavers as valkyries. That identification comes solely from the text of the quoted poem, and it comes indirectly at that. It is indicated by the poem's use of several skaldic-style circumlocutions for valkyries[11] and by the speakers' use of traditional valkyrie-names like Hildr and Gǫndul to refer to themselves. It is the poem alone that makes it clear that the weavers are valkyries. This connection of valkyries with weaving, and specifically with weaving that leads to men's deaths, would probably not have been widely known to the saga writer's audience. It is unique in Old Norse literature and may have been influenced by Celtic or Anglo-Saxon traditions. After the poem has been quoted, the prose narrative reverts to a factual mode of description: the women (designated in the Icelandic text only by the feminine pronoun *þær* 'they') pulled down the 'cloth' they had woven, tore it to pieces, and each kept one piece. They then rode away, six to the south and six to the north, and Dǫrruðr went back home.

This passage reveals a very subtle use of narrative distancing from a paranormal event that a Christian might have considered at best illusory and at worst the work of the devil. In the context of the saga, too, the valkyries' purported actions come to nothing, as King Brian and the forces of Christendom win the battle in spite of the women's magical weaving. However, at no point does the narrator discredit Dǫrruðr's reported eyewitness observations, and in fact, at the conclusion of this episode, he mentions that a similar event was experienced by a certain Brandr Gneistason in the Faroe Islands. On that same

Good Friday, he adds, blood appeared on a priest's cope at Svínafell in Iceland, and another priest had a vision of a deep sea next to the altar, with many terrifying sights in it, a description reminiscent of Christian accounts of Hell. The narrator's addition of three other witness statements to Dǫrruðr's account has the effect of supporting the authenticity of the weaving episode as a paranormal happening, while at the same time not committing him in any way to the identification of the weaving women as valkyries nor to beliefs that such activities could influence fate, in this case the outcome of the Battle of Clontarf. The fact that two of the additional witnesses were priests (Brandr Gneistason's identity is unknown) supports the inference to be drawn from this episode, as well as many other portents associated with the Battle of Clontarf, that all these paranormal events and personages were part of God's plan of Christian history, in which Christianity would conquer paganism, in Scandinavia as elsewhere.

The passage also illustrates another level upon which saga authors could make use of the semiotics of the prosimetrum. The age and provenance of *Darraðarljóð* are uncertain, but the composer of *Njáls saga* probably knew it as an antiquarian work, similar to a number of poems that recount heroic or legendary material that many scholars associate with the late twelfth century. Given its possibly Celtic-influenced theme, it may have originated in the Orkneys or somewhere else in the Hiberno-Norse world. It is found only in manuscripts of *Njáls saga* and in no other source. It is not in the skaldic verse-form *dróttkvætt*, like Kormákr's verses, but rather in the eddic metre *fornyrðislag* 'old story metre', appropriately to its role in the saga at this point. The sub-genre of the saga in which *fornyrðislag* poetry is most common is the *fornaldarsaga*, and the chant of the valkyries in *Darraðarljóð* comes from the conceptual world of the past, not the Christian world of 1014. In this context the saga narrator cannot vouch for its authenticity, but neither does he discredit it. The combination of factual prose, suitable to recording eyewitness experiences, even of a grotesque nature, and highly wrought antiquarian poetry allows the composer of *Njáls saga* to present a dual perspective on events that he represents as showing God's hand in human history.

Ǫrvar-Odds saga, Chapter 42

Lítlu síðar safnar konungr liði handa Oddi, ok eptir þat búa þeir herinn, ok sem Oddr er búinn, tók hann orlof, ok mælti konungr: 'Hér er gjǫf, Oddr! er ek vil þér gefa; þat er ein skjaldmær, er hon ørugg í bardaga ok hefir mér jafnan vel fylgt.' Oddr segir: 'Sjaldan var ek þar, er konur hafi staðit fyrir mér, ok svá mun enn vera, en af því at þér gerit fyrir góðu, þá skal ek þiggja.'

Nú var svá ok fór hon með Oddi.

Svá bar til einn dag, at Oddr fór með her sinn, þar sem mýrótt var, ok varð fen nǫkkut fyrir þeim.

Oddr skapaði skeið ok hljóp yfir fenit. Skjaldmærin skapaði skeið ok ætlaði at hlaupa eptir honum, en er hon kom á bakkan, varð henni bilt.

Oddr mælti: 'Hví fór nú svá?'

Skjaldmær segir: 'Ek skal betr hlaupa í annat sinn.'

Hon ræðr til í annat sinn, ok fór á sǫmu leið.

'Mér sýniz,' segir Oddr, 'sem þú þorir eigi.'

Hon ræðr til enn þriðja sinn ok fór sǫmu leið.

Oddr hljóp þá aptr yfir fenit ok þrífr til hennar ok steypir henni út í fenit, svá at hon kom aldri upp. Oddr mælti þá: 'Far þú nú þar er þik hafi ǫll troll, heldr en ek eiga sigr minn undir þér!'

A short time later the king assembles a fighting force for Oddr, and after that they equip the army, and, when Oddr is ready, he took his leave, and the king said: 'Here is a gift, Oddr, that I want to give you. It is a shield-maiden. She is fearless in battles and has always followed me faithfully.'

Oddr says: 'I have seldom been where women have protected me, and that will continue to be so, but, because you have done this from good intentions, I will take her on.'

Now that happened and she went with Oddr.

It turned out one day that Oddr travelled with his army to a marshy place, and there was a bog in front of them.

Oddr took a running jump and leapt over the bog. The shield-maiden took a running jump, intending to leap after him, but when she came to the slope, she took fright.

Oddr said: 'Why did that happen?'

The shield-maiden says: 'I'll jump better next time.'

She tries a second time, and it turned out the same way.

'It seems to me,' says Oddr, 'that you haven't the courage for this.'

She tries a third time and it turned out the same way.

Oddr then jumped back across the bog and grabs hold of her and flings her out into the bog so that she never surfaced. Then Oddr said: 'Now you go to where all the trolls can have you, rather than that I should owe my victory to you!'[12]

Literary and cultural background

The passage above is a minor episode in the picaresque *fornaldarsaga Qrvar-Odds saga*, 'The Saga of Arrow-Oddr'. The saga's picaresque nature derives from its main plot, which tells the life-history and numerous adventures of the hero, Oddr, who wanders the world to escape the consequences of a prophecy that he will be killed at home in Norway by the skull of his own horse. As his life-span is much longer than that of ordinary men, so the saga accumulates a great many episodes in which the hero travels to exotic lands and encounters a variety of adversaries, human, animal and demonic. The saga exists in a number of versions, some longer than others. The earliest manuscript (Holm perg 7 4°) dates from c. 1300–25, and this is the basis of Boer's edition, quoted above. There is also a version from the second half of the fourteenth century (AM 344 a 4°), while a third redaction, which incorporates episodes that are not present in either of the earlier versions, dates from the fifteenth century. A large number of verses, present in later manuscripts, are absent from the earlier texts. R. C. Boer, who edited the saga twice (1888 and 1892), was of the opinion that the saga's original version may have dated from late in the thirteenth century or from the beginning of the fourteenth.

The episode with the shield-maiden occurs at a point in the saga narrative when Oddr, who has journeyed disguised as an old man named Víðfǫrull 'Widely travelled', has gained acceptance at the court of King Herrauðr of Húnaland 'Land of the Huns' after first having won a series of contests to prove his superior powers. At the beginning of the shield-maiden episode Oddr undertakes yet another test, which the narrative indicates that all other men who had attempted it had failed: to obtain for King Herrauðr tribute from a region called Bjálkaland,[13] ruled over by a certain King Álfr bjálki. If Oddr were to succeed in this mission, he could expect to marry King Herrauðr's beautiful daughter Silkisif. King Álfr was a formidable opponent, as were his wife and son, both pagan sorcerers. At the point where the shield-maiden episode begins, Oddr has just assembled an army to undertake the Bjálkaland mission, from which he eventually returns victorious.

Oddr's mission to some extent assumes the form of a bridal quest, in which the hero must undergo various tests before acquiring his bride, but the saga also represents his journey to Bjálkaland as a cleansing of a hotbed of paganism by a hero who is at least nominally Christian, Oddr having been prime-signed during one of his adventures in Southern Europe (see the discussion in Chapter 5). The longer version of the saga makes a great deal more of the pagan–Christian dimension to this adventure than do shorter texts, like the one quoted here. At all events, the shield-maiden episode, which is totally self-contained, comes between the account of Oddr's various encounters in Húnaland and his journey to the wilds of Bjálkaland. Although their geographical location is vague, the two countries Húnaland[14] and Bjálkaland can be understood to represent oppositional qualities, depending on the version of the saga one reads: respectively the known and the unknown, culture and nature, Christianity and paganism.

The analysis

The modern reader may well find it difficult to understand the point of the shield-maiden episode of *Qrvar-Odds saga*. Is it just a piece of gratuitous misogyny, a way of underlining the stark difference in physical strength between a male hero and a woman, however tough and martial? Is it just thrown into the melting-pot of exotic adventures and equally exotic characters that Oddr encounters in his wandering life-style? Or does it have some point where it is placed in the narrative between the worlds of Húnaland and Bjálkaland? And what exactly is a shield-maiden anyway?

The noun *skjaldmær*, pl. *skjaldmeyjar*, is used in Old Norse texts to refer to women who bear shields and undertake armed conflict. In one instance from *Alexanders saga*, the reference is to Amazons living in the area of the Caucasus, while in a skaldic poem (Stjǫrnu-Oddi Helgason, *Geirviðadrápa* 4/1) a valkyrie seems to be the referent. In *Vǫlsunga saga* the warrior woman Brynhildr refers to herself as a *skjaldmær*, although her self-description here differs little from the conventional presentation of a valkyrie as an armed, mounted 'chooser of the slain' on behalf of the god Óðinn. The most significant piece of evidence, however, comes from the poem *Atlakviða* 'The Lay of Atli', in the Poetic Edda collection, which gives a heroic rendering of a legend based upon the life of the historical Hunnish leader Attila, who was murdered in AD 454. In two places (stanzas 16/9 and 43/8) Hunnish *skjaldmeyjar* are mentioned as a recognisable group within Hunnish society. At the end of the poem, as the temples and homesteads of the Hunnish dynasty rise up in smoke, the shield-maidens are said to burn as well, suggesting their closeness to the centre of Hunnish power. Earlier, Guðrún, Atli's Gothic wife, imagines the defeat of the Huns at the hands of her two brothers, Gunnarr and Hǫgni, including the indignity of Hunnish shield-maidens learning to know the harrow (*hervi kanna*), that is, being forced to give up their lives as warrior women to endure degrading agricultural labour as they pulled the plough like animals.

Atlakviða's two references to shield-maidens indicate that their association with Hunnish warrior society is likely to have been familiar to a medieval Scandinavian audience. My suggestion is that the character of a shield-maiden occurs at this point in *Qrvar-Odds saga* as an appropriate fighting companion to a Hunnish king and that the saga composer, together with his audience, would have had some general awareness of the historical correctness, at least from the point of view of legendary history, in associating the Huns with armed women.

Other kinds of warrior women appear in *riddarasögur* as 'maiden kings' (*meykóngar*), that is, aristocratic women, frequently the daughters of kings, who refuse to marry and go about armed, keen to take on saga heroes in combat. Eventually, they are either tamed into marriage and conventional womanly behaviour by a hero with whom they fall in love, or they come to an unfortunate end in battle. It is generally agreed that representations of such women express a sex-role inversion that can be admired as long as it can ultimately be overturned, but is not socially acceptable in its active form. The shield-maiden episode of *Qrvar-Odds saga* also partakes in this sexualised evaluation of appropriate male and female conduct, as is clear from Oddr's disparaging remarks about never needing the protection of a woman and not wanting to owe any part of his victory to one. To have accepted such a companion, even though she was the gift of a king whose daughter he wished to gain in marriage, would have diminished Oddr's own honour. When she fails a physical test, therefore, the logic of honour requires that she be eliminated, and that is what Oddr does, drowning her in a bog, a location that connotes degradation, if not elimination. On one level, then, the episode reinforces Oddr's masculine qualities, although a modern reader accustomed to a less extreme concept of masculinity may find it hard to tolerate.

As already noted, the shield-maiden episode comes between Oddr's sojourn with King Herrauðr of Húnaland and his journey to the wild Bjálkaland, whose ruler has refused to pay tribute to Herrauðr and whose wife is a practising pagan. The shield-maiden belongs in the world of the Huns, and she herself partakes of the qualities that characterise the Huns in Old Norse literature, particularly in heroic poetry and in *fornaldarsögur*. Traditionally, the Huns were the ancient non-Germanic invaders of Europe in the Migration Age, and they appear as the enemies of Germanic peoples such as the Goths. They are synonymous with weapons, horses and harsh fighting in several poems of the Poetic Edda, including *Atlakviða*, 'The Speech of Hamðir' (*Hamðismál*) and 'The Whetting of Guðrún' (*Guðrúnarhvǫt*). However, although the Huns live on the margin of Europe, they are located within *Qrvar-Odds saga* and other *fornaldarsögur* on a civilised margin, where the culture, though exotic, operates according to norms that also operate in the Old Norse world: Oddr's contests at hunting, swimming and drinking that win him favour with Herrauðr attest to that. This is very much in accordance with the location of the Huns on medieval world maps, where they are placed at the very boundary of Europe. Thus the shield-maiden too partakes of the civilised, in that she is a faithful follower of her Hunnish king.

However, on the level of culture versus nature, she cannot pass the threshold into the world symbolised by Bjálkaland and be effective there, for two reasons: first, she is a woman, and not so physically strong as Oddr; second, even though exotic, she belongs to the world of culture and so cannot take on the forces of nature in Bjálkaland and surmount them, as Oddr can. In several earlier adventures, particularly his first into Bjarmaland 'Permia', Oddr demonstrates his dual capacity to deal with both worlds, and this ability derives from his ancestry, as, like the legendary figures Ketill hœngr 'Salmon' and Grímr loðinkinni 'Hairy-cheek', who are represented in the saga as his father and grandfather, he is of mixed human and Saami descent. The shield-maiden's introduction into the narrative at this point thus externalises the liminal nature of Oddr's quest and the difference between the world he is leaving and that in which his quest must succeed. The shield-maiden must die so Oddr can succeed alone in vanquishing the enemy and winning his bride.

Conclusion

If we compare the shield-maiden episode from *Ǫrvar-Odds saga* with the three passages from sagas of Icelanders analysed in this chapter, we can see that our readerly responses to the *fornaldarsaga* text compared with the others differ to some extent. The principal difference is not, as many analysts have argued, in the degree to which we perceive the sagas as realistic in mode, because we have seen that there are paranormal elements incorporated into each of the four extracts. The key difference is that the literary mode of most *fornaldarsögur* treats all its subject matter on the same level: the narratorial positioning assumes the veracity of the whole narrative, whatever it contains, even though, in some cases, the narrator may adopt a comic or parodic stance, as in 'The Saga of Bósi and Herrauðr' (*Bósa saga ok Herrauðs*), or include direct statements about the truth-value of his story, as in 'The Saga of Hrólfr the Stamper' (*Gǫngu-Hrólfs saga*). The audience – and the modern reader – must accept this assumption of veracity as the basic condition for imaginative entry into the *fornaldarsaga* world. Thus the *fornaldarsaga* is a kind of ethnography of a past world, with the narrator its ethnographer. The translated *riddarasaga* operates in a similar way, although there particular norms and conventions specific to the romance mode are also in play. In other kinds of saga sub-genres, notably sagas of kings, sagas of Icelanders, contemporary sagas and indigenous *riddarasögur*, the narratorial positioning is carefully structured to indicate possible differences in the audience's approach to the world or worlds portrayed, which is why a mixed modality is appropriate to these sub-genres.

In a case like the shield-maiden episode above, the lack of narratorial guid-ance about any changes in the narrative's mode forces us to look for other kinds of interpretative signals, and we have seen that these come from inter-textual and inter-cultural associations (Huns and shield-maidens) and from our ability to understand the *fornaldarsaga*'s deep structure. In effect, the narrator forces the deep structure on the audience because there is no other interpretative guidance to be had. Herein lies the seriousness of the sub-genre and its ability to engage with the central themes of Old Norse culture. We read *fornaldarsaga* texts in terms of recurring narrative patterns and themes, because we have no other mental anchor-points, and we must presume that medieval audiences did so too, at least subconsciously. These patterns and themes explore important social issues, many familiar in different forms from other saga sub-genres, such as family relations between children and parents, children and foster-parents, young men and prospective sexual partners. They also deal in familiar ethical debates, between honour and shame, courage and cowardice, loyalty and treachery. All this takes place, however, in a fantastic world that is presented as real in terms of narrative strategy and structure.

Saga structures

The two previous chapters have been concerned to identify a number of important characteristics of the medieval saga. Chapter 5 dealt with the subject-matter of Icelandic sagas, a topic that included chronological and geographical settings as well as character types, while Chapter 6 analysed their literary modes, styles and points of view. The present chapter investigates the sagas' literary forms, that is, the structural components within and through which the substance of the narrated content is deployed and expressed. Unlike some of the other characteristics of the saga already discussed, some aspects of narrative structure are not always obvious at the level of close literary reading, but rather are immanent in the narrative and sometimes across a number of narratives within the same genre, thus constituting an autonomous layer of meaning, described by Greimas as 'a sort of common structural trunk, at which narrativity is situated and organized prior to its manifestations'.[1]

The twentieth century, from the 1950s onward, has been the great age of analysis of narrative structures, whether of South American myths (Lévi-Strauss), Russian wonder tales (Vladimir Propp) or modern European novels (Barthes, Brémond, Greimas and many others). It is true that some early works, initially of particular interest to anthropologists and psychologists, appeared before that time. One such was *Les rites de passage*, an influential study by Arnold van Gennep (first published in 1909; English translation 1960) of the three-phase schema that he argued always accompanied the phenomenon of initiation in human societies. Another early pre-structuralist classic, which later came to influence some literary analysts of saga literature, was Marcel Mauss's *Essai sur le don (The Gift)*, first published in French in 1922–3 and in English translation in 1954. Although Vladimir Propp's work on the morphology of the folktale appeared in Russian as early as 1928, its influence did not make itself generally felt until it had been translated into other European languages. The first English translation was published in 1958, not long after the writings of the French anthropologist Claude Lévi-Strauss had begun to be widely disseminated in the English-speaking world. Another important area of interest in structure came from those who wanted to discover how long, orally composed epic poetry was created, performed and transmitted to later generations. The study of the Homeric epic and the so-called Serbo-Croatian oral epic by Milman Parry and Albert Bates Lord made many medievalists aware for the first time of how the essential building blocks of medieval literature, particularly poetry, but also prose, could have been put together to make larger wholes. Although this work was begun before the Second World War, it was not widely disseminated until the publication of Lord's book, *The Singer of Tales*, in 1960.

Scholars of Old Norse-Icelandic literature were also strongly influenced by the general mid-twentieth-century interest in the essential structures of narrative, especially those who wrote about sagas of Icelanders. In fact, most of the major contributions to the structural analysis of Icelandic literature have come from scholars in that field, and their work has recently been the subject of an excellent retrospective overview by Lars Lönnroth, himself a key participant in the structuralist debates of the 1960s and 1970s. There have been relatively few structural analyses of other sub-genres of the saga and other medieval Icelandic prose forms like the *Edda* of Snorri Sturluson. In this chapter, just as in the rest of this book, I attempt a broader study of the immanent structures of the various sub-genres of the Icelandic saga, not just the narrative patterns that characterise sagas of Icelanders.

Structure and meaning

In 1986, shortly after the most intense period of structuralist studies of the Icelandic saga had passed, a collection of essays was published by various saga scholars entitled *Structure and Meaning in Old Norse Literature. New Approaches to Textual Analysis and Literary Criticism.* Most of the essays in the volume addressed the question of the relationship between the structure of a literary text and its perceptible meaning. In their different essays the authors drew out the various ways in which the narrative's syntagm, its sequences of surface structures, can articulate certain central thematic paradigms which interrelate to produce the narrative's meaning.[2]

Many scholars, including some of the 1986 volume's contributors, would go further and assert that there are some identifiable basic structures of story-telling, and indeed of human thought in general, that are always present in narrative texts. These tend to be binary categories arranged as sets of oppositional pairs from well-known semantic fields, like male and female, death and life, water and air. Lévi-Strauss, writing about the deep structures of myth, claimed that all myths are structured as four-term homologies in which one pair of opposed mythemes correlates with another.[3] There are also other basic structures, to which we shall return later in this chapter, that combine a set sequence or schema with specific oppositional pairs, such as van Gennep described as the basic structure of initiatory rituals and narratives. These structural patterns, for knowledge of which we are largely indebted to anthropological studies, will be found to be particularly well suited to certain sub-genres of the Icelandic saga, like *fornaldarsögur* and *riddarasögur*, which are closer in some respects, such as characterisation and plot, to myth and folktale than are the other saga sub-genres.

There are other reasons, aside from a search for deep meaning in narrative, that make us want to identify structural patterns in saga literature. As Lönnroth has written in a recent survey, 'one cannot see clearly what is individual or unique in a saga before its traditional elements and conventional narrative strategies have been properly understood'. A comparison between many sagas of the same sub-genre, and indeed across sub-genres, allows us to isolate recurrent structural patterns, large and small, that create the individual saga's syntagm. This in its turn gives us confidence to state whether a specific saga follows a particular structural pattern and expresses specific themes. It may be possible to identify more than one pattern to which a particular saga conforms, or to suggest that structural patterns from non-native sources may have influenced the composer of a particular saga. For example, it is obvious that the so-called *Spesar þáttr* 'The Tale of Spes "Hope"' that concludes the long saga about the famous Icelandic outlaw Grettir Ásmundarson allows the saga writer to end his narrative on a plane far removed from that of the dramatic account of Grettir's desperate last stand and death on the island of Drangey, off the northern coast of Iceland. *Spesar þáttr* belongs in the romance world and is probably influenced by the Tristram legend; it is set in Constantinople and speaks of hope and the continuity of life through its focus on Grettir's brother and avenger, Þorsteinn, and his love affair with the lady Spes. The contrast is stark, but the bold juxtaposition of structures and modes works in terms of the literary dénouement of *Grettis saga*.

The remainder of this chapter will be devoted to an analysis of the different structural syntagms to be found in Icelandic sagas and the thematic paradigms and interrelated meanings these express. Many previous studies of saga structures have concentrated on sagas of Icelanders, as has already been mentioned, and some of them have adopted somewhat of a one-size-fits-all approach to their material, tending either to devalue or ignore those sagas that do not conform to a favoured model. This propensity is particularly strong in the very influential early book by Theodore Andersson, *The Icelandic Family Saga. An Analytic Reading* (1967), which inspired a number of other scholars, many of them former students or close colleagues of Andersson, to undertake research into saga structures. Although Andersson's more recent writings on the saga have abandoned the structuralist approach, the value-judgements that he formed in that process still seem to have affected his literary judgement, witness his continuing low esteem for sagas like *Eyrbyggja saga* and *Vatnsdœla saga* that do not easily conform to the structural model he advocated back in 1967. Because Andersson's views have been so widely influential and have tended to channel discussion into analyses of sagas of Icelanders above all, it remains important to develop a number of structural models that account for a broader range of saga syntagms than simply stories of conflict, which, it cannot be denied, are central to many sagas of Icelanders.

Structures of conflict and resolution

Following Andersson's *The Icelandic Family Saga*, many studies of the structure of Icelandic sagas have seen the conventions of feuding as the underlying substrate of sagas of Icelanders. There is no doubt that the topic of feuding is a central subject, not only of sagas of Icelanders, but also of contemporary sagas, and it plays its part in some other saga sub-genres as well. Saga writers looking back on Icelandic society of the tenth century from the vantage point of the thirteenth or fourteenth centuries may well have represented earlier feuds as more like those of a later day, but the essential structures of feud seem to be recognisable across sub-genres. In Chapter 1 attention was drawn to the importance of both an individual's and a family's sense of honour in the small-scale society of medieval Iceland and also to the likelihood that threats to personal or familial honour and other wrongs perpetrated upon individuals or families would be likely to lead to conflict and, in due course, to retribution and revenge on the part of those who were injured or believed themselves to have been wronged. In the absence of a centralised executive arm of the judiciary, the pursuit of vengeance fell to the individual and his family and supporters.

Life and literature are two different things, however. Andersson's analysis was primarily concerned with the conventions of literature, and he proposed that a typical Icelandic saga could be broken down into six parts, which are in fact predicated on the structure of feud, although Andersson did not stress this. He illustrated his analysis by means of a short tale, 'The Tale of Þorsteinn Staff-struck' (*Þorsteins þáttr stangarhǫggs*), but claimed it applied to the majority of sagas of Icelanders. The six essential parts of the saga's narrative syntagm, according to Andersson, are: '(1) introduction of the protagonists, (2) development of a conflict between them, (3) violent climax of the conflict... (4) attempted revenge... (5) reconciliation, (6) concluding remarks not strictly pertinent to the plot'.[4] The major part of his book is then made up of detailed analysis, following this model, of twenty-four sagas of Icelanders, all of which, Andersson argues, follow the schema he outlined to a greater or lesser extent, with the exception of *Vatnsdœla saga*. What he may have meant by this assessment will be discussed shortly, but the important thing to note about Andersson's postulated structure is that the theme of conflict is central to it:

> It is a very nearly universal rule... that a saga is built around a
> conflict... It is the conflict that gives the saga its special character, its
> narrative unity, and its dramatic tension. It is the conflict that polarizes
> whatever else is in the saga, it is the sense of the saga and the organizing
> concept. This is an instance where a reduction to a single principle is not
> a case of oversimplification. The usual definitions and characterizations
> of the sagas have become mired in details of subject matter and have
> described the sagas as stories of families, feuds, Icelandic life, as
> biographies, family chronicles, or district chronicles. Such definitions
> are accurate enough but peripheral; the backbone of the saga, its formal
> principle, is the conflict.[5]

This manifesto, although it does not use the vocabulary of structuralism, essentially claims that, while the six-point schema is the saga narrative's syntagm, its paradigm explores the theme of conflict, and Andersson adds that 'the conflict is most often between two men', although it can also be between an individual man and a group or between two male groups. There are indeed many sagas of Icelanders that represent conflict and the eventual resolution of that conflict, but one of the problems raised by Andersson's analysis is that conflict in itself could be considered a theme as superficial as the various definitions of the saga that he rejected. People do not usually enter into conflicts with others about nothing. It is arguable that it is not the conflicts themselves, but the pressures that motivate them, that constitute the deep structure of sagas of Icelanders. A case could be made, and has been by the Danish scholar Preben Meulengracht Sørensen, for arguing that the core themes of sagas of Icelanders are honour and its opposite, shame.

The other fundamental problem with Andersson's schema is the limited extent to which it really takes account of all the non-superficial elements in sagas of Icelanders, leaving aside for the moment the fact that it manifestly does not fit other saga sub-genres. A review of his analysis and comments on individual sagas, which makes up the bulk of his 1967 book, reveals that a great deal of the narrative must in many cases be passed over as superficial or non-functional in terms of the plot if the six-point schema is to be seen as central and the theme of conflict between men the saga's main focus.

One of the sagas to which Andersson applied his schema was *Laxdœla saga*. The first twenty-four chapters, up to the account of Óláfr pái's 'Peacock''s building of his house at Hjarðarholt, is regarded as part of the Introduction, with the material only being functional in that it sets the stage for the birth of Kjartan and Bolli. We are told then that the conflict section, which is represented as one between these two men, who are cousins and foster-brothers, 'is built with near-perfect economy'. Most readers would be likely to disagree with this view, because, in order to fit the saga into the standard conflict pattern he has identified, Andersson has deflected attention from the richly nuanced and quite slowly built-up character of Guðrún Ósvífsdóttir, the woman whom both men love and want to marry. Although it is true that the immediate cause of Bolli and Kjartan's conflict is their rivalry over Guðrún, the seeds of that jealous rivalry are sown in earlier parts of the saga when they are shown growing up together, with Bolli always overshadowed by Kjartan's brilliance. Further, Guðrún's role in this love triangle, with its echoes both of heroic poetry and of courtly romance, is far from superficial or perfunctory, and an account of the saga's structure that sees it primarily as a conflict between men is unsatisfactory in many respects.

It could easily be argued that *Laxdœla saga*'s structure involves an inter-section between Andersson's conflict schema and a schema based on the life-history of Guðrún, a schema whose syntagm traces her troubled series of marriages, something foreshadowed by her extraordinary dreams, which are recounted shortly after she herself comes into the saga (Chapters 32–3), and concludes with her exchange of domicile with Snorri goði 'the Priest', her residence at Helgafell, her conversion to Christianity and her becoming Iceland's first nun and anchoress. A fuller analysis would expand this schema to include other female characters in *Laxdœla saga*, like Jórunn, legal wife of Hǫskuldr Kollsson; Melkorka, the concubine he buys in Sweden, who turns out to be an enslaved Irish princess, and who becomes the mother of Óláfr pái, father of Kjartan; and Hrefna, the woman Kjartan marries to spite Guðrún. The themes articulated by Guðrún's biographical schema also appear in miniature in the narratives concerning the other female characters.

This syntagm then sets up a paradigm that explores several important themes which interact with those of the conflict schema but yet are distinct from them. Among them are the oppositional pairs male and female; active and passive; dominance and subordination; love and hate; honesty and deception; home (Iceland) and away (Norway); pagan and Christian. The resonances from Germanic legend in the form of eddic poetry, with its implicit parallel between Brynhildr and her lovers, Sigurðr and Gunnarr, and Guðrún and hers, Kjartan and Bolli, emphasise the cruel frustration that fate and male deception bring to a woman in a male-dominated world, however strong-minded she is. Thus Brynhildr is deceived into marrying Sigurðr's sworn-brother Gunnarr, just as Guðrún is deceived by Bolli into marrying him on the pretext that Kjartan has stayed behind in Norway to pursue his dalliance with Ingibjǫrg, sister of King Óláfr Tryggvason. At the same time, the saga's insistence that its protagonists, particularly Kjartan, are courtly (*kurteis*), both in their behaviour and their appearance, sets up a contrast between the foreign world of romance and the reality of life in Iceland, a society in which concepts of honour and shame, conflict, vengeance and resolution dominate the lives of both men and women.

Studies of saga structure that followed Andersson's pioneering work avoided the narrow confines of his six-point schema in two ways. First, some of them looked at smaller narrative units rather than the whole narrative syntagm of a saga. In his 1972 article 'Genre and Narrative Structure in some *Íslendinga þættir*' Joseph Harris, for example, developed a different six-point schema for analysing short tales (*þættir*) about Icelanders who visit Norway and other foreign lands, returning home with enhanced reputations or wealth. Harris's schema, which incorporates a travel pattern in two of its phases, will be discussed further below. Two years later Carol Clover also concentrated on smaller narratives, although she was to subsequently (1982) propose a rather different structural framework for the Icelandic saga as a whole, one influenced by foreign interlace patterns. This will also be discussed below. Her 1974 study 'Scene in Saga Composition' was of the formal structural unit of the scene, which she argued had a simple tripartite form of preface, dramatic encounter and conclusion, and which she presented as an underlying mental template not only of sagas of Icelanders but of other Old Norse narrative prose.

The second means by which scholars with an interest in saga structure avoided too narrow a schema was to develop a broader and more diverse basis for analysis, as Lars Lönnroth did in his 1976 book *Njáls Saga. A Critical Introduction*, or to propose a far more detailed framework for the analysis itself, like Tommy Danielsson's 1986 *Om den isländska släktsagans uppbyggnad* ('On the Construction of the Icelandic Family Saga'). These scholars built on Andersson's work but created a more finely grained analytical tool. They were perhaps in part indebted to the excellent second chapter of Andersson's study, on the rhetorical conventions that saga writers habitually employed to create narrative sequences and to bind them together, techniques such as the foreshadowing of events, retardation or escalation of the plot, necrologies for dead heroes and what he called posturing, the flamboyant last stand of saga characters at the moment of doom.

A structuralist of a different kind is Jesse Byock. Perceiving some of the structural inflexibilities of the Anderssonian six-point schema, Byock proposed in his *Feud in the Icelandic Saga* (1982) that saga literature imitates life, that is, social life in Iceland in the Saga Age, not by using a fixed narrative syntagm, but rather by combining three active elements that he argued were present in all Icelandic feuds, but in a variable order, as happened in real life. These three elements were conflict, advocacy and resolution, and the narrative elements that expressed these elements Byock termed 'feudemes', the minimal elements of feud stories. His feudeme of advocacy, for example, laid emphasis on the roles played by men who acted as brokers of conflict, as go-betweens who had ties with both sides of the feuding groups. Byock's approach has been useful in drawing attention to the social conventions presupposed by sagas of Icelanders and in clarifying the nature of feud in small-scale societies, but, although it may throw light on some aspects of the sagas' narrative syntagm, it says nothing very much about the paradigmatic themes that the syntagm expresses. The legal historian and theorist William Ian Miller has explored a number of these thematic paradigms in various of his writings, while adopting the same basic approach to saga literature as Byock.

Life-histories: structures of biography and genealogy

The arguable presence of a schema in the form of Guðrún Ósvífdóttir's life-history in *Laxdœla saga* introduces a narrative syntagm that is at least as widely distributed in Icelandic saga literature as the conflict schema, if not more so. It is likely, as we have seen in earlier chapters, that the ubiquitous medieval genres of hagiography and biography provided the impetus for the development of the vernacular saga genre. If so, it is understandable that the life-history, whether inclining to the secular biography or the hagiographical *vita*, should remain a major schema of saga literature. In the case of some sagas of Icelanders, as we have seen, the life-history is often combined with other schemas, but there are at least two sub-classes among sagas of Icelanders in which the life-history predominates. These are sagas of poets (*skáldasögur*) and sagas of outlaws.

Kings' sagas are also largely biographical in their structure, following the life-history of a king from childhood to adulthood, assumption of the throne, sometimes after a conflict or series of conflicts, and concluding with an account of his death, usually in battle. Sometimes the biography begins before the king's birth and describes his mother's pregnancy or her premonition that she will give birth to an exceptional individual. Because the lives of Scandinavian kings of the Viking Age and the following centuries involved a great deal of movement from place to place, both within their own territories and outside them, often in order to engage in warfare with their military and political opponents, kings' sagas necessarily also involve travel patterns, which, as we shall see below, constitute yet another major structural schema of Icelandic saga literature.

Saga accounts of the Norwegian King Haraldr harðráði 'Hard-rule' Sigurðarson's life, for example, usually begin by telling something of his family connections, and then of how he escaped from the battle of Stiklastaðir, where his half-brother, King Óláfr Haraldsson, was killed, eventually making his way overland into Sweden and so to Russia, where he took refuge at the court of King Jaroslav in Kiev. After staying in Russia for several years, Haraldr travelled to Constantinople, where he took service with the Byzantine Emperor under an assumed name. The sagas then give varying accounts of Haraldr's adventures during his time in the East, in many cases backed up by verses composed by a number of the skalds who accompanied him as well as some of his own composition.

A journey to Jerusalem was the culmination of Haraldr's eastern adventures, and this is followed in the saga accounts by his imprisonment in Constantinople as a consequence of some trumped-up charges brought against him by the Empress Zoe. Then follows his escape from prison and his journey north across the Black Sea and so to Kiev again, now in possession of a great deal of wealth in the form of gold that he had won during his years in Constantinople. He so impressed Jaroslav that he was given permission to marry his daughter Ellisif, after which Haraldr set sail from the east for Sweden, where he formed a short-lived political alliance with the Danish king Sveinn Úlfsson, who was an enemy of the reigning Norwegian king, Haraldr's nephew Magnús inn góði 'the Good' Óláfsson. Magnús gathered a large army in Norway against Sveinn, who was burning and looting in Denmark, but offered his relative a deal, a half-share in the throne of Norway in return for a half-share of Haraldr's wealth. The two kinsmen ruled jointly for some time but eventually fell out. Magnús died after invading Denmark, and Haraldr then claimed the throne of both Norway and Denmark. After this point, the saga accounts aggregate a series of episodes detailing Haraldr's activities: his expeditions to Denmark, his fallings out with various Norwegian magnates and his punitive expeditions against them, his sexual liaisons and children, and his battles outside Norway designed to extend his rule beyond his native land, in Denmark, and finally in England, where he met his death in 1066 at the Battle of Stamford Bridge.

The bare bones of the narrative of *Haralds saga* certainly do not do justice to the varying character of the different extant saga accounts. The version of the saga in Snorri Sturluson's *Heimskringla* is much barer than that in *Morkinskinna*, where a number of separate anecdotes and *þættir*, both about Haraldr himself and about men associated with him, including some of his poets, render the narrative much more elaborate. However, in all cases, the main narrative schema is essentially biographical and linear. The side-narratives attach to the main schema like branches of a tree.

The main narrative schema of *fornaldarsögur* and *riddarasögur* is also frequently biographical, beginning with the hero's parentage and childhood and soon moving to a series of narrative adventures, in which he performs feats of strength and bravery against a variety of opponents, many of them monstrous or supernatural. In many cases, but not all, the hero wins himself a bride as a reward for one of his struggles against hostile opponents of a friendly ruler into whose territory he happens to travel. The conclusion to such life-histories varies; usually the hero returns home to success both political and domestic, but by no means always. He may return home, like Ǫrvar-Oddr, to fulfil a prophecy of his death or die away from home in foreign parts, like Yngvarr in *Yngvars saga víðfǫrla*, although in the latter case Yngvarr's surviving companions are returned to Sweden.

As we shall see, there is a comparison to be drawn between many *fornaldarsögur* and *riddarasögur* and Proppian folktale structures, not least in their linear, biographical syntagms. Unlike sagas of Icelanders, whose narrative structures are often more complex, with several interwoven syntagms, the main structures of kings' sagas, *fornaldarsögur* and *riddarasögur* tend to be simpler. The great achievements of the kings and the adventures of the heroes are usually encoded as episodic narratives arranged along the main narrative syntagm at chronological intervals that correspond to stages in the protagonist's life-history, although this statement is less true of the group of *fornaldarsögur*, like *Hervarar saga* and *Vǫlsunga saga*, that deal with successive generations of legendary royal dynasties and their family problems.

The *þáttr* or short tale, which typically focusses upon a single individual, usually an Icelander, also conforms to the pattern of the life-history, as it traces the hero's life and personal development from youth and obscurity to maturity and fame. It is no accident that many *þættir* have been recorded in manuscripts alongside sagas of Norwegian kings, for they both share the biographical mode, and the protagonists of the *þættir* are typically shown interacting with kings and the royal court. As we have already seen, Joseph Harris developed a narrative schema for the commonest type of the *þáttr*, which necessarily involves a travel pattern, from Iceland to Norway (and sometimes beyond) and back again. Although Harris incorporated the travel pattern as points two and five of his six-point schema, it may be better regarded as an interrelated but separate syntagm that is frequently involved in narratives that are life-histories. The protagonists of these life-histories are almost always male and usually young when their adventures start. Where the protagonists are female, as in the case of Guðrún Ósvífsdóttir discussed above, mobility is blocked, even if the woman wants to travel (*Laxdœla saga*, Chapter 40) or, in a few instances, she is represented as exceptional, like the settler women Unnr (or Auðr) in djúpúðga 'the Deep-minded', also mentioned in *Laxdœla saga* (Chapters 4–7).

The narrative syntagm of the life-history is capable of expressing a number of different themes, depending on the character and status of the protagonist and the environment in which he (or less often she) is placed. Environments are both generic (meaning that they are within the literary conventions of the genre or sub-genre) and representational, relating to the time and space within which the protagonist moves. Let us consider in this context the cases of the protagonists of sagas of poets and of outlaws, both distinctive sub-classes of the sub-genre of sagas of Icelanders. There are three major sagas of outlaws, *Gísla saga Súrssonar*, *Grettis saga Ásmundarsonar* and 'The Saga of Hǫrðr Grímkelsson' (*Harðar saga Grímkelssonar*), while the core of the poets' sagas comprises *Kormaks saga Ǫgmundarsonar*, *Hallfreðar saga vand-ræðaskálds*, *Bjarnar saga Hítdœlakappa* and *Gunnlaugs saga ormstungu*. *Egils saga Skallagrímssonar* and *Fóstbrœðra saga* share some of the dominant themes of the poets' sagas and have poets as their protagonists, but also deal with a range of other themes.

Both poets and outlaws have certain qualities in common, at least in their depiction in Icelandic saga literature, and in fact all three outlaws are also represented in their sagas as composing poetry, although they are not known for that capacity outside the sagas of Icelanders, in contrast to the members of the *skáldasögur* group. In their early lives both the poets and the outlaws are difficult, hot-tempered and assertive, in several cases to such a pronounced degree that they can be classed as anti-social. Most have poor relationships with their fathers but are doted on by their mothers.[6] In the poets' cases, their unruly behaviour is accompanied by early manifestations of poetic talent; in the case of two of the outlaws, Grettir and Hǫrðr, their early unruliness leads to lives of bad luck and misfortune in which even well-intentioned acts turn bad. Gísli's misfortunes are more complex, however, because they are precipitated by unusually convoluted family and affinal relations for which he is not fully responsible. There is a suggestion in one version of the saga that he is over-solicitous of his sister's honour, but this alone would not normally be expected to have precipitated the sequence of events that leads to his outlawry.

Both the outlaws and the poets have temperaments that set them at variance with normal society; in the case of the poets this is manifested largely through their disastrous relationships with the women they love, disastrous because they provoke conflict with the women's male relatives, usually by failing to observe the proper procedures involved in Icelandic betrothal and marriage customs. An instance of this kind in *Kormáks saga* has been analysed in detail in Chapter 6. Thus in these sagas conflict patterns are embedded sequentially within the protagonist's life-history, which is spent both in Iceland and abroad, as he practises his profession at royal courts overseas or undertakes foreign adventures. The sagas of outlaws, on the other hand, express the troubled life-history syntagm somewhat differently. In each case the first part of the outlaws' sagas describes the events that lead up to the protagonist's outlawry, while, after the outlawry has been proclaimed, each saga consists of a series of adventures in which the hero escapes those who try to capture and kill him. An important difference between the poets and the outlaws here is that, once they have been outlawed, Gísli, Grettir and Hǫrðr do not seek to go abroad, which would have been the only way of saving themselves under Icelandic law, but remain on the run in Iceland for a varying number of years until they are finally caught and killed. They are temperamentally flawed and unlucky, tragic figures who bring misfortune upon themselves that is out of proportion to their offences, captured by morally inferior men, but, in two cases, Gísli and Hǫrðr, aided by loyal wives.

One of the most distinctive narrative elements in Icelandic sagas is the genealogy, usually of the protagonists, but sometimes of other characters as well. Genealogies appear, in one form or another, in all sub-genres of the saga, are of greater or lesser complexity, and are more or less extensive as syntagmatic structures. The syntagmatic and paradigmatic values of genealogies may also cross sub-generic boundaries of the saga, as, for example, is the case with *Egils saga, Bjarnar saga Hítdœlakappa, Ketils saga hœngs, Gríms saga loðinkinna, Áns saga bogsveigis* and *Qrvar-Odds saga*, whose protagonists are all said to descend from the prehistoric Norwegian chieftain Úlfr inn óarga 'the Un-cowardly' of Hrafnista (Ramsta), an island off the coast of Norway. This particular genealogical syntagm has paradigmatic importance beyond its establishment of family connections: it reveals the underlying assumption that particular traits of character in these sagas' protagonists (in this case the ability to engage with the paranormal world) are carried down family lines. Hence in this cluster of sagas their narrative syntagms as well as their paradigmatic themes are comparable.

Other genealogies foreshadow the saga protagonists' inheritance of the status and power of their illustrious ancestors, as happens in the first chapter of *Laxdæla saga*, where the adjectives *ríkr* 'powerful', *kynstórr* 'high-born, of noble kin' and *ágætr* 'excellent, noble' are all used of the immediate ancestors of the first generation of settlers in Iceland whose descendants are the subject of the saga and who are particularly noteworthy for their sense of self-importance and nobility. Still others look forward to the importance of the descendants of the saga protagonists, as is the case in 'The Saga of Eiríkr the Red' (*Eiríks saga rauða*), where the descendants of Guðríðr Þorbjarnardóttir are said to include bishops and other important members of the early Icelandic Church. This connection has paradigmatic significance in *Eiríks saga*, because the narrative gives an account of the establishment of an Icelandic colony in Greenland, then a heathen society, and with that the spread of Christianity westwards from Europe.

In the view presented here, the genealogies within sagas are not mere flourishes that do not contribute to the main narrative; on the contrary, they project the life-historical syntagm of a saga either backwards in history or forwards to the future, or both, and carry a number of the saga's key themes. There is no doubt that the genealogical turn of mind, that saw history as a narrative of interrelated family and dynastic connections, was a general predisposition of medieval European literature and not only characteristic of Icelandic writing. Nor, within Icelandic writing, was it a characteristic of the saga alone, for it can be found in historical texts, like Ari Þorgilsson's *Íslendingabók*, in the Preface to Snorri Sturluson's *Edda*, and in a large number of other works which are indebted to the general medieval idea that European culture of the Middle Ages, including its social and political structures, derived from that of the ancient world, and particularly from the society of ancient Troy. The progenitors of medieval European polities were refugees from Troy, according to this hypothesis, and accordingly derived their family trees from the heroes of the Trojan war.

Structures of travel and the acquisition of knowledge

The narrative syntagm of the life-history is very often interwoven with the closely related syntagm of travel away from home, experience abroad and later return home again. In most sagas of Icelanders and *þættir* where this syntagm is present, the traveller is a man, usually a young man, who leaves Iceland and travels to Norway, and sometimes to other, more distant lands. There he has one or more transforming experiences, frequently but not always involving conflict, and later returns to Iceland with enhanced honour or great material wealth. A good example of the travel pattern is 'The Tale of Auðunn' (*Auðunar þáttr*), the story of a poor young man from the West fjords of Iceland who has bought a polar bear, a rarity in medieval Europe, while he is in Greenland. He travels to Norway and offers it as a gift to two rulers, first to King Haraldr harðráði of Norway and then to King Sveinn Úlfsson of Denmark, eventually reaping the rewards of his bold manipulation of the obligations of gift-giving and returning home a rich man. Central to this *þáttr* is the idea that the poor Icelander from the margins of society must travel abroad to improve his prospects and must use his wits to do so.

A set of binary oppositions underlies this and many other narratives that utilise the travel schema. It comprises oppositional pairs that involve a transformation of terms suggestive of qualities like isolation, inexperience and youthfulness into another set indicative of cosmopolitanism, experience, wisdom and maturity. On a geographical plane this transformation is usually expressed as a movement from west to east, particularly from Iceland to Norway, but also from Scandinavia to mainland Europe, and further east to the Mediterranean world and Asia. In some sagas, however, especially in *fornaldarsögur*, the hero travels north rather than east, usually in search of some powerful or numinous object. After Scandinavia's conversion to Christianity, the west-to-east spatial direction gained even greater importance because it marked the movement towards the Christian centre of the world, Jerusalem and the Holy Land. It can be seen that, at its core, the travel schema involves its protagonists in the getting of wisdom and experience, and this can be expressed through various personae, including those of poets, pilgrims, mercenary soldiers and adventurers and in various sub-genres of the saga, including sagas of Icelanders, *þættir*, kings' sagas, *fornaldarsögur* and *riddarasögur*.

The travel pattern is extremely important to the two last-named sub-genres. Virtually all sagas of these sub-genres involve a travel schema combined with a biographical syntagm focalised through the persona of a young male hero. Whereas in the case of the *fornaldarsaga* this combination of travel and biography is comparable with the fundamental structures of the wonder tale (or fairy tale, depending on one's nomenclature) as analysed by Vladimir Propp,[7] the indigenous *riddarasögur* are more playful and even sometimes frivolous in their exploitation of the syntagms' common themes. Many of them involve the hero's quest for a bride, and it has been argued by Marianne Kalinke that the bridal quest is the fundamental distinguishing feature of most indigenous *riddarasögur* and some *fornaldarsögur*. One cannot deny the ubiquity of bridal quests in these sagas, nor, of course, in many other kinds of narrative, like Proppian wonder tales. The question really is whether the bridal quest is a fundamental narrative syntagm or rather, the view espoused here, a variant of the travel schema, which is often treated as a pretext for the narrator's display of his mastery of learned, encyclopedic lore.

The travel schema is extant in one significant variant whose paradigm is arguably based, at least in its original form, on the fundamental religious structures of initiation as a rite of passage, as defined by Arnold van Gennep and recently applied by Jens Peter Schjødt to a number of Old Norse texts, including some of the stories of Saxo grammaticus and *fornaldarsögur* like *Vǫlsunga saga* and *Hrólfs saga kraka*. Van Gennep subdivided rites of passage into rites of separation, rites of transition and rites of aggregation. In the case of initiation these rites involve separation of children (usually boys) from their mothers and family group, with adult males then taking them to a place away from home where, as initiands, they undergo a series of trials in a liminal state between youth and maturity, and are finally reunited with their natal society as adult initiates, having successfully attained some form of secret or numinous knowledge or a magically powerful object. It is not hard to see that the initiatory pattern has a great deal in common with the travel pattern, especially the form of the travel pattern that has the gaining of knowledge or the quest for a precious object at its core. There are also considerable similarities with the Proppian wonder-tale schema. Before leaving this schema and its variants, however, it is important to assert that a distinction must be made between possible religious rites, such as those from Australian Aboriginal and other then contemporary societies upon which van Gennep based his analysis, and the quite attenuated literary manifestations of these structures that Schjødt has argued for in his 2008 study.

Structural complexity in the Icelandic sagas

This chapter has been concerned to reveal a variety of structural syntagms in the Icelandic saga and to indicate that certain structural schemas are especially common in particular sub-genres. It has also become clear that some schemas, like the biographical and travel patterns, are often found in combination. Smaller-scale schemas, which some scholars have termed building blocks, such as stereotyped character portraits, whetting patterns, and others, many of which were identified by Andersson and by Lönnroth in the latter's study of the structure of *Njáls saga*, are also identifiable as constituents of the complex structures that form individual saga narratives. The degree of structural complexity is probably at its greatest within sagas of Icelanders, and it has been argued by Clover (*The Medieval Saga*) that what she detects as an interlace structural patterning of narrative stranding within that sub-genre owes a considerable debt to the use of such structures in medieval European narratives of various genres, including historical works and romances. This hypothesis is not new and it has much in common with the views of the twentieth-century Icelandic school of saga scholarship, which saw the evolution of the saga as largely dependent on the Icelanders' knowledge of foreign literary forms. However, it has been counterbalanced, particularly in recent years, by scholars' insistence that oral narrative structures also played their part in the evolution of the Icelandic saga form and may indeed have been primary in its development. The question of the likely relationship between oral and literate impulses in the development of the Icelandic saga was discussed in Chapter 3. Here, at the conclusion to a chapter on saga structures, it is important to state that most of the structures analysed here need not be characterised *a priori* as either of oral or of literate origin; the question of the origin of these structures is largely speculative and dependent on various hypotheses about their relationships to ancient narrative forms in Scandinavian and European culture.

Chapter 8

The material record: how we know the sagas

The material means that enables us, in the twenty-first century, to be able to read and understand medieval Icelandic sagas is unique. It is fundamentally dependent on the hand copying of medieval texts by Icelanders, initially on vellum and then in paper manuscripts, from the Middle Ages until the late nineteenth century. This in its turn is dependent on the Icelanders' determination to preserve knowledge of their sagas from generation to generation. The history of the preparation of printed editions of saga texts is also important, although it did not gather momentum until the late eighteenth and nineteenth centuries. The way in which the academic study of Old Norse-Icelandic literature developed is also unique but not unrelated to larger intellectual movements within Western society after the Middle Ages, as people sought to understand their own cultural roots and began to prize the earliest written texts that had survived in European languages.

Without some inkling of both these topics, the history of texts and the history of Old Norse literature, a modern reader may fail to understand certain basic issues within saga studies: why many sagas are extant only in post-medieval paper manuscripts when they are assumed to have been composed in the thirteenth or fourteenth centuries; why there are variant versions of saga texts; why so many manuscripts have disappeared or been destroyed; why it is so difficult to date many sagas; how these sagas have been transmitted to modern times; how they were disseminated outside Iceland and outside Scandinavia; what role translations into Latin and various European vernaculars played in the dissemination of these texts; what post-medieval changes in cultural values have led to changes in readerly tastes for certain kinds of sagas over others; what principles have guided editors of the Icelandic sagas when preparing the texts for the use of modern readers.

This and the following chapter are designed to answer some of those fundamental questions. Chapter 9 takes up questions relating to the reception of saga literature from the end of the Middle Ages to the present time, tracing changing tastes across the centuries and suggesting reasons for such changes. The present chapter is concerned with the material record, that is, the manuscripts and later the printed books in which texts of Icelandic sagas have been recorded, the nature of those records, and their likely provenance and usage. This chapter will also consider the activities of patrons, scribes and collectors, how the modern collections of medieval Icelandic and Norwegian manuscripts were formed, and where they are now to be found. Finally, it will look at the nature of modern editions of Icelandic sagas and discuss the types of editions the reader may encounter.

Medieval Icelandic manuscripts and manuscript copying

Since the early 1990s scholars of medieval literatures have placed greater emphasis than they usually did before that time on the material circumstances of the texts they study, on the nature of the manuscript witness or witnesses in which the texts were recorded, and on anything about their material nature that might assist them in understanding the status and usage of those particular texts at the time or times they were recorded and subsequently. For example, the company a particular text keeps within a manuscript compilation, in which a variety of works are preserved, may tell us something of how people classified it in earlier times. The renewed (rather than wholly new) interest in the material circumstances of medieval textual production has been called 'the new philology', a phrase promoted and an approach first widely advocated in a special issue of the American journal *Speculum* in 1990. This renewed emphasis has slowly made itself felt in Old Norse-Icelandic studies, although it might be argued by some that they had been practising the new philology all along, especially as a great deal of the scholarship in the field has been devoted to the editing of texts of Old Norse-Icelandic literature, rather than to the new philological study of those texts as works of literature.

In the case of the Icelandic saga it is necessary to know about the history of a text's material manifestations from the earliest witnesses to the most recent, particularly because there has been an unusually high continuity of manuscript hand copying of vernacular texts in Iceland compared with much of the rest of Europe. One reason for this has to do with the fact that, after the printing press had been introduced to Iceland in the first half of the sixteenth century, its use was largely restricted to the production of Christian Bibles and other essential religious books. Vernacular texts, on the other hand, continued to be copied by hand beyond the Middle Ages and into the early twentieth century in many cases.

The mid-sixteenth-century Reformation in Iceland, as in most other European countries where it occurred, caused a disruption in manuscript book production and the abandonment, devaluation or destruction of many books and other items associated with Roman Catholicism, a movement that undoubtedly led to a now unquantifiable loss of medieval Icelandic texts. Yet by the seventeenth century, influenced by Renaissance humanism, those medieval vernacular texts that had survived the Reformation came to be highly valued and much sought-after by European scholars intent on discovering authentic sources of early Northern literary culture. As most of them knew no Icelandic, they necessarily depended on Icelanders both to copy old manuscripts for them and to tell them what the texts meant. These circumstances explain in part why a number of texts of medieval origin, like Ari Þorgilsson's *Íslendingabók*, usually dated to *c.* 1122–32, exist only in seventeenth-century and later copies.

In Iceland, as in the rest of Europe, the technology of writing using the Roman alphabet on animal skins accompanied the introduction of Christianity. It involved the production of parchment or vellum[1] from dried and treated animal skins, the making of quill pens and ink,[2] and the folding of the vellum to produce gatherings of leaves in smaller or larger sizes.[3] These gatherings were placed together and sewn, using threads of animal gut, onto cross-straps, the whole manuscript book being then bound either between wooden boards or sewn into a leather binding, which in Iceland was often made of sealskin. The fact that substantial economic resources were required for the production of manuscripts – a whole calf skin would have been needed to produce two manuscript sheets of vellum – suggests that only wealthy farmers or religious houses would have been likely to have been able to afford to divert their resources in this way. A contrary view was presented, albeit half-humorously, by Sigurður Nordal, who argued that young calf skins were in plentiful supply in Iceland, as was time to write, and that this conjunction explains the abundance of medieval Icelandic manuscript production.

Some Icelandic manuscripts, many of them only fragments, date from *c.* 1200 or slightly earlier, but these are relatively few in number and are mostly vernacular translations or adaptations of well-known Christian texts, like the theological handbook *Elucidarius*, saints' lives, homilies, and legal and computistical texts. Hreinn Benediktsson (in his *Early Icelandic Script* of 1965) gives a practical introduction to early Icelandic manuscripts with facsimiles of sample texts, transcriptions and a valuable account of their scripts and the foreign influences that shaped them. The earliest known manuscripts of sagas of Icelanders date from the middle of the thirteenth century, and these are also mostly fragments. As we saw in Chapter 4, the fragment AM 162 A θ fol of *Egils saga* is the earliest of these. There are also a few manuscripts and fragments from the late thirteenth century, like the fragment AM 162 D 2 fol of *Laxdœla saga*, but by far the majority of saga texts are extant only in manuscripts of the fourteenth century and later. It is this phenomenon, as we saw, that is one of the reasons why it very difficult to date one saga relative to others, especially if that saga exists in more than one manuscript version and the versions are of different ages.

The fourteenth century was the period in Iceland that saw the production of large vellum codices (sg. codex), or manuscript compilations, containing a variety of texts, many of them religious. It has been proposed by Stéfan Karlsson that some wealthy farmers, together with some of the monasteries, principally Viðey, Helgafell and Þingeyrar, made fortunes during the period that Iceland was under direct Norwegian rule (1265–1380) through the export to Norway of dried cod or stockfish, and that they used some of the profits from this trade to fund the production of manuscript books, many of which they also exported to Norway.

A number of Icelandic codices from the first half of the fourteenth century have survived and bear witness to contemporary tastes in saga literature. They demonstrate that the tastes of those for whom the compilations were made were often eclectic when it came to sagas, evidently preferring a mix of sagas belonging to different sub-genres. For example, the manuscript Holm perg 7 4° of c. 1300–25, now in the Royal Library, Stockholm, contains a mix of indigenous romances (*Konráðs saga keisarasonar* 'Saga of Konráðr, the Emperor's son', *Hrólfs saga Gautrekssonar*), an historical saga with legendary qualities (*Jómsvíkinga saga*), two *fornaldarsögur* (*Ásmundar saga kappabana* 'Saga of Ásmundr the Champion-slayer' and *Qrvar-Odds saga*) and a fragment of a saga of Icelanders, namely *Egils saga*.

An early fourteenth-century codex of a different character, *Hauksbók* 'Haukr's Book', was compiled by and for an Icelandic lawman, Haukr Erlendsson, who lived a large part of his life in Norway. The codex, which was separated into three parts after the Middle Ages, was probably compiled between 1306 and 1310 by Haukr himself and several Norwegian and Icelandic scribes to form Haukr's private library. The texts in this codex are many and various, but Haukr clearly had a sense of Christian universal history and how Scandinavian and particularly Icelandic history mapped onto it. The sagas included in this compilation relate to that vision, and include *Fóstbrœðra saga* and *Eiríks saga rauða*, both of which are partly set in Greenland.

The first extant codex containing sagas of Icelanders alone and nothing else is the compilation *Möðruvallabók* 'The Book of Möðruvellir', named for the farm of Möðruvellir in Eyjafjörður in the north of Iceland. It is likely that the manuscript was produced in the north of Iceland, probably for the owner of the farm. In 1628 the manuscript was still there, and the farmer at that time wrote his name in it. In the late seventeenth century the manuscript was brought to Copenhagen, where it came into the possession of Árni Magnússon, the most important collector of Icelandic manuscripts there has ever been (see below). In 1974 *Möðruvallabók* was returned to Iceland along with other manuscripts following a lengthy court case in Denmark for the restitution of the Icelanders' cultural property, which in harsher colonial times had been deliberately removed from Iceland to preserve it.

Möðruvallabók (AM 132 fol) is thought to have been written between 1330 and 1370. It contains eleven sagas of Icelanders, the first seven of which are arranged in a significant geographical order, following the Quarters of the island of Iceland, beginning in the south and ending in the east, the same trajectory as was followed by the original *Landnámabók*. Thus the collection begins with *Njáls saga*, set in the south, and was to have continued with another now lost southern saga that was never copied into the manuscript, **Gauks saga Trandilssonar* 'The Saga of Gaukr, son of Trandill'. It continues tracking west, then north, and east, with *Egils saga*, 'The Saga of Finnbogi the Strong' (*Finnboga saga ramma*), *Bandamanna saga*, *Kormáks saga*, *Víga-Glúms saga* and *Droplaugarsona saga*; then, breaking the geographical order, come 'The Saga of Ale-hood' (*Ǫlkofra saga* or *Ǫlkofra þáttr*, as it is also known), *Hallfreðar saga*, *Laxdœla saga* with *Bolla þáttr* 'The Tale of Bolli', and *Fóstbrœðra saga*.

Möðruvallabók is the most significant surviving manuscript containing sagas of Icelanders, and it records some sagas in whole or in part that are not found elsewhere. Other saga compilations suffered a less favourable transmission history or have only survived by report or in summary in post-medieval sources. One such is the late fourteenth-century codex* *Vatnshyrna* 'The [manuscript] from Vatnshorn', which now no longer exists. Information about its contents can, however, be gleaned from various later sources. This codex also contained sagas of Icelanders, including 'The Saga of the men of Flói' (*Flóamanna saga*), 'The Saga of Bárðr Snæfell-deity' (*Bárðar saga Snæfellsáss*), 'The Saga of Þórðr the Menace' (*Þórðar saga hreðu*), *Laxdœla saga*, *Hœnsa-Þóris saga*, *Vatnsdœla saga*, *Eyrbyggja saga*, 'The Saga of the people of Kjalarnes' (*Kjalnesinga saga*), 'The Saga of Refr the Sly' (*Króka-Refs saga*), 'The Dream of Star-Oddi' (*Stjǫrnu-Odda draumr*), 'The Tale about Mountain-dwellers' (*Bergbúa þáttr*), 'The Tale about Cairn-dwellers' (*Kumlbúa þáttr*) and 'The Dream of Þorsteinn son of Síðu-Hallr' (*Þorsteins draumr Síðu-Hallssonar*). It is obvious from a number of the titles of these works that whoever compiled or ordered the collection to be made must have had a taste for the marvellous and the supernatural, and this is likely to have reflected the interests of the codex's patron, probably Jón Hákonarson of Víðidalstunga in the north of Iceland, whose genealogy and that of his wife were apparently originally given at the end of both *Flóamanna saga* and *Þórðar saga hreðu*.

There are a great many Icelandic manuscripts of the late fourteenth and fifteenth centuries that contain sagas of various kinds. The only two extant vellums of *Sturlunga saga*, *Reykjarfjarðarbók* 'Book of Reykjafjörður' (AM 122 b fol) and *Króksfjarðarbók* 'Book of Króksfjörður' (AM 122 a fol), date from 1375–1400 and 1350–70 respectively. Many collections of *riddarasögur* and *fornaldarsögur* from the fifteenth century show that the taste for these sub-genres must have been very fashionable at that time. A good example is the manuscript AM 343 a 4°, dated to some time in the fifteenth century. It contains fifteen texts, a mixture of *riddarasögur* and *fornaldarsögur*, and offers the best and earliest text of a number of these works, including 'The Saga of King Flóres and his sons' (*Flóres saga konungs ok sona hans*) and 'The Saga of Saulus and Nikanor' (*Saulus saga ok Nikanors*), among the *riddarasögur*. It also contains several sagas of the Hrafnistumenn, including *Ketils saga hœngs* and *Qrvar-Odds saga*.

The copying and collecting of Icelandic manuscripts after the Middle Ages

After the Reformation the impetus to collect and copy medieval Icelandic manuscripts came from both within and outside Iceland, when a general humanistic interest in the medieval Northern past as a key to the ethnic origins and identities of several European nations of the sixteenth and seventeenth centuries began to grow. One of the first Icelanders to signal to the outside world that Iceland and Icelandic writings might legitimately be considered among the most ancient in Europe was Arngrímur Jónsson, whose two Latin publications about Iceland, Icelandic history and literature, *Brevis commentarivs de Islandia* ('Short Commentary on Iceland', Copenhagen, 1593) and *Crymogaea sive rerum Islandicarvm libri tres* ('Ice-land or three books of Icelandic matters', Hamburg, 1609), attained wide circulation in Europe and whetted people's appetites for the whole texts of which he provided some abstracts in his books. *Brevis commentarivs* was reprinted with an English translation in Hakluyt's *Collections of Early Voyages* (1599), while *Crymogaea* appeared in English translation in *Purchas his Pilgrimage* (1625).

Royal and noble collectors from other parts of Scandinavia, especially Denmark and Sweden, soon began to send emissaries to Iceland to collect medieval manuscripts or sought them as presents from Icelanders at home and abroad who were themselves collectors. The seventeenth-century king of Denmark, Frederick III (r. 1648–70), gained a number of important Icelandic manuscripts by this means, and they passed into the royal collection in Copenhagen (*Den kongelige samling, Det kongelige bibliotek*), where they mostly remained until the late twentieth century. The most notable Icelandic manuscript collectors of the seventeenth century were Bishop Brynjólfur Sveinsson of the southern bishopric of Skálholt (d. 1675) and Bishop Þorlákur Skúlason of the northern see of Hólar (d. 1656). These men and others in Iceland had copies made of many medieval manuscripts which have since disappeared or been destroyed, and we owe our knowledge of a number of important texts to these seventeenth-century copyists.

By far the most important collector and preserver of medieval Icelandic manuscripts was the Icelander Árni Magnússon (1663–1730). Without him, it is true to say that a large proportion of the texts, including sagas, that we now know would have vanished from the cultural record. His central importance to the study of Old Icelandic literature of all kinds is reflected in the title of a lecture delivered in 2002 by Benedikt S. Benedikz, *Árni Magnússon – Where Would We Be Without Him?* Árni was important for several reasons: he was himself a man who had a wide and deep knowledge of medieval Icelandic literature and could read and understand the handwriting of old manuscripts. In his early years in Iceland he had been educated at home by his maternal grandfather, Ketill Jörundsson, himself a manuscript copyist and scholar.

Many copies or annotations of early manuscripts in Árni's own hand still exist, together with anthologies he created of important texts, especially poetry. The first public sign of his familiarity with the texts themselves, however, came from the assistance he provided in Copenhagen to Thomas Bartholin the Younger, newly appointed Royal Antiquarian of Denmark, who wrote a history of Northern culture and religion, and ascribed the contempt of death he attributed to the ancient Danes to their beliefs in the transmigration of souls. This work, published in Copenhagen in 1689 with the title *Antiqvitatum danicarum de causis contemptæ a danis adhuc gentilibus mortis libri tres* ('Three books of Danish antiquities concerning the causes of the contempt of death hitherto [felt] by the Danish peoples') proved enormously influential in Europe, not only for Bartholin's bold hypotheses, but also because, for the first time, substantial Icelandic texts accompanied by Latin translations appeared within it. These were Árni's work, and they introduced many in Europe for the very first time to the richness of medieval Icelandic literature, particularly poetry.

In 1701 Árni Magnússon was appointed by the new king Frederick IV to a Chair of Danish Antiquities at the University of Copenhagen and shortly thereafter gained a second appointment, one that was to change his life for a good ten years (1703–13) and more and the face of Icelandic manuscript studies for ever. King Frederick appointed two commissioners, Árni Magnússon, as the senior, and Páll Vídalín, to conduct a thorough survey of the state of Iceland, its economy and society, and report back to him with suggested improvements so he could assess the plight of his Icelandic subjects and his own not inconsiderable income from the island. The *jarðarbók* 'land register' that resulted was a meticulous work that provided details of every dwelling in Iceland, together with its livestock and other resources.[4] Among other things, Árni's commission included a clause enabling him to collect documents from religious foundations and private households that might assist the work of reviewing the state of Iceland at that time. Thus it was, as Benedikt Benedikz put it, that Árni 'swept the country as clean of manuscripts as if he had employed a vacuum cleaner' and eventually transferred those manuscripts from Iceland to Copenhagen.

Ever since he had come to Copenhagen as a student at the age of 20, Árni had been collecting Icelandic, Norwegian and Danish manuscripts and developing detailed notes on their provenance and history for the benefit of posterity, so that he had come to build up the most comprehensive library of such manuscripts then in existence. To this library he added the manuscripts that he had collected during his years as a royal commissioner in Iceland, although these were not transported to Copenhagen until 1720. Right up to the time of his death in 1730 Árni continued to study and annotate his manuscripts, employing amanuenses to make copies of them. Unfortunately, most of Árni's printed books, many paper manuscripts and documents, and some of his notes were destroyed in the great fire of Copenhagen of 1728, but the majority of his vellum manuscripts were saved, including those containing many saga texts. When he died, he bequeathed his collection to the University of Copenhagen, together with a large sum of money to fund its preservation and the copying and eventual publication of manuscripts by Icelandic amanuenses.

Árni Magnússon's material legacy, his manuscripts and notes, were (and still are to some extent) housed in a special institute, now known as *Den arnamagnæanske samling* 'The Arnamagnæan Collection' within the University of Copenhagen's *Nordisk Forskningsinstitut* 'Institute for Nordic Research'. However, a large number of the Icelandic manuscripts that were sent to Denmark in the seventeenth and eighteenth centuries, whether part of Árni's collection or that of the Danish king in the Royal Library, have now been returned to

Iceland after a landmark legal case conducted by the Icelandic government in the Danish courts for the restitution of their cultural property. This was one of the first such cases in international law. A committee was formed, half of Danish and half of Icelandic scholars, to oversee the orderly return to Iceland of all manuscripts (with a few notable exceptions) written by Icelanders that concerned the island, and the gradual return of the manuscripts took place, beginning in 1971.[5] The University of Iceland, which had been founded in 1911, had built a special manuscript institute, the *Stofnun Árna Magnússonar á Íslandi* 'The Árni Magnusson Institute in Iceland', to house its part of Árni Magnússon's collection, with the remainder remaining in the Copenhagen institute. In 2006 the Institute became part of an umbrella body, funded directly by the Icelandic Ministry of Education, called *Stofnun Árna Magnússonar í íslenskum fræðum* 'The Arnamagnæan Institute for Icelandic Studies', whose remit is the study of Icelandic language and literature generally, in addition to manuscript studies. The institute's webpage at www. arnastofnun.is gives information in Icelandic and English about its activities and publications.

Both Arnamagnæan manuscript collections, in Reykjavík and Copenhagen, hold comprehensive photographic records of Old Norse manuscripts, and it is increasingly possible for anyone to access images of the manuscripts on-line. Many manuscripts from the collection in Reykjavík are now available in digital form and may be viewed on the Institute's website. Other digital resources are to be found on Saganet, a collaborative enterprise combining digitised manuscripts from the National Library of Iceland, which holds many paper manuscripts of Icelandic sagas, with the rich array of printed works of relevance to Icelandic studies from the Fiske Collection in the Cornell University Library at Ithaca, New York. Saganet is freely available on the web.

The two Arnamagnæan collections are the most important modern resources for the study and preservation of medieval Norse, particularly Icelandic, manuscripts. However, there are other important collections in Scandinavia, in Norway, Denmark and Sweden. The most important Norwegian collection of medieval Norwegian and Icelandic manuscripts is in the *Riksarkiv* 'the National Archive' in Oslo, while both the Royal Library (*Kungliga Biblioteket*) in Stockholm and the University Library in Uppsala (*Uppsala Universitetsbibliotek, Carolina Rediviva*) hold important collections in Sweden, many of which were acquired by gift or purchase in the seventeenth and eighteenth centuries. Outside Scandinavia there are fewer manuscripts of medieval date, more of post-medieval paper, and these can be found in various European libraries, in Austria, France, Germany, Holland, Russia and the British Isles.

In Chapter 4 it was mentioned that manuscripts are normally referred to by abbreviated forms of the name of the collection to which they belong and a unique alphanumeric reference, together with an indication of their size. Thus the manuscript AM 343 a 4°, mentioned earlier in this chapter, indicates by its abbreviation AM (standing for Árni Magnússon) that it belongs in the Arna-magnæan collection, which is now split between Copenhagen and Reykjavík, while the abbreviation 4° indicates that it is a quarto-sized book. The former collection of the Royal Library in Copenhagen is now also split between Copen-hagen and Reykjavík. Manuscripts from these latter collections are designated either GKS (*Den gamle kongelige samling* 'The old royal collection') or NKS (*Den nye kongelige samling* 'The new royal collection'). The collection in the National Library of Iceland, which holds a large number of paper manuscripts, is abbreviated Lbs for *Landsbókasafn Íslands*. Other important collections are abbreviated NRA (*Riksarkivet*, Oslo), Holm (*Kungliga Biblioteket*, Stockholm), with a further designation in the latter case of whether the manuscripts are parchment or vellum (Holm perg) or paper (Holm papp), and either UUB or UppsUB for *Uppsala Universitetsbibliotek*.

Saga editions: principles and practice

Although Árni Magnússon made a major contribution to manuscript studies, he did very little in his lifetime to further the production of printed editions of medieval Icelandic texts, including sagas. However, his bequest helped fund the publication of editions after his death, beginning with the Arnamagnæan Commission's publication of some of the earliest editions of sagas of Icelanders from 1772 onwards. The Commission continues to publish editions in its series *Editiones Arnamagnæanae*, Series A (1958–) and B (1960–). Until editions of saga texts became generally available in the form of printed books, Icelandic literature remained the preserve of Icelanders and the very small number of non-Icelanders who had access to manuscripts and could read and understand them. The production of the first editions of Icelandic texts, which began in the seventeenth century, was therefore an essential step in the dissemination of medieval Icelandic literature to the world at large.

Many of the first published editions were bi- or tri-lingual, with parallel translations of the Old Norse texts into a modern Scandinavian language (Swedish or Danish) and Latin. Some translations were only done into Latin, as the *lingua franca* of the educated world in Europe, for which these early editions were intended rather than for a popular audience. The question of the changing reception of the various sub-genres of the saga will be discussed further in Chapter 9; here it is worth noting in passing that the first types of saga to be edited and/or translated were historical works, like Snorri Sturluson's *Heimskringla* and a number of *fornaldarsögur* and *riddarasögur*. Publication of the texts of sagas of Icelanders did not get underway until the second half of the eighteenth century.

Many of the first printed editions were based on whatever manuscripts happened to be accessible to early editors, rather than upon a considered comparison of a variety of manuscript witnesses. For one thing, the early editors usually had access to only a limited number of manuscripts: the Swede Olaus Verelius, for example, based the first edition (1672) of the *fornaldarsaga* 'The Saga of Hervǫr and Heiðrekr' (*Hervarar saga ok Heiðreks*) on the paper manuscript UppsUB R 715 in the University Library at Uppsala. This is not usually used as the base manuscript of this saga by modern editors, but it was the manuscript closest to hand. Secondly, the principles of editing that involve the comparison of manuscripts of the same text in order to determine their relationship to each other and to a postulated original by means of the study of errors and their distribution had not yet been developed. Eighteenth- and nineteenth-century classical scholars, like Richard Bentley in England and Karl Lachmann in Germany, evolved the methodology of textual criticism and applied it to the surviving witnesses of the works of classical authors. Their practice was then taken over by editors of vernacular texts such as Icelandic sagas, many of whom had had a classical education.

The nineteenth century was the first age of professional editing of Old Norse-Icelandic texts of all kinds, not just sagas, by scholars using the comparative method and with a sound philological training. Many editions from this early period were what Odd Einar Haugen has termed eclectic, that is, although they did not provide an exhaustive comparison of all known manuscripts of a text, they did consider more than just a single, best manuscript. They then pieced the text together from several sources with the aim of reconstructing the work as it originally was. During the last 150 years, however, most editions of Old Norse texts have been based on a critical recension of all available manuscripts, which has led the editor to construct a stemma or family tree showing the relationship of existing manuscripts to the postulated original text. In this respect editors have followed the Lachmannian approach of classical scholarship.

More recently, however, there has been an appreciable change towards an editorial approach that is sometimes termed the 'best-manuscript' tradition. This may be in part because many scholars are now sceptical about whether it is possible to reconstruct 'original' forms of a text, preferring to give value to the versions of the text that actually exist. In the case of Icelandic sagas, as we have seen in previous chapters, many existing manuscripts are very much younger than the original texts, if these can be dated at all accurately. The 'best-text' approach involves the editor in choosing a 'best' manuscript, usually on the grounds that it is the earliest and the most complete, and basing the edition on this alone, sometimes together with the parallel publication alongside the main text of significant variant versions. As Haugen has argued with some justice, a considerable number of modern editions of Old Norse texts use the 'best-text' method for their presentation of the text itself, but adopt a Lachmannian approach in the Introduction to the edition, where they review and assess the extant manuscript witnesses for their closeness to a postulated original text and often create a stemma based on the relationships between the manuscripts.

Another important type of edition, which is favoured particularly by the Editiones Arnamagnæanae series published by the Arnamagnæan Commission, is a diplomatic edition, which aims to reproduce a text as close as possible to its appearance in a specific manuscript, copying the unnormalised spelling of the manuscript and its medieval punctuation (which usually differs from modern usage), though normally expanding and italicising the scribal abbreviations that are ubiquitous in medieval and some later manuscripts. In some cases the diplomatic edition may reproduce several manuscripts in parallel; in others several manuscript witnesses to a particular text (e.g. *Egils saga*) are published seriatim, each in a separate volume. Even where the diplomatic edition reproduces a single manuscript, however, the editor's Introduction usually adopts a Lachmannian approach, assesses manuscript witnesses and constructs a stemma, if it is possible to do so.

The diplomatic edition, while very useful to a scholar wishing to come to grips with what a particular manuscript actually reads on the page, is of little use to a reader who does not already know a great deal about the text. Not only does the unnormalised spelling make for hard going (a training in palaeography is required here), but the lack of notes (except for variant readings) and contextualisation of all kinds gives no help to the novice. Assuming always that an individual can read and understand Icelandic (otherwise a translation is required), the most helpful kind of edition for the student and general reader is a best-text edition equipped with an Introduction that explains not only the textual side of the edition and the text's manuscript context, but also something of the context in which the work is thought to have been produced, along with a short account of its literary qualities and its relationship to other literary works. Textual and general notes are also important, as is a comprehensive glossary, if the edition is intended for students. Perhaps most important, from a practical point of view, is the price: students cannot be expected to buy a book that is too expensive. Good examples of editions useful to students are Bjarni Einarsson's edition of *Egils saga* (2003), published by the Viking Society for

Northern Research in London, and the *Nordisk filologi* series of texts published in Norway, Sweden and Denmark in the 1950s and 1960s under the general editorship of Jón Helgason, although the latter do not have glossaries.

There are many issues to do with the editing of Old Norse-Icelandic sagas (and other texts) that have no easy answer. One such is the question of language and spelling. Given that most sagas exist in manuscripts that are thought to have been written later, sometimes much later, than the sagas were originally composed and written down (and the question of whether we can speak of an original inscription of a saga is itself a difficult issue), what sort of orthographical standard should we use to normalise these texts, that is, to change them from the manuscript spellings to something more useable for the reader? In Iceland itself there has long been a tradition of converting the Old Icelandic texts to a Modern Icelandic orthography, and this is now sometimes followed even in semi-scholarly editions (for example, in the *Svart á hvítu* 'Black on White' series). Unfortunately, the not insignificant differences between the medieval and modern forms of the language are lost in this process. The *Íslenzk fornrit* series of editions of sagas has adopted a normalisation appropriate to the Icelandic language in the first half of the thirteenth century, and this has been the dominant scholarly practice over the last eighty years or so. However, it ignores the likelihood that many of the sagas converted to this standard probably took shape either in the late thirteenth or in the fourteenth century, possibly in some cases in the fifteenth, when language and orthography had changed considerably. Very few editors normalise to a late thirteenth- or fourteenth-century standard, although it would be logical to do so in many cases.

The business of editing a written text is complex, just as the product is. It is important for users of editions to be aware of what an editor actually does with and to the edited text, especially if that text has been created long ago, as is the case with Icelandic sagas, and possibly exists in several variant versions of differing ages. However much an editor's work with a text is based upon empirically verifiable evidence and practices, what that person does to the text alters the raw material upon which the edition is based in some way or other and to a greater or lesser extent. The product that results from the editor's activities is different from the manuscript or manuscripts that he or she used to produce it. Ideally, the user needs to be in a position to understand how and why the editor acted as he did, and the editor should ideally make his editorial activities transparent to the user. The diplomatic edition alters least, but it requires most in terms of the user's input.

Chapter 9

Changing understandings of the sagas

The reception of sagas in post-medieval Iceland

In previous chapters we have touched from time to time both on the continuity of interest among Icelanders in their medieval sagas and on differences in taste for the various sub-genres that particular manuscript compilations and rates of manuscript copying reveal. The very large number of extant paper manuscripts of a good many sagas of different sub-genres indicates that they remained popular well beyond the Middle Ages in Iceland. When considering the post-medieval reception of saga literature in Iceland itself, it is necessary to make a distinction between the interests of educated Icelandic scholars and antiquarians and the more general popular interest among the farming community in the countryside. While many priests, lawmen and other intellectuals continued to study, copy and add to the corpus of Icelandic texts that had been composed during the Middle Ages, and from the mid eighteenth century to publish the first Icelandic editions of medieval sagas, popular interest was sustained mainly by sagas that were intended to be read aloud at the *kvöldvaka* (pl. *kvöldvökur*) or 'evening wake', the evening work period that took place on Icelandic farms during the winter months up to the end of the nineteenth century. A good many of the stories read at these gatherings were post-medieval compositions rather than versions of medieval sagas. Some were translations from Danish, German or Dutch chapbooks, but the majority were original Icelandic romances, to which the term *lygisǫgur* 'lying sagas' is often applied. These romances were the most popular sagas among the general Icelandic population until the end of the nineteenth century.

It is likely that the oral circulation of medieval saga stories, with or without written texts, was their principal means of dissemination in Iceland from the late Middle Ages onwards and that they were also read aloud for entertainment at the *kvöldvökur*, alongside other entertainments such as *rímur*. These latter were stanzaic narrative poems, often with romance subjects, that were a dominant form of entertainment in Iceland until the early twentieth century. The entertainment involving saga reading would have taken the form of an oral performance in which the reciter or reader is likely to have introduced variations to the text and comments of his own, often value-judgements on the saga characters themselves and their actions. Some saga manuscripts introduce such comments into the text and so indicate that the Icelandic audience often thought about the saga plot in black-and-white terms of heroes and villains.

The popular interest in *lygisǫgur* and *rímur* met with considerable opposition from the more conservative clergy of the Icelandic Reformed Church during the period from the mid sixteenth to the nineteenth centuries. Attempts were made at various times to ban saga reading and *rímur* chanting on the farms, and Bible readings were actively promoted instead of the reading of traditional stories. Given the strong association between popular tastes and *lygisǫgur*, it is not surprising that a sharp distinction was drawn by the educated classes in Iceland between romances and other sagas of a clearly fictional nature, which were regarded as disreputable, and sub-genres with an apparently historical foundation, which were thought of with approval. As we saw in Chapter 4, the division of sagas into realistic and fictional kinds was to play a very important part in the Icelandic school's evaluation of the various sub-genres of the saga in the early twentieth century, and it is hard not to see a continuity here from pre-twentieth-century attitudes.

In the middle of the nineteenth century what Jürg Glauser (in his 1994 article 'The End of the 'Saga') has described as 'the quasi-medieval tradition of manuscript circulation' in Iceland of sagas and *rímur* gave way to the popular circulation of inexpensive printed books, which in many cases adopted certain of the features of the manuscript tradition. These books were intended for a popular rather than a scholarly audience. Between about 1850 and 1920 seventy-seven popular editions of Icelandic sagas were published in Iceland, many of them late medieval or post-Reformation original romances, relatively few sagas of Icelanders, and hardly any kings' sagas, chivalric sagas or pseudo-historical sagas. In his 1994 study Glauser provides a list of the titles published and their place of publication, the majority being published in Reykjavík, others coming out in Akureyri, Copenhagen and Winnipeg, Canada, to where a number of Icelanders had emigrated in the nineteenth and early twentieth centuries.

There is good evidence that up to the early twentieth century Icelanders at large looked upon sagas of Icelanders as heroic literature in which the male and female characters served as role models for ordinary people whose personal circumstances were anything but heroic. The examples of these larger-than-life characters buoyed people up and gave them courage to face adversity and poverty on the one hand and feel proud of their ancient heritage on the other. The saga stories also provided role-play material for children. Twentieth-century surveys, quoted by Jón Karl Helgason (in his 2005 article 'Continuity?'), reveal that this uncritically romantic attitude towards the narratives of sagas of Icelanders underwent a change during the early twentieth century, and that people, especially women, born between 1900 and 1930 were much less likely to empathise with saga heroes; on the contrary, some of them actually repudiated the violence represented in the sagas or claimed the sagas were of no interest to them. Around the same time beliefs in the historicity of the sagas also waned and the advent of new media, like the radio and cheap popular books, led to a decline in popularity of traditional forms of entertainment.

Another, equally important dimension to the influence of the sagas upon the Icelandic people was political. It was bound up with Iceland's position as first a Norwegian and then a Danish colony after a period in which it had been independent, lasting from the original settlement until 1262–4. In tune with the many independence movements in Europe in the eighteenth and nineteenth centuries, Icelanders began to press for independence from their Danish masters. The movement for political independence began among Icelandic students and intellectuals in Copenhagen in the nineteenth century, the so-called Fjölnismenn,[1] and then spread to Iceland itself. By the early twentieth century the movement for independence was in full swing, particularly among the urban intellectuals of Reykjavík. In this context, the sagas came to be seen as proof of Icelandic society's golden age of independence, proof also of the high status of Icelandic culture during the Middle Ages, and symbolic of pride in nationhood, typified by the refusal of Gunnarr Hámundarson in *Njáls saga* to leave 'the lovely hillsides' (*fǫgr... hlíðin*) of his home at Hlíðarendi for the uncertainties of exile abroad. It has been argued that the strong attraction that early twentieth-century Icelandic scholars felt towards the bookprose theory of saga composition (see Chapter 3) can be accounted for in part because they wanted to advance the cultural standing of Iceland in comparison with other Scandinavian countries by pointing to the sophistication of the written saga tradition. At the same time, and in a somewhat contradictory manner, they also wanted to maintain that the sagas of Icelanders, which were for them the most important saga type, were largely Icelandic in inspiration.

The reception of the Icelandic sagas outside Iceland

In Chapter 8 we saw how the reception of Icelandic sagas outside Iceland depended initially on the mediation of Icelanders like Arngrímur Jónsson as interpreters of their own culture and literature to a European world that was largely ignorant of it. For the sagas to become known to a wide audience it was also necessary for them to be published in book form rather than to be transmitted only in manuscript. And, in general, because most non-Icelanders were ignorant of the Icelandic language, it was normal in the first period of the sagas' reception to provide the Icelandic texts with a facing Latin translation. In early editions published in the Scandinavian countries, a translation into contemporary Swedish or Danish was provided for Scandinavian readers, together often with a Latin translation for the learned world of non-Scandinavians.

In the sixteenth century and for much of the seventeenth there were no true editions of Icelandic sagas to be had. Extracts and plot summaries from Old Norse prose and poetic sources were embedded in discursive histories, geographical compendia and treatises on the religion and beliefs of the ancient pagan Scandinavians. These were intended for an educated, even antiquarian audience. The main purpose of these works, which include Olaus Magnus's *Historia de gentibus septentrionalibus* ('History of the Northern Peoples', 1555), Arngrímur Jónsson's *Brevis commentarivs de Islandia* (1593) and *Crymogaea* (1609), Ole Worm's *RUNIR seu Danica literatura antiqvissima* ('Runes, or the Most Ancient Danish Literature', 1636), Thomas Bartholin's *Antiqvitatum danicarum de causis contemptæ a danis adhuc gentilibus mortis libri tres* (1689) and several works by Þormóður Torfason, was not primarily literary. Rather, most of them advanced hypotheses about the relation of Scandinavian culture, history and religion to better-known European and classical cultures and concepts. Whatever literary examples were to be found in these works were there in support of their authors' theories about the antiquity of Nordic culture, not there in their own right. Nevertheless, extracts and synopses from Old Norse poetry and prose aroused the curiosity and enthusiasm of many European readers.

Many of the works mentioned above, as well as others like the Swede Olaus Rudbeck's *Atland eller Manheim* (1679–1702), had a political or ethnically motivated purpose, sharpened in the cases of Danes and Swedes by the fact that their countries were at war during much of the seventeenth century. The fundamental aim of these writers was to show that their own culture had played a vital role in world history in the distant past. Thus Swedish authors argued that their ancestors were one and the same as the ancient Goths, who were thought to have originated in Götaland in Sweden. Rudbeck went further and claimed that

Sweden was Plato's lost Atlantis. Swedish writers sought proof of the antiquity of their culture in the language of 'Gothic' texts, as they wrongly considered the Old Norse-Icelandic sources to be. Thus scholars such as Verelius, Peringskiöld and others published a number of early editions of *fornaldarsögur*, many set in Sweden or involving Swedish protagonists, including *Gautreks saga*, *Hrólfs saga Gautrekssonar*, *Hervarar saga ok Heiðreks* and *Bósa saga*, during the years 1664–1740, seeking to provide evidence of early 'Gothic' history.

Danish authors held similar views, except that for them the Danes, not the Swedes, were the true antique Scandinavians. When Thomas Bartholin wrote of the Danes' fearlessness in the face of death his sources were Icelandic, like the poem *Krákumál* 'Lay of Kráka',[2] often termed 'The Dying Ode of Ragnarr loðbrók 'Hairy-breeches', but he glossed over the lack of evidence associating many of the ancient customs and beliefs he wrote about with the Danes of Denmark. Similarly, when Ole Worm put forward the view that all Old Norse literature was written in runes in his *RUNIR seu Danica literatura antiqvissima*, his influential but incorrect argument was made to apply to all the Nordic peoples, but much of the supporting evidence came from Icelandic sources, principally poetry.

Aside from *fornaldarsögur*, few texts of any other saga type were published before the second half of the eighteenth century. An exception was Snorri Sturluson's *Heimskringla*. As this work was a history of the kings of Norway it was naturally of particular interest to Norwegians, especially a group of Bergen humanists, who had access to several of the manuscripts of *Heimskringla*, which were then in Bergen. Mattis Størssøn translated extracts from the work into Danish, and they were published in Copenhagen in 1594. In 1633 a second Norwegian, Peder Claussøn Friis, published another Danish translation of the whole text, again in Copenhagen, edited by Ole Worm. The first edition of the Icelandic text was that of Johan Peringskiöld (Stockholm, 1697), which had a parallel Icelandic text with a Swedish translation, together with a Latin version at the bottom of each page. Another important work to have been published in the seventeenth century, though not a saga, was Snorri Sturluson's *Edda* in the trilingual Icelandic-Danish-Latin edition of Peder Resen (1665). The publication of Snorri's *Edda* in Latin translation gave an enormous boost to the growing European interest in Norse mythology and poetry.

By the middle of the eighteenth century the quest of many Europeans, inside and ouside Scandinavia, for what the English writer Thomas Percy was to call 'northern antiquities'[3] had gained new momentum and began to reach a wider reading public. This new momentum was bound up with the pre-Romantic and Romantic desire to trace national origins to their earliest roots and to discover the most ancient and sublime literature of the ancestors of modern

European nations. It was generally held that the most ancient literature took the form of poetry, and that the pagan Scandinavians, like the pagan Celts (with whom they were sometimes confused), possessed the most sublime and the wildest poetry. The evidence for this view came, by and large, from the pages of the very works, like those of Bartholin, Verelius, Peringskiöld and Ole Worm, that had been published during the seventeenth century, together with the new, exciting and very popular volumes on 'Danish' culture and history by Paul-Henri Mallet (1755–6). A small number of poems, mainly of heroic kind, became the standard examples of the Nordic sublime and appeared again and again, in translation and sometimes in the original Icelandic, in all the major European languages in both books and literary periodicals. Although several of these poems had been preserved within prose sagas, the sagas themselves were usually of secondary importance to the late eighteenth-century readership.

In line with the new and growing European interest in national origins and the primitive sublime in the late eighteenth century, going into the nineteenth, readers outside Scandinavia began to assert their ethnic links with the Nordic world and its early literature. This was particularly true in England and Scotland in the British Isles, and in Germany, all societies whose intelligentsia had become aware of their linguistic affiliation with Scandinavians, as speakers of cognate Germanic languages. In North America too, many people of ethnic Scandinavian descent were keen to claim affiliation with the Viking heroes of old and to exploit the claim that medieval Icelanders may have been the first Europeans to reach America. Although these sentiments were to become much stronger in the nineteenth century, they began in the eighteenth and served as the basis of a sense of ownership that English- and German-speakers could feel for the heroic age of the North, its heroes and its literature.

It was not until the last decades of the eighteenth century that editions of individual sagas became at all common in Europe, and even then some of them would have been difficult for the ordinary reader to obtain. From the 1770s onwards the first editions of sagas of Icelanders made their appearance, both in Iceland and in Denmark. Among the earliest was an edition of *Njáls saga*, edited by an Icelander named Olavus Olavius (Copenhagen, 1772) and later translated into Latin (published 1809) by another Icelander, Jón Johnsonius. Like the Icelandic texts published in the seventeenth century, this edition was valued for its historical and legal rather than its literary content. The earliest edition of *Egils saga* was published in Iceland (*Sagan af Eigle Skallagríms Syne*, Hrappsey, 1782), probably based on a manuscript similar to the version of the saga in *Möðruvallabók*. Although it is a printed book, its layout is similar to that of a manuscript, and it presents the poetry, of which there is a great deal in this saga, in prose form, just as medieval manuscripts do.

From 1772 onwards the Arnamagnæan Commission, the body set up to administer Árni Magnússon's estate, published a series of editions of sagas of Icelanders in Copenhagen, and others were published by Det Nordiske Oldskrift-Selskab in the same city. The corpus of sagas that are now termed *fornaldarsögur* also saw publication in this period. The Danish philologist Carl Christian Rafn (1795–1864) brought together from various manuscripts a collection of three volumes of these sagas, which he published in Copenhagen in 1829–30 with the title *Fornaldarsögur Nordrlanda* 'Sagas of the Ancient Time of Northern Lands', thus giving this group of sagas a collective identity and a name that they still bear.

Latin translations of Icelandic sagas, which were still provided in many late eighteenth- and early nineteenth-century editions, continued to be important in making the contents of these works known to a readership unable to read Icelandic. A good example of the galvanising effect of a Latin translation is provided by Sir Walter Scott's 1814 English abstract of *Eyrbyggja saga*, based on the Latin translation in Grímur J. Thorkelin's 1787 Copenhagen edition of the saga.[4] Scott's abstract was the first (partial) translation into English of a family saga, although James Johnstone's 1780–2 translations of parts of Sturla Þórðarson's *Hákonar saga Hákonarsonar* is likely to have been the first English translation of any saga by a native speaker of English.[5] Although Scott's was not a full translation and was based on the Latin translation rather than the Icelandic text of *Eyrbyggja saga*, it struck a new note in the reception of saga literature by showing an interest in the *realia* of medieval Icelandic social life and the characters depicted in the saga. That interest was to develop during Scott's career as a successful author of historical novels, many of them set in the Middle Ages in Scotland. One novel, *The Pirate*, published in 1821–2, was set in the Shetland Islands and drew freely on the works of Olaus Magnus, Bartholin and the poetic translations from Old Norse of the English poet Thomas Gray.

The nineteenth century not only saw the height of Romantic nationalism in Europe and in America, but also the rise of the professional, academic study of Old Norse-Icelandic language and literature in the universities. On the one hand, there was a proliferation of editions and translations of Old Norse-Icelandic literature, including sagas, compared with what there had been earlier, and, on the other, a range of creative works in various media, plays, opera, poetry and novels, only some of which were directly inspired by sagas. Still equally if not more important remained the Poetic Edda, the *Edda* of Snorri Sturluson and the whole subject of pagan Norse mythology and heroic legend. This dimension of Old Norse culture has remained popular and productive of new creative works throughout the twentieth century and into the twenty-first, especially in fantasy literature, new media and New Age religions. It also provided the basis for the ideology of a special Germanic national character that was the foundation for the Nazi policies and practices of the Third Reich in Germany.

Nineteenth-century tastes for Icelandic sagas were mixed. Among the most popular were, on the one hand, the late romantic Viking adventure story 'The Saga of Friðþjóf the Bold' (*Friðþjófs saga hins frækna*), and, on the other, the longest of the sagas of Icelanders, *Njáls saga*. The popularity of *Friðþjófs saga* grew from the Swedish Bishop Esaias Tegnér's poetic paraphrase of the saga, published in 1825, which was itself translated into other European languages. Nineteenth-century readers appreciated *Friðþjófs saga* for the great beauty of its story, in which the young Friðþjófr falls in love with a princess, Ingibjǫrg, but his wish to marry her is thwarted by various enemies and vicissitudes. After Friðþjófr's many adventures in various parts of the Nordic world, though not in Iceland, the saga has a happy ending: the lovers are reunited and Friðþjófr becomes a king. Although a number of scholars of the period regarded this saga as ahistorical rubbish (in *The Vikings and the Victorians* Wawn provides the evidence), the general public did not share their views.

It is hard not to see the growing popularity of *Njáls saga* – and indeed other sagas of Icelanders – in the nineteenth century as part of the general literary popularity of the realistic novel as the dominant literary mode of the age. The fine-grained detail of daily life, the large cast of characters and the geographically specific settings to be found in nineteenth-century novels prepared Victorian readers well for some aspects of the sagas of Icelanders, although there were others that did not fit at all. The lack of psychological internalisation of character in the saga as contrasted with the novel is one of the most obvious, the apparently non-committal narrative persona another, the concern with genealogy still another. The general nineteenth-century interest in realistic detail was further strengthened by the fact that by now a number of admittedly privileged individuals had actually travelled to Iceland and seen the saga-steads for themselves, written about their journeys and thus involved the reading public as armchair travellers in their personal experiences of the very places where the saga characters were represented as having lived and died.

The early twentieth century inherited many of the later nineteenth-century tastes for saga literature, though arguably moderating the sense of identification that Victorian readers felt with Viking heroes and their deeds. It is hard to know how the general reader reacted to the various scholarly debates about the origin and nature of the Old Norse-Icelandic saga that were occupying many academics, both in Iceland and elsewhere, in the first half of the twentieth century. For many general readers, the introductions to individual saga translations and popular translation series, like the Thule series in Germany[6] or the Penguin Classics series in the English-speaking world (1960–), would have provided their most likely entrée into these debates. Certainly, however, the general interest in sagas of ancient time and romances, which had been so strong in the seventeenth, eighteenth and much of the nineteenth centuries, was in decline. We have seen that, in Iceland, this interest was largely at the popular level, while among the educated such stories were frowned upon. Outside Iceland, national Romanticism, together with a somewhat uncritical attitude to the likely historicity of non-realistic sagas, ensured their popularity with a larger audience. However, once the pressure of a leaning towards literary realism came to be felt among the general, novel-reading public, non-realistic sub-genres like the *fornaldarsögur* fell out of favour or, in the case of the romances, had never really been in favour outside Iceland itself. The evidence of English translations from the period 1914–50, however, suggests that translated romances like *Tristrams saga ok Ísöndar* 'The Saga of Tristram and Ísönd' maintained a certain interest, at least among medievalists, doubtless because they were part of the pan-European Arthurian literature of the Middle Ages.

If the sagas that were translated into English in the second half of the twentieth century reflected the tastes of the majority, then sagas of Icelanders were the runaway favourites of the period between 1950 and 2000. A reasonable number of historical works, such as *Jómsvíkinga saga, Heimskringla, Landnámabók, Orkneyinga saga, Ágrip af Nóregskonungasögur* and *Morkinskinna* were also translated during this period, as was *Sturlunga saga* and other kinds of literature, like saints' lives, legal and religious texts, and grammatical literature, some of which had not previously been available in English translation. As John Kennedy observes in *Translating the Sagas*, his 2007 survey of saga translations into English, some *fornaldarsögur* were published in translation in the second half of the twentieth century, but the titles of these translations, such as *Arrow-Odd: A Medieval Novel* (Paul Edwards and Hermann Pálsson, 1970), highlight what the translators hoped was their novel-like entertainment value.

The general character of many twentieth-century translations of sagas, at least into English, reinforced the dominant sense of what Heather O'Donoghue has called 'their novelistic fictionality'. These translations emphasise the undoubtedly laconic and understated character of many saga exchanges, but are often not very sensitive to rhetorical registers that are mannered or learned. To quote O'Donoghue again, 'the alterity, or "otherness", of saga narrative has been effaced by a novelistic presentation, but its naturalness and humour have been made appealingly accessible'.[7] By contrast, another later twentieth-century approach to saga translation, typified by Andersson and Miller (*Law and Literature in Medieval Iceland*), 'urges that the sagas be refocused as historical documents', both by attempting 'to tie the sagas more closely to medieval literature and oral literature in general' and by attempting 'to define the relationship between the sagas and the social systems in which they evolved', such that 'the case can plausibly be made that the sagas at times surpass the quality of other, more "historical" sources for purposes of historical enquiry'.[8]

Because most contemporary sagas' translators are also professional academics or individuals who have studied Old Norse-Icelandic literature at university, translators as well as editors of saga texts now reflect current or near-current approaches to the sagas in their work. Thus Andersson and Miller's scholarly book (the Introduction alone is 118 pages) reflects a view that seeks to redefine the nature of the historicity of sagas of Icelanders, not by claiming that everything in *Ljósvetninga saga* and *Valla-Ljóts saga* is accurate in terms of exactly what happened to a certain group of Icelanders in the tenth century, but rather in terms of the way the saga authors built up the social context in which the sagas' actions unfolded, giving the sort of ethnographic detail that allows someone with a basic understanding of how the kinship and feuding systems worked within the context of medieval Icelandic law, for example, to follow the main themes of these sagas in a manner that approximates to the position of a historically informed participant observer. Given that one cannot actually go back in time and space to the tenth century, such an approach is the next-best thing, it could be argued.

It is possible to extend the sort of approach advocated by scholars with anthropological or legal-historical interests to other cultural fields relevant to the historically aware understanding of medieval Icelandic sagas. A most important field in this regard concerns medieval Christian attitudes and religious beliefs and their informing presence in saga literature of all sub-genres, something that both scholars and general readers of the past have often ignored. Another, closer to the anthropological field, is the dynamics of family relations, including relationships between parents and children, fosterage practices and pseudo-kinship bonds of other kinds, like trading partnerships and blood-brother relations. With care and caution, the insights of a modern, socially and culturally historical awareness can be extended to the interpretation of themes and deep structures of saga texts, in the manner suggested in Chapters 5–7 of this book. Such an approach offers one of the most promising ways of rehabilitating the non-realistic sub-genres of the saga for a twenty-first-century audience and of giving them due value as literary works.

There are many recent signs that the focus of scholarly interest in the Icelandic sagas has shifted from sagas of Icelanders and kings' sagas to the once ignored or despised kinds of late medieval prose fiction, the *riddarasögur* and *fornaldarsögur*. There have now been three international conferences on *fornaldarsögur* (2003, 2006 and 2009), organised by younger scholars keen to encourage new approaches to this sub-genre, and, at the recent fourteenth International Saga Conference held in Uppsala (August 2009), there were many papers on aspects of late medieval Icelandic sagas, most of them intent upon moving beyond the notion that these literary kinds are mere escapist fiction to explore a variety of approaches, structuralist, psychoanalytic and fantastic, that are better able to reveal the role these sagas are likely to have played in Icelandic society during the later thirteenth, fourteenth and fifteenth centuries.

The wheel of fortune for these sub-genres within saga studies has thus come full circle. As we saw earlier in this chapter, *fornaldarsögur* and historical sagas were the most popular types of the Icelandic saga in the seventeenth and eighteenth centuries, when this kind of literature first became known to educated European readers, although the reasons for their popularity then were rather different from the reasons they are beginning to regain the attention of scholars now. It is a fair assumption that interest in the sagas of Icelanders, in particular, will never wane, because their subject-matter has an affinity with the modern condition and is particularly compatible with the literary conventions of the modern novel, although, as we have seen throughout this book, the saga is very different from the novel in many ways. A new approach to the less realistic sub-genres of the saga is likely to benefit future studies of sagas of Icelanders and kings' sagas as well as reviving the fortunes of the more overtly fictional sub-genres, and bodes well for the future of saga studies and the general appreciation of the Icelandic sagas as works of the human imagination.

Notes

1 Medieval Iceland

1 This and all other translations from Old Norse-Icelandic are my own, unless otherwise attributed. The Icelandic text of 'The Book of the Land-Takings' (*Landnámabók*), from which this passage quoted, is in *ÍF* I, 1, pp. 41–2. There is an English translation of 'The Book of the Land-Takings' (*Landnámabók*) and 'The Book of the Icelanders' (*Íslendingabók*) cited later in this chapter by Hermann Pálsson and Paul Edwards, trans. *The Book of Settlements. Landnámabók.* [Winnipeg]: University of Manitoba Press 1972. 'The Book of the Icelanders' is also available in the translation of Siân Grønlie, *Íslendingabók. Kristni saga. The Book of the Icelanders. The Story of the Conversion.* Viking Society for Northern Research Text Series, vol. XVIII. University College London: Viking Society for Northern Research. 2006.

2 *Landnámabók, ÍF* I, 1, pp. 34–8, trans. Pálsson and Edwards, *The Book of Settlements. Landnámabók*, pp. 16–18.

3 This text, which may derive from the lost early thirteenth-century *Styrmisbók* version of 'The Book of the Land-Takings', is printed in *ÍF* I, 1, p. 336, n. 1. A partial English translation is provided by Pálsson and Edwards, *The Book of Settlements. Landnámabók*, p. 6.

2 What is an Old Norse-Icelandic saga?

1 All citations from the second edition of *The Oxford English Dictionary* have been taken from the online version, unless otherwise noted. The entry 'Norse' was accessed on 8 July 2008.

2 The term eddic (or eddaic) refers primarily to heroic and mythological poetry in Norse versions of the common Germanic alliterative verse form preserved in a single manuscript, the Codex Regius GKS 2365 4° of *c.* 1275, and by extension to other poetry in these metres. Many of the heroic subjects of eddic poetry seem originally to have been common to all the Germanic peoples. Skaldic poetry (named from ON *skald*, later *skáld* 'poet') is usually characterised by stanzaic form, syllable-counting metres with internal rhyme and elaborate diction. This uniquely Scandinavian

poetry seems to have originated at the courts of Norwegian kings and aristocrats during the ninth century.

3 As far as I am aware, the term 'Old Norse-Icelandic' made its first appearance in the title of the *Bibliography of Old Norse-Icelandic Studies* (1964–), edited by the Danish scholar Hans Bekker-Nielsen and published in English by the publisher Munksgaard and the Royal Library in Copenhagen, but gained wider currency from the title of Carol Clover and John Lindow eds. *Old Norse-Icelandic Literature. A Critical Guide*. Islandica 45. Ithaca and London: Cornell University Press. 1985.

4 *OED* online: 'A narrative having the (real or supposed) characteristics of the Icelandic saga; a story of heroic achievement or marvellous adventure. Also, a novel or series of novels recounting the history of a family through several generations, as *The Forsyte Saga*.'

5 See *Fritzner: saga* 1 for examples of this sense.

6 Cf. *Fritzner: saga* 3: *nú ferr tveim sögunum fram* 'now it [the narrative] goes forward in two stories'.

7 See a number of examples cited in *CVC:* '*saga* B. A story, tale, legend, history'.

8 Some such titles, like *Veraldar saga* 'History of the World', an Icelandic chronicle of world history, are modern and therefore cannot be used in support of medieval naming practices.

9 The commonest verb used to express the mental effort of composing a saga is *samansetja/setja saman* 'to bring together, compile' (probably influenced by the Latin verb *componere* 'to collect, put together'), while the verb most often used of poetic composition is *yrkja* '(literally) to work, to compose poetry'. Both verbal uses are exemplified in the quotation from 'The Saga of Þorgils and Hafliði', and it also demonstrates that composers of sagas could sometimes compose some at least of the poetry within them. *Samansetja* is also used of the compilation of historical, educational and didactic works, like Snorri Sturluson's *Edda*.

10 A *flokkr* was a long skaldic poem without a refrain (*stef*), distinguishing it thus from a *drápa*, which was a long poem with one or more refrains.

11 The Icelandic text is taken, with some omissions, from the edition of Ursula Brown, *Þorgils saga ok Hafliða*, pp. 17–18. London: Geoffrey Cumberlege for Oxford University Press. 1952.

12 *Bæði lǫg ok áttvísi eða þýðingar helgar eða svá þau hin spakligu frœði er Ari Þorgilsson hefir á bœkr satt af skynsamligu viti.* The Icelandic text is based on the edition of Hreinn Benediktsson, *The First Grammatical Treatise*, p. 208. University of Iceland Publications in Linguistics 1. Reykjavík: Institute of Nordic Linguistics. 1972.

13 The Latin text is taken from the edition of Gustav Storm, *Monumenta historica Norvegiæ. Latinske kildeskrifter til Norges historie i middelalderen*, pp. 21–2. Kristiania (Oslo): Brøgger. 1880. The English translation is by David and Ian McDougall, *Theodoricus Monachus. Historia de Antiquitate Regum Norwagiensium. An Account of the Ancient History of the Norwegian Kings*, p. 17. University College London: Viking Society for Northern Research. 1998.

14 It is difficult to translate the word *hamrammr*; *hamr* is a skin or shape, which some people were thought capable of sloughing off, frequently in the evening, as here. It implies that Úlfr was a werewolf.

15 Bjarni Einarsson ed., *Egils saga Skallagrímssonar*, p. 1. University College London: Viking Society for Northern Research. 2003.

16 For details of the text and citation, see McDougall and McDougall, *Theodoricus*, p. 72, n. 102.

17 References to texts containing these terms can be found in *CVC: saga* 1. B.

18 There is an English translation of this passage by Theodore M. Andersson, *The Saga of Olaf Tryggvason. Oddr Snorrason*, p. 35. Islandica 52. Ithaca and London: Cornell University Press. 2003.

3 The genesis of the Icelandic saga

1 B. Colgrave and R. A. B. Mynors eds., *Bede, Ecclesiastical History of the English People*, pp. 566–7. Oxford: Clarendon. 1969.

2 Gabriel Turville-Petre, *Origins of Icelandic Literature*, p. 142. Revised from 1st edn of 1953. Oxford: Clarendon. 1967.

4 Saga chronology

1 Theodore M. Andersson, *The Growth of the Medieval Icelandic Sagas (1180–1280)*, p. 1. Ithaca and London: Cornell University Press. 2006. See Further Reading (Chapter 3).

2 For the Icelandic text of *Landnámabók*, see *ÍF* I, 1, p. 199, trans. Hermann Pálsson and Paul Edwards, *The Book of Settlements. Landnámabók*, p. 76. [Winnipeg]: University of Manitoba Press. 1972; cf. *Grettis saga*, Chapter 84, *ÍF* VII, p. 70; trans. Bernard Scudder, 'The Saga of Grettir the Strong', in Viðar Hreinsson *et al.* eds., *The Complete Sagas of Icelanders including 49 Tales*, vol. II, p. 180. Reykjavík: Leifur Eiríksson Publishing. 1997. For a translation of Oddr Snorrason's saga of Óláfr Tryggvason, see Theodore M. Andersson trans., *The Saga of Olaf Tryggvason. Oddr Snorrason*. Islandica 52. Ithaca and London: Cornell University Press. 2003.

3 For the texts of these runestones, see Judith Jesch, *Ships and Men in the Late Viking Age. The Vocabulary of Runic Inscriptions and Skaldic Verse*, pp. 102–7. Woodbridge: The Boydell Press. 2001. The date of 1041 is given for Yngvarr's death in two Icelandic annals.

4 For the Icelandic text of *Gísla saga*, Chapter 16, see *ÍF* VI, pp. 52–4; for a translation, see George Johnston, *The Saga of Gísli*, pp. 22–4. 2nd edn. London: Dent and University of Toronto Press. 1963. The Icelandic text of the passage from *Droplaugarsona saga*, Chapter 13 is cited from *ÍF* XI, pp. 168–75, and the translation is that

of Rory McTurk, 'The Saga of Droplaug's Sons', in Viðar Hreinsson *et al.* eds. *The Complete Sagas of Icelanders*, vol. IV, pp. 372–5.

5 The Icelandic bed closet, *lokrekkja* or *lokhvíla*, could be closed or locked, both to give its occupants some privacy and to provide protection from unexpected attack.

6 The Icelandic text is cited from *ÍF* VI, pp. 127–8, the English translation from Martin S. Regal, 'The Saga of the Sworn Brothers', in Viðar Hreinsson *et al.* eds. *The Complete Sagas of Icelanders*, vol. II, pp. 332–3. The reference to Lönnroth's argument is from his *Njáls Saga. A Critical Introduction*, pp. 107–13. Berkeley, Los Angeles and London: University of California Press. 1976. Further Reading (Chapter 3).

7 *Alexanders saga* is an Old Norse prose version of the Latin poem *Alexandreis* of Walter of Châtillon (*c.* 1180). It was translated by the Icelander Brandr Jónsson, Bishop of Hólar, at the request of the Norwegian King Magnús Hákonarson, probably in the years 1262–3.

5 Saga subjects and settings

1 Beryl Smalley, *Historians in the Middle Ages*, p. 28. London: Thames and Hudson, 1974.

2 Richard Kieckhefer, *Magic in the Middle Ages*, p. 9. Cambridge and New York: Cambridge University Press. 1990.

3 Theodore M. Andersson, *The Saga of Olaf Tryggvason. Oddr Snorrason*, pp. 92–4 and 108–9. Islandica 52. Ithaca and London: Cornell University Press. 2003. The Icelandic text is in *ÍF* XXV, pp. 249–54 and 288–90.

4 Guðni Jónsson ed., *Fornaldar sögur Norðurlanda*, 4 vols., vol. II, p. 269. Akureyri: Íslendingasagnaútgáfan. 1954. This passage is taken from a younger version of the saga than that cited in Chapter 6.

5 Marianne Kalinke ed. and trans., *Ívens saga*, in Kalinke ed., *Norse Romance*, II. *The Knights of the Round Table*, pp. 38–9. Arthurian Archives IV. Cambridge: D. S. Brewer. 1999.

6 The Icelandic text is cited from *ÍF* XXVI, p. 5.

7 *ÍF* XXVIII, pp. 96–8, trans. Magnus Magnusson and Herman Pálsson, *King Harald's Saga. Harald Hardradi of Norway*, pp. 69–70. Harmondsworth: Penguin Books. 1966.

8 The text and translation of *Sexstefja* is cited from Diana Whaley, ed., 'Þjóðólfr Arnórsson, *Sexstefja*', in Kari Ellen Gade ed., *Skaldic Poetry of the Scandinavian Middle Ages*. II. *Poetry from the Kings' Sagas 2*. Part 1, p. 122. Turnhout: Brepols. 2009.

9 *ÍF* VI, p. 125.

10 The Icelandic text is cited from Jón Jóhannesson *et al.* eds. *Sturlunga saga*, 2 vols., vol. I, pp. 492–4. Reykjavík: Sturlunguútgáfan. 1946. There is an English translation by Julia H. McGrew, *Sturlunga saga*, 2 vols., vol. I, pp. 401–3, *The Saga of*

Hvamm-Sturla and The Saga of the Icelanders. New York: Twayne Publishers, Inc. and The American-Scandinavian Foundation. 1970.

6 Saga mode, style and point of view

1 I am using the term 'register' in its linguistic sense of a form of language associated with a particular social situation or subject matter. Cf. the definition (*register* n.[1]) of the *OED* 2nd edn on-line (accessed 10 May 2009): 'A variety of a language or a level of usage, *spec.* one regarded in terms of degree of formality and choice of vocabulary, pronunciation, and (when written) punctuation, and related to or determined by the social role of the user and appropriate to the particular need or context.'

2 The Icelandic text is cited from *ÍF* VIII, pp. 222–4, and the English translation is by Rory McTurk, 'Kormak's saga', in Viðar Hreinsson *et al.* eds., *The Complete Sagas of Icelanders including 49 Tales*, vol. I, pp. 187–8. Reykjavík: Leifur Eiríksson Publishing. 1997.

3 Compensation (*manngjöld*) was money or other valuables payable to the kin of a person who had been killed or maimed by another. The obligation to pay devolved upon the perpetrator and his kin. In this instance, there were presumably no male kin to prosecute the case against Kormákr on behalf of Þórveig's sons, and they had clearly been the aggressors in the fight, so Kormákr was on reasonably safe ground in refusing to pay compensation. However, he did not reckon with the effect of Þórveig's weapon, sorcery.

4 Kari Ellen Gade, 'The Dating and Attribution of Verses in the Skald Sagas', in Russell Poole ed., *Skaldsagas. Text, Vocation, and Desire in the Icelandic Sagas of Poets.* Ergänzungsbände zum Reallexikon der Germanischen Altertumskunde 27, pp. 50–74. Berlin and New York 2001.

5 It is necessary to understand that in medieval Iceland marriage involved two distinctive rites, the betrothal, at which the male kin of both the woman and the man agreed to the marriage and sealed their agreement with a handshake and the promise of *brúðkaup* 'bride-price', and the wedding proper, which followed some time later and took the form of a feast at the house of the bride's family, during which further sureties were exchanged and the marriage was consummated.

6 The Icelandic text is cited from *ÍF* IX, pp. 244–6, and the translation is by Paul Acker, 'Valla-Ljot's Saga', in Viðar Hreinsson *et al.* eds., *The Complete Sagas of Icelanders*, vol. IV, pp. 137–8.

7 The noun *geit* can refer to a male or a female animal, but the female is clearly intended here.

8 Theodore M. Andersson and William Ian Miller, *Law and Literature in Medieval Iceland. Ljósvetninga saga and Valla-Ljóts saga*, p. 269, n. 244. Stanford University Press. 1989.

9　The Icelandic text is cited from *ÍF* XII, pp. 454–9, and the translation is by Robert Cook, *Njal's Saga*, pp. 303–7. London: Penguin Books. 2001. Previously published in Viðar Hreinsson *et al.* eds., *The Complete Sagas of Icelanders*, vol. III, pp. 1–220. A helpful plot summary is on pp. 344–53 of Cook's 2001 translation.

10　Only the first of the verses has been reproduced here. The saga writer's use of the personal name Dǫrruðr probably derives from the poem's refrain, which first appears in stanza 4: *Vindum, vindum* | *vef darraðar* 'let us wind, let us wind, the web of the banner', where *darraðr* is a poetic word for 'banner', 'pennant', or possibly 'spear', not a proper name. The metaphorical parallel between weaving cloth and the magical weaving of the favoured outcome of a battle, using human body parts, originates from the poem.

11　For example *vinur Randvés bana* 'female friends of Randvér's slayer' (Óðinn) [valkyries] (1/8, 10), *sóknvarðar* 'battle-wardens' [valkyries] (9/7) and *geirfljóðar* 'spear-women' [valkyries] (10/7).

12　The Icelandic text is cited from R. C. Boer ed., *Qrvar-Odds saga*, pp. 87–8. Altnordische Saga-Bibliothek 2. Halle a. S.: Niemeyer. 1892. The translation is my own. There is an English translation of this saga, based on a longer version than that cited here, by Hermann Pálsson and Paul Edwards, 'Arrow-Odd', in *Seven Viking Romances*, pp. 25–137. Harmondsworth: Penguin Books. 1985.

13　The precise geographical location of this country is not made clear in the saga, but the first element of the compound, *Bjálka-* (or *Bjalka-*), is probably cognate with Russian *bĕlka* 'squirrel, fur-bearing animal'. Thus Bjálkaland is probably to be envisaged as located somewhere in Eastern Europe where hunting for wild, fur-bearing animals is common.

14　In the later, fifteenth-century versions of the saga, King Herrauðr's kingdom is in Greece, not Húnaland, and King Álfr is supposed to have lived in Antioch.

7 Saga structures

1　Algirdas J. Greimas, 'Elements of a narrative grammar', *Diacritics* 7 (1977): 23. Originally published in French in 1969.

2　The terms 'syntagm' and 'paradigm', used a great deal in narratology, are borrowed from twentieth-century linguistics. In linguistics, combinations of words that are arranged in a sequence in natural discourse are called syntagms (see *OED* 2nd edn, 2. *syntagm*, on-line edition accessed 5 July 2009), while the term 'paradigm' in linguistics describes patterns, as, for example, inflectional forms of a word which can be presented in a table.

3　The term 'mytheme' is also based upon a term from linguistics. In linguistics a phoneme is a minimal phonetic unit; in mythological studies, a mytheme is a minimal unit of myth.

4　Andersson, *The Icelandic Family Saga*, pp. 4–5.

5　Ibid., p. 11.

6 *Harðar saga* is an exception here. As a 3-year-old boy, Hǫrðr is abnormally slow to walk, and, as he takes his first stumbling steps, he falls into his mother's lap, breaking a precious necklace. She curses him roundly for this and predicts a bad end for him.

7 The basic structure of Propp's schema is as follows: there is an Initial Situation into which the Hero is introduced. He is under some kind of Prohibition or Command, which he disobeys or neglects, and this leads to an encounter with his Antagonist, which in turn leads either to a Misdeed or Wrong being caused to the Hero or his family that has to be rectified, or the Hero experiences a Lack (which may be of a bride, magic object etc.), which he needs to satisfy. The Hero must then set out on a Journey, which may take the form of a Quest. He leaves home and usually encounters Tests, Difficult Tasks, Interrogations or Attacks along the way. He also meets possible Helpers (Providers) and may receive a Magic Object or some other form of assistance. He journeys to his destination, the place where the object of his quest is to be found, with or without companions. Usually he engages in Combat with his Antagonist and receives a Mark (wound, ring, kiss etc.). He is victorious and rights the original Misdeed or Wrong, takes the object of his Quest and returns home. He is sometimes pursued but is able to evade his pursuers.

8 The material record: how we know the sagas

1 In English usage, the term 'vellum' refers strictly to the skins of calves, while 'parchment' is used for other animal skins, usually from sheep or goats.

2 In most of medieval Europe, ink was produced from galls that grow on trees, especially oaks, but these were not available in Iceland, so the boiled juice of the bearberry (*Arctostaphylos uva-ursi*, Icelandic *sortulyng*) mixed with willow twigs is thought to have been used instead.

3 The commonest page sizes were, from larger to smaller, folio (fol, usually 28+ cm. high), quarto (4to, 4°, 18–28 cm.) and octavo (8vo, 8°, 9–20 cm.).

4 The land register remained in the Danish royal treasury in manuscript form until it was finally published in thirteen volumes in the twentieth century (1913–90).

5 A clear account of the complexities of the conditions of transfer of the manuscripts can be accessed on the website of *Den arnamagnæanske samling* under the heading 'transfer_to_iceland'. See http://nfi.ku.dk/english/collections/arnamagnaean_collection

9 Changing understandings of the sagas

1 They were named for the periodical *Fjölnir* (in Norse myth, one of the names of the god Óðinn), in which they expressed their radical views on politics and literature, and much else besides.

2 The name Kráka 'Crow' was the nickname of the Viking hero Ragnarr loðbrók's second wife Áslaug, according to his saga. *Krákumál* achieved paradigmatic status in the seventeenth and eighteenth centuries as the wildest and most sublime Old Norse poem, and was translated and anthologised repeatedly.

3 Percy's *Northern Antiquities or, A Description of the Manners, Customs, Religion and Laws of the Ancient Danes*... (London, 1770) was a translation, with a great deal of supplementary material, of Paul-Henri Mallet's *Introduction à l'histoire de Dannemarc* and *Monumens de la mythologie et de la poesie des Celtes* (Copenhagen 1755–6, 2nd edn Geneva, 1763).

4 Scott's abstract was published as an appendix to the miscellany *Illustrations of Northern Antiquities*, edited by Henry Weber and Robert Jamieson (Edinburgh, 1814).

5 In all likelihood, Johnstone had been assisted by the native Icelander, resident in Copenhagen, Grímur J. Thorkelin, who had himself produced partial English translations of *Laxdœla saga*, *Eyrbyggja saga* and *Ragnars saga loðbrókar* in his *Fragments of English and Irish History in the Ninth and Tenth Century* (London, 1788).

6 The original Thule series (ed. Felix Niedner) comprised twenty-four volumes and was published between 1912 and 1930; a second edition came out between 1963 and 1967. An additional series (1978–), excellently translated and with very good notes, was Saga: Bibliothek der altnordischen Literatur, series editor Kurt Schier (Munich: Diederichs), but this series is now finished.

7 *Old Norse-Icelandic Literature. A Short Introduction*, p. 134. Malden Mass. Oxford and Carleton, Victoria: Blackwell Publishing 2004.

8 These quotations are taken from the front and back flaps of the dust-jacket of Theodore M. Andersson and William Ian Miller, *Law and Literature in Medieval Iceland. Ljósvetninga saga and Valla-Ljóts saga*. Stanford University Press. 1989.

Glossary of technical terms

All terms that are likely to be unfamiliar to the reader are glossed on first mention, and titles of works in languages other than English (including Old Norse-Icelandic) are translated upon first mention, and sometimes subsequently, if they recur at a distance from the first mention. The list below is not exhaustive, but includes the most commonly used terms, arranged alphabetically.

Age of Settlement: in Icelandic history, refers to the period between AD c. 870–930 when the island was settled by people from Scandinavia and the British Isles

Age of the Sturlungs: the period of civil unrest in Iceland during the first half of the thirteenth century, named for one of the most powerful families, the Sturlungar

bookprose theory of saga composition: refers to the views of scholars who emphasised the influence of written texts on the development of the Icelandic saga

Commonwealth Iceland: refers to the period between the settlement and the Icelanders' loss of political independence to the Norwegian king in 1262–4

fornaldarsaga (**pl.** *-sögur*): 'saga(s) of ancient times', sub-genre of the Icelandic saga usually set in Scandinavia before the settlement of Iceland

freeprose theory of saga composition: refers to the views of those scholars who considered sagas to derive from oral narratives which were later written down

Íslendingasaga (**pl.** *-sögur*): 'saga(s) of Icelanders', family sagas, sub-genre of the Icelandic saga set in Iceland in the Age of Settlement or shortly afterwards

konungasaga (**pl.** *-sǫgur*): 'saga(s) of kings', vernacular biographies of Norwegian and Danish kings

lausavísur: 'loose verses', single stanzas of poetry in skaldic metres quoted in the texts of Icelandic sagas

lygisaga (**pl.** *-sǫgur*): 'lying saga(s)', term applied to entertaining but fictitious stories, possibly to be identified as *fornaldarsögur*

Old Norse: term referring primarily to the Scandinavian language group (Norwegian and its offshoots, including Icelandic; Swedish and Danish) and the cultures of Norse-speaking peoples

Old Norse-Icelandic: use of this term occurs when a phenomenon (text, custom etc.) is not exclusively Icelandic, but may also be Norwegian

Poetic (or Elder) Edda: collection of heroic and mythological poems in alliterative verse mainly found in a single Icelandic manuscript, GKS 2365 4° of *c.* 1275

riddarasaga (pl. *-sögur*): 'saga(s) of knights', romances both translated (from French, Anglo-Norman etc.) and indigenous

saga: 'something said, a story', as a literary term applied to an oral and/or written prose narrative in Old Norse-Icelandic, often incorporating poetry

samtíðarsaga (pl. *-sögur*): 'contemporary saga(s)', sagas about Icelanders set in the twelfth and thirteenth centuries

skáld: 'poet', a term usually applied to someone who composes verse in skaldic metres (syllable-counting, with both internal rhyme and alliteration and complex diction)

skáldasögur: 'sagas of poets', term applied to a sub-set of the sagas of Icelanders dealing with the lives of Icelandic poets

Snorri Sturluson's Edda: treatise on poetics and Old Norse myth, composed by the Icelandic chieftain Snorri Sturluson *c.* 1225

þáttr (pl. *þættir*): a short tale (literally 'strand of a rope') often associated with characters who appear in kings' sagas

Guide to further reading

1. Medieval Iceland

Brink, Stefan, in collaboration with Neil Price. *The Viking World*. London and New York: Routledge. 2008. Wide-ranging and informative study of Viking Age society, material and intellectual culture by a large number of international specialists.

Byock, Jesse. *Viking Age Iceland*. London and New York: Penguin Books. 2001. Accessible study of Iceland in the Viking Age and later.

Clover, Carol and John Lindow eds. *Old Norse-Icelandic Literature. A Critical Guide*. Islandica 45. Ithaca and London: Cornell University Press. 1985. Although now slightly out of date, this book contains excellent survey chapters on most major saga sub-genres, on eddic and skaldic poetry and on myth, by leading American researchers in the field.

Clunies Ross, Margaret ed. *Old Icelandic Literature and Society*. Cambridge Studies in Medieval Literature 42. Cambridge University Press. 2000. Contains thirteen chapters on a range of topics, from myths, poetry and sagas to Biblical writing and saints' lives.

Foote, Peter G. and David M. Wilson. *The Viking Achievement*. 2nd edn. London: Sidgwick and Jackson. 1980. A very good general study of the Viking Age across the whole of Scandinavia, with a strong emphasis on material culture.

Gunnar Karlsson. *Iceland's 1100 Years. History of a Marginal Society*. London: Hurst & Company. 2000. The best general introduction in English to the history of Iceland from the beginnings to the present day.

Hastrup, Kirsten. *Culture and History in Medieval Iceland. An Anthropological Analysis of Structure and Change*. Oxford University Press. 1985. The first specifically anthropological study of medieval Icelandic society and culture.

Lindow, John. *Handbook of Norse Mythology*. Santa Barbara, Calif., Denver, Colo. and Oxford, England: ABC Clio. 2001. Informative and succinct; arranged alphabetically.

McTurk, Rory ed. *A Companion to Old Norse-Icelandic Literature and Culture*. Malden, Mass., Oxford and Carlton, Victoria: Blackwell Publishing. 2005. A recent Companion volume, with chapters on history, geography, archaeology, society, language and literature of early Scandinavia, especially Iceland.

Meulengracht Sørensen, Preben, trans. Joan Turville-Petre. *The Unmanly Man. Concepts of Sexual Defamation in Early Northern Society*. The Viking Collection 1. Odense University Press. 1983. Incisive short study of the key concepts of honour and shame in early Scandinavia and its literature.

Orri Vésteinsson. *The Christianization of Iceland. Priests, Power, and Social Change 1000–1300*. Oxford University Press. 2000. The most comprehensive treatment of this topic.

Pulsiano, Phillip and **Kirsten Wolf** eds. *Medieval Scandinavia. An Encyclopedia*. New York and London: Garland Publishing, Inc. 1993. An invaluable reference tool on all aspects of early Scandinavia, including saga literature.

Stefán Karlsson, trans. Rory McTurk. *The Icelandic Language*. University College London: Viking Society for Northern Research. 2004.

Viðar Hreinsson *et al.* eds. *The Complete Sagas of Icelanders including 49 Tales*. 5 vols. Reykjavík: Leifur Eiríksson Publishing. 1997. An excellent translation of all sagas of Icelanders and some *þættir*. Some of the individual translations (but not all) were later published in paperback by Penguin.

The following references are for those interested in modern genetic evidence for the origins of the Icelandic population:

Agnar Helgason, E. Hickey, S. Goodacre, V. Bosnes, Kári Stefánsson, R. Ward and **B. Sykes**. 'mtDNA and the Islands of the North Atlantic: Estimating the Proportions of Norse and Gaelic Ancestry'. *American Journal of Human Genetics* 68 (2001): 723–37.

Gísli Sigurðsson. *Gaelic Influence in Iceland: Historical and Literary Contacts. A Survey of Research*. 2nd edn. Reykjavík: University of Iceland Press. 2000. Originally published in 1988 as Studia Islandica 46. Reykjavík: Bókaútgáfa Menningarsjóðs.

Price, T. Douglas and **Hildur Gestsdóttir**. 'The First Settlers of Iceland: An Isotopic Approach to Colonisation'. *Antiquity* 80 (2006): 130–44.

2 What is an Old Norse-Icelandic saga?

Clunies Ross, Margaret. *A History of Old Norse Poetry and Poetics*. Cambridge: D. S. Brewer. 2005. An accessible study of the various kinds of Old Norse-Icelandic poetry from the Middle Ages.

Harris, Joseph. 'Genre and Narrative Structure in some *Íslendinga þættir*'. *Scandinavian Studies* 44 (1972): 1–27. A seminal study of the *þáttr* or short narrative, also relevant to Chapter 7.

O'Donoghue, Heather. *Skaldic Verse and the Poetics of Saga Narrative*. Oxford and New York: Oxford University Press. 2005. Discusses the developing

relationship between verse and prose in Old Norse-Icelandic historical
writing and saga literature.

Schier, Kurt. *Sagaliteratur.* Sammlung Metzler 78. Stuttgart: Metzler. 1970. A
compact and informative German study of the saga genre.

Vésteinn Ólason, trans. Andrew Wawn. *Dialogues with the Viking Age. Narration
and Representation in the Sagas of the Icelanders.* Reykjavík:
Heimskringla. 1998. An excellent general study of the saga genre, which
puts its main emphasis on sagas of Icelanders. Also relevant to Chapters
4, 6 and 7.

3 The genesis of the Icelandic saga

Andersson, Theodore M. *The Growth of the Medieval Icelandic Sagas
(1180–1280).* Ithaca and London: Cornell University Press. 2006. Lays
emphasis upon the development of the Icelandic family saga out of early
native historical writing and oral tradition.

Byock, Jesse. 'Modern Nationalism and the Medieval Sagas'. In Andrew Wawn
ed., *Northern Antiquity. The Post-Medieval Reception of Edda and Saga,*
pp. 163–87. Enfield Lock, London: Hisarlik Press. 1994. Discusses the
influence of Icelandic nationalism on theories of saga origins and
development. Also relevant to Chapter 9.

Clover, Carol. 'The Long Prose Form'. *Arkiv för nordisk filologi* 101 (1986): 10–39.
Argues for the 'immanent' character of the Icelandic saga in its oral state.

  The Medieval Saga. Ithaca and London: Cornell University Press. 1982.
Important study of the genesis of the Icelandic saga, stressing the
influence of learned literary techniques and structures. Also relevant to
Chapter 7.

Einar Ól. Sveinsson, trans. G. Turville-Petre. *Dating the Icelandic Sagas. An Essay
in Method.* London: Viking Society for Northern Research. 1958. One of
the key bookprosist manifestos.

Gísli Sigurðsson, trans. Nicholas Jones. *The Medieval Icelandic Saga and Oral
Tradition. A Discourse on Method.* Publications of the Milman Parry
Collection of Oral Literature No. 2. Cambridge, Mass. and London,
England: Harvard University Press. 2004. Originally published in 2002
as *Túlkun Íslendingasagna í ljósi munnlegrar hefðar. Tilgáta um aðferð.*
Rit 56. Reykjavík: Stofnun Árna Magnússonar. A major reassessment of
the importance of oral traditions in the creation and development of the
Icelandic saga.

Gordon, E. V. 'On Hrafnkels saga Freysgoða'. *Medium Ævum* 8 (1939): 1–32.
Argues for this saga's lack of historical reliability.

Guðrún Nordal. *Tools of Literacy. The Role of Skaldic Verse in Icelandic Textual
Culture of the Twelfth and Thirteenth Centuries.* Toronto, Buffalo and
London: Toronto University Press. 2001. An important study of the role
of skaldic poetry in Icelandic society during the twelfth and thirteenth

centuries; argues that skaldic poetry as well as Latin verse were studied in medieval Icelandic schools.

Heusler, Andreas. 'Die Anfänge der isländischen Saga'. In Stefan Sonderegger ed., *Kleine Schriften*, 2 vols., vol. II, pp. 388–459. Berlin: de Gruyter. 1969. Rpt from *Abhandlungen der Königlichen Preussischen Akademie der Wissenschaften, phil.-hist. Klasse 9*. Berlin: Königl. Akademie der Wissenschaften. 1913 [published 1914]. The classic discussion of the 'bookprose' versus 'freeprose' theories of Icelandic saga composition.

Liestøl, Knut, trans. A. G. Jayne. *The Origin of the Icelandic Family Sagas*. Oslo: H. Aschehoug & Co and Harvard University Press. 1930. Rpt Westport, Conn.: Greenwood Press. 1974. First published in Norwegian in 1929 as *Upphavet til den islendske ættesaga*. Oslo: Aschehoug. The most sustained freeprosist approach to the Icelandic saga from the early twentieth century.

Lönnroth, Lars. *Njáls Saga. A Critical Introduction*. Berkeley, Los Angeles and London: University of California Press. 1976. A critical introduction to one of the greatest sagas of Icelanders, incorporating analysis of saga structures on macro and micro levels. Relevant also to Chapters 6 and 7.

Maurer, Konrad. 'Ueber die Hœnsa-Þóris saga'. *Abhandlungen der philos.-philol. Classe der königlichen bayerischen Akademie der Wissenschaften* 12.2 (1871): 157–216. Seminal bookprosist analysis and textual criticism applied to an Icelandic saga.

Ong, Walter J. *Orality and Literacy. The Technologizing of the Word*. New York and London: Methuen. 1982. Although now nearly thirty years old, this is still one of the best short introductions to the salient findings of worldwide research into oral literatures and cultures.

Sigurður Nordal. *Hrafnkatla*. Studia Islandica 7. Reykjavík: Ísafoldarprentsmiðja. 1940. Translated by R. George Thomas as *Hrafnkels saga Freysgoða*. Cardiff: University of Wales Press. 1958. Argues that *Hrafnkels saga* (and probably other sagas) is a plausible historical fiction.

4 Saga chronology

Arnold, Martin. *The Post-Classical Icelandic Family Saga*. Scandinavian Studies 9. Lewiston, Queenston and Lampeter: The Edwin Mellen Press. 2003. A useful critical analysis of sagas of Icelanders from the late thirteenth and fourteenth centuries (or later).

Einar Ól. Sveinsson. *Sturlungaöld. Drög um íslenzka menningu á þrettándu öld*. Reykjavík: nokkrir Reykvíkingar. 1940. Translated by Jóhann S. Hannesson as *The Age of the Sturlungs*. Islandica 36. Ithaca: Cornell University Press. 1953. Rpt New York: Kraus Reprint Corp. 1966. The classical statement of the nexus between the Sturlung Age and saga writing.

Hofmann, Dietrich. 'Die *Yngvars saga víðfǫrla* und Oddr munkr inn fróði'. In Ursula Dronke, Guðrún Helgadóttir, Gerd Wolfgang Weber and Hans Bekker-Nielsen eds., *Specvlvm Norrœnvm: Norse Studies in Memory of Gabriel Turville-Petre*, pp. 188–222. Odense University Press. 1981. Argues that Oddr Snorrason wrote *Yngvars saga víðfǫrla*.

Jónas Kristjánsson. *Um Fóstbræðrasögu*. Stofnun Árna Magnússonar á Íslandi, Rit 1. Reykjavík: Stofnun Árna Magnússonar. 1972. Argues that this saga is a work of the late thirteenth century; English summary on pp. 311–26.

Torfi Tulinius, trans. Randi Eldevik. *The Matter of the North. The Rise of Literary Fiction in Thirteenth-Century Iceland*. The Viking Collection 13. Odense University Press. 2002. The best recent account of the development and character of the *fornaldarsaga*. Also relevant to Chapters 5 and 6.

Vésteinn Ólason. 'Family Sagas'. In Rory McTurk ed., *A Companion to Old Norse-Icelandic Literature and Culture*, pp. 101–18. Malden, Mass., Oxford and Carlton, Victoria: Blackwell Publishing. 2005. A clear and useful survey of saga chronology as well as other characteristics of the Icelandic family saga. Also relevant to Chapters 5 and 6.

Örnólfur Thorsson. '"Leitin að landinu fagra": Hugleiðing um rannsóknir á íslenzkum fornbókmenntum'. *Skáldskaparmál* 1 (1990): 28–53. A dispassionate survey of the evidence for the chronology of the medieval Icelandic saga in the light of the manuscript evidence.

5 Saga subjects and settings

Andersson, Theodore M. 'The Displacement of the Heroic Ideal in the Family Sagas'. *Speculum* 45 (1970): 575–93.

Ármann Jakobsson. 'Royal Biography'. In Rory McTurk ed., *A Companion to Old Norse-Icelandic Literature and Culture*, pp. 388–402. Malden, Mass., Oxford and Carlton, Victoria: Blackwell Publishing. 2005. Stresses the importance of concepts of kingship in kings' sagas.

Barnes, Geraldine. 'The Riddarasögur: A Medieval Exercise in Translation'. *Saga-Book of the Viking Society* 19 (1977): 403–41. Discusses the differences between Norse translations of French romances and the originals.

'Riddarasögur 2. Translated'. In Phillip Pulsiano and Kirsten Wolf eds., *Medieval Scandinavia. An Encyclopedia*, pp. 531–3. New York and London: Garland Publishing, Inc. 1993.

Faulkes, Anthony. 'Descent from the gods'. *Mediaeval Scandinavia* 11 (1982) [1978–9]: 92–125. Analyses the construction of myths of Scandinavian rulers' descent from the gods of paganism and Christianity.

Glauser, Jürg. 'Romance (Translated riddarasögur)'. In Rory McTurk ed., *A Companion to Old Norse-Icelandic Literature and Culture*, pp. 372–87. Malden, Mass., Oxford and Carlton, Victoria: Blackwell Publishing. 2005.

Guðrún Nordal. *Ethics and Action in Thirteenth-Century Iceland*. The Viking
Collection 11. Odense University Press. 1998. A study of Sturla
Þórðarson's *Íslendinga saga*.

Kalinke, Marianne E. *Bridal-Quest Romance in Medieval Iceland*. Islandica 46.
Ithaca and London: Cornell University Press. 1990. Also relevant to
Chapter 7.

'Riddarasögur 1. Indigenous'. In Phillip Pulsiano and Kirsten Wolf eds.,
Medieval Scandinavia. An Encyclopedia, pp. 528–31. New York and
London: Garland Publishing, Inc. 1993.

Kalinke, Marianne E. ed. *Norse Romance I. The Tristan Legend. II. The Knights of
the Round Table. III. Hærra Ivan*. Arthurian Archives III–V. Cambridge:
D. S. Brewer. 1999.

Lindow, John. 'The Social Semantics of Cardinal Directions in Medieval
Scandinavia'. *Mankind Quarterly* 34 (1994): 209–24.

Lönnroth, Lars. 'The Noble Heathen: A Theme in the Sagas'. *Scandinavian
Studies* 41 (1969): 1–29.

Ney, Agneta, Ármann Jakobsson and Annette Lassen eds., *Fornaldarsagaerne.
Myter og virkelighed*. Copenhagen: Copenhagen University, Museum
Tusculanums Forlag. 2009. Proceedings of a conference on
fornaldarsögur; it contains many chapters in English showcasing new
research into this sub-genre.

Úlfar Bragason. 'Sagas of Contemporary History (*Sturlunga saga*): Texts and
Research'. In Rory McTurk ed., *A Companion to Old Norse-Icelandic
Literature and Culture*. pp. 427–46. Malden, Mass., Oxford and Carlton,
Victoria: Blackwell Publishing. 2005.

Whaley, Diana. 'A Useful Past: Historical Writing in Medieval Iceland'. In
Margaret Clunies Ross ed., *Old Icelandic Literature and Society*,
pp. 161–202. Cambridge Studies in Medieval Literature 42. Cambridge
University Press. 2000.

6. Saga mode, style and point of view

Andersson, Theodore M. and William Ian Miller. *Law and Literature in Medieval
Iceland. Ljósvetninga saga and Valla-Ljóts saga*. Stanford University Press.
1989. A detailed analysis of these two sagas and the culture that
underpinned them, together with English translations.

Bartlett, Robert. *The Natural and the Supernatural in the Middle Ages*. The Wiles
Lectures. Cambridge University Press. 2008. A discussion of medieval
attitudes to the supernatural.

Clunies Ross, Margaret. 'Realism and the Fantastic in the Old Icelandic Sagas'.
Scandinavian Studies 74 (2002):4, 443–54. An earlier attempt of the
author to define saga modality.

Poole, Russell ed. *Skaldsagas. Text, Vocation, and Desire in the Icelandic Sagas of
Poets*. Ergänzungsbände zum Reallexikon der Germanischen

Altertumskunde 27. Berlin and New York: de Gruyter. 2001. Contains a number of chapters by leading scholars all investigating different aspects of the sagas of poets.

Gísli Sigurðsson, trans. Nicholas Jones. 'The Immanent Saga of Guðmundr ríki'. In Judy Quinn *et al.* eds., *Learning and Understanding in the Old Norse World. Essays in Honour of Margaret Clunies Ross*, pp. 201–18. Turnhout: Brepols. 2007. Discusses various and varying saga presentations of the chieftain Guðmundr the Powerful and the implications of that variability for understanding how sagas came into being.

Lönnroth, Lars. *Njáls saga*. 1976. See full entry under further reading for Chapter 3.

Sävborg, Daniel. 'Avstånd, gräns och förundran. Möten med de övernaturliga i islänningasagan'. In Margrét Eggertsdóttir *et al.* eds., *Greppaminni. Rit til heiðurs Vésteini Ólasyni sjötugum*, pp. 323–49. Reykjavík: Hið íslenska bókmenntafélag. 2009. Analysis of the various ways saga authors represented the paranormal in sagas of Icelanders.

7 Saga structures

Andersson, Theodore M. *The Icelandic Family Saga. An Analytic Reading.* Harvard Studies in Comparative Literature 28. Cambridge, Mass.: Harvard University Press. 1967. The first and most influential anlysis of the structure of sagas of Icelanders.

Byock, Jesse L. *Feud in the Icelandic Saga*. Berkeley: University of California Press. 1982. Argues that the typical structures of Icelandic feuds shaped their literary representation.

Clover, Carol. J. 'Scene in Saga Composition'. *Arkiv för nordisk filologi* 89 (1974): 57–83.

Faulkes, Anthony. 'Outlaws in Medieval England and Iceland'. In Margrét Eggertsdóttir *et al.* eds., *Greppaminni. Rit til heiðurs Vésteini Ólasyni sjötugum*, pp. 139–51. Reykjavík: Hið íslenska bókmenntafélag. 2009. Analyses structural and thematic patterns in sagas of outlaws.

Gennep, Arnold van. *Les rites de passage. Étude systématique des rites.* Paris: Nourry. 1909. English translation by Monika B. Vizedom and Gabrielle L. Caffee as *The Rites of Passage*. London: Routledge and Kegan Paul. 1960.

Hume, Kathryn. 'Beginnings and Endings in the Icelandic Family Sagas'. *Modern Language Review* 68 (1973): 593–606. Looks at the part played by beginnings and endings, and especially genealogies, in conveying meaning in saga literature.

Lévi-Strauss, Claude. *Structural Anthropology.* Garden City, NY: Doubleday Anchor Books. 1968. Originally published in French in 1958.

Lindow, John, Lars Lönnroth and Gerd Wolfgang Weber eds. *Structure and Meaning in Old Norse Literature. New Approaches to Textual Analysis and*

Literary Criticism. The Viking Collection 3. Odense University Press. 1986.

Lönnroth, Lars. 'Structuralist Approaches to Saga Literature'. In Judy Quinn *et al.* eds., *Learning and Understanding in the Old Norse World. Essays in Honour of Margaret Clunies Ross*, pp. 63–73. Medieval Texts and Cultures of Northern Europe 18. Turnhout: Brepols. 2007. A useful summary account of the subject.

Miller, William Ian. *Audun and the Polar Bear. Luck, Law and Largesse in a Medieval Tale of Risky Business*. Leiden: Martinus Nijhoff. 2008. Analysis of this short tale's structure, inspired by Marcel Mauss's study of reciprocal gift-giving.

Propp, Vladimir, trans. Lawrence Scott. *Morphology of the Folktale*. Philadelphia: American Folklore Society. 2nd edn 1968 (1st edn 1958). Austin and London: University of Texas Press. Originally published in Russian in 1928. The major study of the structure of folktales.

Schjødt, Jens Peter, trans. Victor Hansen. *Initiation between Two Worlds. Structure and Symbolism in Pre-Christian Scandinavian Religion*. The Viking Collection 17. Odense: University Press of Southern Denmark. 2008. Argues that structures of initiation can be detected in some *fornaldarsögur*.

8 The material record: how we know the sagas

Benedikt S. Benedikz. *Árni Magnússon – Where Would We Be Without Him?* The Fell-Benedikz Lecture delivered in the University of Nottingham 24 October 2000. University of Nottingham: Centre for the Study of the Viking Age. 2002. On the importance of Árni Magnússon to Icelandic studies today.

Bjarni Einarsson ed. (with Anthony Faulkes) *Egils saga Skallagrímsonar*. University College London: Viking Society for Northern Research. 2003. Example of an accessible, informative student edition of a saga text.

Brown, Michelle P. *The British Library Guide to Writing and Scripts. History and Techniques*. London: The British Library. 1998. A very useful practical guide to the technical aspects of manuscript production, though not focussed on Icelandic manuscripts.

Guðvarður Már Gunnlaugsson. 'Manuscripts and Palaeography'. In Rory McTurk ed., *A Companion to Old Norse-Icelandic Literature and Culture*, pp. 245–64. Malden, Mass., Oxford and Carlton, Victoria: Blackwell Publishing. 2005. Good overview of medieval Icelandic manuscripts and handwriting.

Haugen, Odd Einar. 'Stitching the Text Together: Documentary and Eclectic Editions in Old Norse Philology'. In Judy Quinn and Emily Lethbridge eds. *Creating the Medieval Saga. Versions, Variability and Editorial Interpretations of Old Norse Saga Literature*, pp. 37–63. The Viking

Collection 18. Odense: University Press of Southern Denmark. 2010. Discusses major approaches to editing Icelandic sagas.

Hreinn Benediktsson ed. *Early Icelandic Script as Illustrated in Vernacular Texts from the Twelfth and Thirteenth Centuries.* Íslenzk handrit. Icelandic Manuscripts. Series in Folio II. Reykjavík: The Manuscript Institute of Iceland. 1965. Discusses and exemplifies early Icelandic scripts and manuscripts.

Nichols, Stephen G. 'Introduction: Philology in a Manuscript Culture'. *Speculum* [Special Issue 'The New Philology'] 65 (1990): 1–10.

Sigurður Nordal. 'Time and Vellum'. *M. H. R. A. Annual Bulletin of the Modern Humanities Research Association* 24 (1952): 15–26. Surmises that the Icelandic practice of slaughtering many calves each autumn (because they could not be fed through the winter) and the fact that people had time on their hands over winter may have helped create the right circumstances for writing and copying sagas.

9 Changing understandings of the sagas

Clunies Ross, Margaret. *The Norse Muse in Britain 1750–1820.* Trieste: Edizioni Parnaso. 1998. Documents the reception of Old Norse literature in Britain from the mid eighteenth century to the 1820s.

Driscoll, Matthew J. 'Traditionality and Antiquarianism in the Post-Reformation *Lygisaga*'. In Andrew Wawn ed., *Northern Antiquity. The Post-Medieval Reception of Edda and Saga*, pp. 83–99. Enfield Lock, London: Hisarlick Press. 1994.

The Unwashed Children of Eve. The Production, Dissemination and Reception of Popular Literature in Post-Reformation Iceland. Enfield Lock, London: Hisarlik Press. 1997.

Glauser, Jürg. *Isländische Märchensagas. Studien zur Prosaliteratur im spätmittelalterlichen Island.* Beiträge zur nordischen Philologie 12. Basel and Frankfurt am Main: Helbing und Lichtenhahn. 1983.

'The End of the Saga: Text, Tradition and Transmission in Nineteenth- and Early Twentieth-Century Iceland'. In Andrew Wawn ed., *Northern Antiquity. The Post-Medieval Reception of Edda and Saga*, pp. 101–41. Enfield Lock, London: Hisarlick Press. 1994.

Jón Karl Helgason. 'Continuity? The Icelandic Sagas in Post-Medieval Times'. In Rory McTurk ed., *A Companion to Old Norse-Icelandic Literature and Culture*, pp. 64–81. Malden, Mass., Oxford and Carlton, Victoria: Blackwell Publishing. 2005.

Kennedy, John. *Translating the Sagas. Two Hundred Years of Challenge and Response.* Making the Middle Ages 5. Turnhout: Brepols. 2007.

Wawn, Andrew, ed. *Northern Antiquity. The Post-Medieval Reception of Edda and Saga.* Enfield Lock, London: Hisarlik Press. 1994.

'The Post-Medieval Reception of Old Norse and Old Icelandic Literature'. In Rory McTurk ed., *A Companion to Old Norse-Icelandic Literature and Culture*, pp. 320–37. Malden, Mass., Oxford and Carlton, Victoria: Blackwell Publishing. 2005. A concise review of the post-medieval reception of sagas, providing handy lists of the earliest text editions and translations of Old Norse literature (1500–1750) and the general works mentioned in Chapter 9.

The Vikings and the Victorians. Inventing the Old North in Nineteenth-Century Britain. Cambridge: D. S. Brewer. 2000.

Zernack, Julia. *Bibliographie der deutschsprachigen Sagaübersetzungen 1791–1955.* Berliner Beiträge zur Skandinavistik 4. Berlin: Freie Universität Berlin. 1997.

Geschichten aus Thule. Íslendingasögur in Übersetzungen deutscher Germanisten. Berliner Beiträge zur Skandinavistik 3. Berlin: Freie Universität Berlin. 1994. A study of German translations of Icelandic sagas and their motivations.

References to volumes in the Íslenzk fornrit editions of Icelandic sagas

ÍF = Íslenzk fornrit, vols. I–. Reykjavík: Hið íslenzka fornritafélag (cited by volume and page numbers).

ÍF I = Jakob Benediktsson ed. *Íslendingabók. Landnámabók*. Parts 1 and 2. 1968. Rpt. in one vol. 1986. Reykjavík: Hið íslenzka fornritafélag.

ÍF II = Sigurður Nordal ed. *Egils saga Skalla-Grímssonar*. Reykjavík: Hið íslenzka fornritafélag. 1933.

ÍF III = Sigurður Nordal and Guðni Jónsson eds. *Borgfirðinga sǫgur*. Reykjavík: Hið íslenzka fornritafélag. 1938.

ÍF IV = Einar Ól. Sveinsson and Matthías Þórðarson eds. *Eyrbyggja saga*. Reykjavík: Hið íslenzka fornritafélag. 1935.

ÍF VI = Björn K. Þórólfsson and Guðni Jónsson eds. *Vestfirðinga sǫgur*. Reykjavík: Hið íslenzka fornritafélag. 1943. (Contains *Gísla saga Súrssonar*, pp. 1–118 and *Fóstbrœðra saga*, pp. 119–276)

ÍF VII = Guðni Jónsson ed. *Grettis saga Ásmundarson*. Reykjavík: Hið íslenzka fornritafélag. 1936.

ÍF VIII = Einar Ól. Sveinsson ed. *Vatnsdœla saga*. Reykjavík: Hið íslenzka fornritafélag. 1939. (Contains *Kormáks saga*, pp. 201–302)

ÍF IX = Jónas Kristjánsson ed. *Eyfirðinga sǫgur*. Reykjavík: Hið íslenzka fornritafélag. 1956. (Contains *Valla-Ljóts saga*, pp. 231–60)

ÍF XI = Jón Jóhannesson ed. *Austfirðinga sǫgur*. Reykjavík: Hið íslenzka fornritafélag. 1950. (Contains *Droplaugarsona saga*, pp. 135–80)

ÍF XII = Einar Ól. Sveinsson ed. *Brennu-Njáls saga*. Reykjavík: Hið íslenzka fornritafélag. 1954.

ÍF XXV = Ólafur Halldórsson ed. *Færeyinga saga, Óláfs saga Tryggvasonar eptir Odd munk Snorrason*. Reykjavík: Hið íslenzka fornritafélag. 2006.

ÍF XXVI–XXVIII = Bjarni Aðalbjarnarson ed. *Snorri Sturluson Heimskringla*. 3 vols. Reykjavík: Hið íslenzka fornritafélag. 1941–51.

Index

Note: All personal names of Icelanders are alphabetised by first name followed by last name; all other persons listed here are alphabetised by last name, followed by first name or initials.

The Cambridge Introduction to...

AUTHORS

Margaret Atwood Heidi Macpherson

Jane Austen Janet Todd

Samuel Beckett Ronan McDonald

Walter Benjamin David Ferris

J. M. Coetzee Dominic Head

Samuel Taylor Coleridge John Worthen

Joseph Conrad John Peters

Jacques Derrida Leslie Hill

Charles Dickens Jon Mee

Emily Dickinson Wendy Martin

George Eliot Nancy Henry

T. S. Eliot John Xiros Cooper

William Faulkner Theresa M. Towner

F. Scott Fitzgerald Kirk Curnutt

Michel Foucault Lisa Downing

Robert Frost Robert Faggen

Nathaniel Hawthorne Leland S. Person

Zora Neale Hurston Lovalerie King

James Joyce Eric Bulson

Herman Melville Kevin J. Hayes

Sylvia Plath Jo Gill

Edgar Allan Poe Benjamin F. Fisher

Ezra Pound Ira Nadel

Jean Rhys Elaine Savory

Edward Said Conor McCarthy

Shakespeare Emma Smith

Shakespeare's Comedies Penny Gay

Shakespeare's History Plays Warren Chernaik

Shakespeare's Tragedies Janette Dillon

Harriet Beecher Stowe Sarah Robbins

Mark Twain Peter Messent

Edith Wharton Pamela Knights

Walt Whitman M. Jimmie Killingsworth

Virginia Woolf Jane Goldman

William Wordsworth Emma Mason

W. B. Yeats David Holdeman

TOPICS

The American Short Story Martin Scofield

Comedy Eric Weitz

Creative Writing David Morley

Early English Theatre Janette Dillon

English Theatre, 1660–1900 Peter Thomson

Francophone Literature Patrick Corcoran

Literature and the Environment Timothy Clark

Modern British Theatre Simon Shepherd

Modern Irish Poetry Justin Quinn

Modernism Pericles Lewis

Narrative (second edition) H. Porter Abbott

The Nineteenth-Century American Novel Gregg Crane

The Novel Marina MacKay

The Old Norse-Icelandic Saga Margaret Clunies Ross

Postcolonial Literatures C. L. Innes

Postmodern Fiction Bran Nicol

Russian Literature Caryl Emerson

Scenography Joslin McKinney and Philip Butterworth

The Short Story in English Adrian Hunter

Theatre Historiography Thomas Postlewait

Theatre Studies Christopher Balme

Tragedy Jennifer Wallace

Victorian Poetry Linda K. Hughes

Made in the USA
Middletown, DE
20 April 2016